"An introduction to the world of unions and their enemies. . . . McAlevey's writing is an attempt to circulate organizers' skills, breathing life into the long-quiescent labor movement. . . . *A Collective Bargain*, like the rest of McAlevey's work, is indispensable."
—Alex Press, *Bookforum*

"Incisive, brilliant, and combined with trenchant strategic analysis. If we had more organizers like Jane McAlevey, we'd be winning."
—Van Jones, CNN host and author of *Beyond the Messy Truth: How We Came Apart, How We Come Together*

"A half century ago, the Koch family targeted workers' collective power with so-called right-to-work laws. Now they and their allies have expanded their agenda to shackling democracy writ large so as to achieve society-wide corporate supremacy. Jane McAlevey shows us how workplaces provided a laboratory for this audacious project of domination—and better still, she explains how following the strategies and tactics of savvy union organizers could help save America from an ever more ruthless right. With young climate activists embracing strikes as a tool of struggle, this empowering book could not be more timely."
—Nancy MacLean, author of *Democracy in Chains: The Deep History of the Radical Right's Stealth Plan for America*

"Jane McAlevey has devoted her life to reining in the destructive power of concentrated wealth, and she is consumed with one overarching question: How do we win? In this essential book, she draws on decades of organizing experience to make an overwhelming case that the new face of working-class power is female and fiercely feminist. It's past time to listen up."
—Naomi Klein, author of *This Changes Everything: Capitalism vs. the Climate*

"Jane McAlevey is a brilliant strategist, rousing organizer, and razor-sharp critic inside the labor movement. In this critical moment when labor is resurgent, McAlevey's small *d* democratic spirit, and her humane and deeply informed reporting and analysis are needed more than ever."
—Katrina vanden Heuval, editorial director
and publisher of *The Nation*

"Read this book! It's full of effective strategies for overcoming voter suppression against even the stiffest odds. Jane McAlevey is the type of experienced organizer the current White House fears."
—Benjamin Todd Jealous, former national president and CEO of the NAACP

"Democracy is when the many can rule over the powerful few. Americans haven't been able to vote for this kind of power for decades. But what Jane McAlevey shows, with gripping reportage and deep analysis from the front line of national union struggles, is that Americans have increasingly forged democracy in their workplaces. At the very same moment that the Trump administration seeks to snuff unions out of existence, hundreds of thousands of workers are discovering what democracy feels like by winning labor fights across the country. For anyone wanting a surge of hope in the fight for democracy, McAlevey shows us that the best place to find an America of hope, equality, justice, and good plans isn't the ballot box but a union hall."
—Raj Patel, research professor at the University of Texas at Austin and author of *Stuffed and Starved: The Hidden Battle for the World Food System*

"A battle cry for union rights in a time hostile to labor organizations."
—*Kirkus Reviews*

"Labor activist McAlevey delivers a persuasive argument that the power of 'strong, democratic' trade unions can fix many of America's social problems in this timely cri de coeur. . . . She offers a useful primer on how labor organizing works and effectively refutes common assumptions about unions. . . . McAlevey's . . . humor and contagious confidence in the efficacy of organized labor give this succinct volume an outsize impact."
—*Publishers Weekly* (starred review)

A Collective
Bargain

A Collective Bargain

Unions, Organizing, and the Fight for Democracy

Jane McAlevey

ecco

An Imprint of HarperCollinsPublishers

*To the brilliant people who went on strike in 2018 and 2019:
the educators from West Virginia to California; the Marriott and
Stop & Shop workers; the many nurses and health care workers
in Massachusetts, Pennsylvania, and beyond. You've helped one
another, your families, your communities, and the nation, raising
expectations that life should and can be better. Keep going!*

#lajf

HarperCollins books may be purchased for educational, business, or sales promotional use. For information, please email the Special Markets Department at SPsales@harpercollins.com.

Ecco® and HarperCollins® are trademarks of HarperCollins Publishers.

A hardcover edition of this book was published in 2020 by Ecco, an imprint of HarperCollins Publishers.

FIRST ECCO PAPERBACK EDITION PUBLISHED 2021

Designed by Michelle Crowe

Library of Congress Cataloging-in-Publication Data

Names: McAlevey, Jane, author.
Title: A collective bargain : unions, organizing, and the fight for democracy / Jane McAlevey.
Description: First edition. | New York, NY : Ecco, [2019] | Includes index.
Identifiers: LCCN 2019028863 (print) | LCCN 2019028864 (ebook) | ISBN 9780062908599 (hardcover) | ISBN 9780062908605 (paperback) | ISBN 9780062908612 (Digital Edition)
Subjects: LCSH: Collective bargaining—United States—History. | Labor unions—United States—History.
Classification: LCC HD6508 .M228 2019 (print) | LCC HD6508 (ebook) | DDC 331.890973—dc23
LC record available at https://lccn.loc.gov/2019028863
LC ebook record available at https://lccn.loc.gov/2019028864

23 24 25 26 27 LBC 7 6 5 4 3

Contents

Thirty-six Weeks

THE ORIGINAL PUBLICATION OF *A COLLECTIVE BARGAIN*, IN JANUARY 2020, coincided with one of many recent events that has revealed our threadbare democracy: the impeachment trial of Donald Trump. Soon after proceedings started, the first ravaging pandemic in a century revealed an equally threadbare social safety net in a country where, from March 18 to November 25, U.S. billionaires' wealth increased by $1 trillion dollars—a whopping 34 percent—while a quarter million people died and 33 million filed for unemployment. Amazon CEO Jeff Bezos's wealth alone grew by $70 billion, while demands from his employees for personal protective equipment and a hazard-pay raise were deflected and denied.

At nearly the same time, from March 2 to November 3, the Democratic Party shirked two progressive candidates and consolidated its support around Joe Biden. George Floyd's horrifying execution by the Minneapolis police invigorated a new civil rights movement, and Trump continued to incite white nationalist fervor. In a historic election turnout, nearly half of voters opted for a candidate and party that couldn't care less about killing them—literally—and Democrats won the Electoral College by a thin 44,000-vote margin.

Analyzing the subjects of these deeply disturbing and intertwined thirty-six weeks could—and no doubt will—fill entire books. My focus, however, is on why *this* book is even more relevant than ever. The year 2020 has shown us that the corporate class will stop at nothing to exploit and divide workers. In this book are stories of workers winning big. In each, workers learned that they could exercise a power that some say is "outdated" but that remains as effective now as ever: the power to withhold their labor by going on strike. The solidarity they built among themselves and their communities in the course of preparing for these strikes also prepared workers for the political fight against the anti-worker regime of Donald Trump. All the victories described in this book happened in the four years from Trump's Electoral College stunner in 2016 until his Electoral College loss in 2020. This was by design: As an organizer, I understood that with Trump's win—and a worsening climate crisis—a deep sense of despair had gripped progressives. Despair is demobilizing, so I set out to raise people's expectations that with smart strategy, workers and their communities *can* still win, even under difficult conditions.

Though few will give them credit, unions were central to defeating Trump. *Every* union I chronicle played a huge, if not decisive, role in pulling Biden across the finish line in each swing state the Democrats won. From Atlanta, Detroit, and Las Vegas to Milwaukee, Philadelphia, and Phoenix, it was unions and allied grassroots groups who had the know-how and capacity that day in and day out drove enough voters to the polls to deliver the country from four more years of a Mitch McConnell–led senate or a Trump presidency.

Though Trump is about to leave the White House, Trumpism won't leave with him. He amassed 74 million voters (47.3 percent of the electorate), and plenty believe the election was stolen from him—and, more important, from them. It is entirely reasonable to conclude that, had there not been a global pandemic and had Trump not catastrophically failed to address it, he could have won. To these sobering results, add down-ballot defeats for Democrats and a baffling mix of wins and losses on key ballot measures, and one observation is clear: there is huge confusion about who, and which policies, are culpable for the significant decline in many Americans' quality of life over the past few decades, and the pain inflicted in 2020 in particular.

Trump came much closer to winning than he should have. An obvious conclusion from these dismal thirty-six weeks is that progressives in general, and unions in particular, must recommit to base expansion using the key strategies I outline in this book. What actually wins meaningful change is organizing that shifts people's understanding of *us versus them*. Because of the power of Fox News and antisocial media, people need help making sense of what's happening to them and why. *How* we do this matters. It requires a recommitment to union organizing that recognizes the triple crises of race, gender, and class are inseparable. This approach deeply integrates the sum of those three forces into the theory of power and thus the theory of winning.

In chapters five and six, I walk the reader through specific methods that successful organizers have used to win against powerful employers that are often connected to a larger, more powerful political elite. Supermajority strikes are central to each of these successes, and the stories illustrate how workers can fight against rapacious income incquality, a by-product of a power imbalance so skewed that essential workers, who keep others alive, risk death while serving the corporate class, who shelter at home.

If we want to have a fighting chance at reviving our democracy, we must look to the base-building and political-education efforts of unions. And unions, in turn, must come to see themselves not merely as a solution to workplace troubles but also as part of the broader community in which workers live, worship, gather, and play. The organizing strategies that help workers win big *and* understand who and what divides and oppresses them make up what I call "whole worker organizing." This method starts by identifying informal or organic leaders in the workplace and engages them in what organizers call structure tests, or mini-campaigns, that build and assess active participation among the ranks on immediate issues like excessive overtime, too few employees, and mistreatment. Structure tests force unions to regularly engage 100 percent of the workforce in two-way conversations instead of talking only with workers who already support the union, and they are much more reliable than polls at showing us where workers really stand on key issues.

Crucially, whole worker organizing extends the same methods into the workers' communities. Once workers have built enough trust and organization inside their workplaces, union organizers among the ranks then map the broader structures of power in the labor market in which those workers live, so workers come to understand the relationships their employers have to the political elite in the area. More important, workers then upend those relationships by dividing and conquering those forces and forging new alliances with their communities' organized social sectors, such as faith leaders and civil rights groups, which often have more power than today's unions in any single labor market.

Such alliances need to be built by the workers themselves through their own community connections, not union officials handing out contributions to local church groups. Forging strong alliances with their communities helps workers neutralize their employers in union elections and strikes, allowing more victories while uniting unions with movements fighting for more affordable housing and environmental and climate justice, and combatting violence against people of color and women. As workers come to see the network of power relationships at work and in their broader communities, they become highly educated voters—not just new union members or union members winning better contracts. In this type of union campaign, workers build a broader working-class resilience across an entire community.

In chapter five, "How Do Workers Get a Union?," I tell the story of nurses who formed new unions in seven hospitals in Philadelphia in 2016 and 2017. I dive deep into the campaign at Einstein Medical Center, where I served as campaign director and eventually chief contract negotiator. One story that illustrates the whole-worker-organizing approach is that of Joyce Rice.

When the Einstein campaign began, Rice was already a well-respected nurse in the labor and delivery department. Because Einstein is a safety-net hospital, it serves a disproportionately high percentage of the significant black population in America's fifth largest city. The more tenured nurses in those units had helped birth what sometimes felt like half of Philadelphia's population—and most of its power structure. Despite having built a strong work-site organization and high levels of participation, they still hadn't developed sufficient power to compel the CEO to take them seriously at the bargaining table.

Meanwhile, union staff had undertaken the research for a "geographic power structure analysis," in which they studied who and which entities held what kind of power in the broader labor market of Philadelphia. Just as the nurses were getting frustrated at the lack of progress in the talks, we held a large strategy meeting with nurse leaders from each newly unionized hospital across the city. The four-hour strategy retreat began with staff presenting what they had learned about the power analysis.

As we kicked off the meeting, we asked everyone to hold their questions until the end, except for clarifying questions. About forty minutes in, after a slide that showed graphically how power was distributed among one of many types of organized social groups—the faith community—Joyce Rice raised her hand. Did she have a clarifying question? we asked. "I think it might be helpful to the discussion," she said. "But I'm not sure." The room had been nearly silent until then, with rapt faces engaged in the presentation. She went on to point out that when she saw the name of one of the many faith-based organizations whose power we had assessed as strong—the Baptist Pastors and Ministers Conference of Philadelphia and Vicinity—she thought she had seen in her church newsletter that her minister had recently been elected as its president. Rice said she had just been texting him to ask if she was correct; was he the president? In the course of their back and forth, he said he would like to hear from the nurses about their fight for better lives and better patient care.

Mic drop!

Not only did Rice have a connection to just the type of power institution she and the nurses needed to tip the balance of power, but she was *texting* with him! As an organizer or strategist, you couldn't pay a Bezos-billion stolen from his workers for this pivotal type of dynamic in an organizing meeting. This moment gets to the heart of what whole worker organizing is: a process to help workers see the power they can have when they understand the power structure around them, how it works and how they can tap into it. After Rice shared this gem of information with the group, everyone started murmuring about people they knew in that same power structure. After an hour of small-group discussions over lunch, the nurses then decided to systematically chart their connections to their own community's power structure, one worker at a time. Within weeks, we had hundreds of straight-line connections—what sociologists and economists call strong ties—between the nurses and many of Philadelphia's power brokers.

At the invitation of her pastor and the new president of BPMC, Darrian A. Brown Sr., Joyce Rice took a delegation of nurses to a meeting of the BPMC's leadership to share the details of their struggle to get hospital management to take their demands seriously. Days later, Brown wrote a strongly worded letter on BPMC letterhead to the hospital's CEO, advising him to listen carefully to the congregants of the organization's one hundred churches, many of them nurses at his hospital.

There are millions of connections that one nurse in one campaign in one city put to work, helping her and thousands more win a great contract. She and her colleagues went from being nurses to nurse leaders to community leaders capable of changing the city. They went on to play a role in helping increase the turnout in one of the most watched cities in the 2020 presidential election.

Every untapped connection is power left on the table, in fights where workers desperately need way more to win. This is the kind of organizing that, scaled up, *can* build a better democracy. Success stories like this fill the pages of this book, and workers everywhere can build the power to win like Joyce Rice did.

Twelve Years of Freedom (Almost)

UNIONS ARE SUCH A PAIN IN THE ASS. REALLY.

Anyone who has dealt with a union understands. Then again, so is trying to get through to customer service at your bank, or the warranty division of a company that made one of your household appliances. Unions can be bureaucratic and hard to navigate in the same way dealing with the permit process to build a house or a building, or opening a child-care center is. Paying union dues can feel as exciting as paying taxes. Going to a badly run union meeting may be every bit as painful as attending an interminable city council meeting or a public hearing on just about anything. But unions, Americans may finally be coming to realize, are absolutely essential to democracy. Wild levels of income inequality have led to wild levels of political inequality. Turns out that when you destroy the most effective tool that ordinary people have to challenge the powerful elite in their workplaces, you destroy democracy itself.

Chapter 2 of Timothy Snyder's bestselling 2017 book, *On Tyranny: Twenty Lessons from the Twentieth Century,* is a directive titled "Defend Institutions." It begins with his summary of why institutions matter to ward against tyranny.

> It is institutions that help us to preserve decency. They need our help as well. Do not speak of "our institutions" unless you make them yours by acting on their behalf. Institutions do not protect themselves. They fall one after the other unless each is defended from the beginning. So choose an institution you care about—a court, a newspaper, a law, a labor union—and take its side.

In a world of widening income inequality, the foundering of the democratic electoral process, and rampant sexual and racial inequality, I take the side of unions. Despite their numerous problems, unions alone have the potential to match the power of giant corporations and massive wealth and solve the many social problems we face now.

This book is about how unions can get us out of the mess we're in today. Although its focus is on the United States, the analysis and strategies have implications for Brexit-stung England, yellow-vested France, the rest of the trending right-wing populist Europe, and the world—on which the aforementioned countries have long trampled with even less regard than they currently treat their own workers. My firm belief that only strong, democratic unions can get us out of the myriad crises engulfing the United States, and large parts of the world, is based on my twenty-five years as an organizer in the field, running and winning hard campaigns—including strikes, negotiating hard-fought collective agreements, and more recently reinforced by five years of later-in-life doctoral research at the City University of New York and two years as a postdoc at Harvard Law School. The chapters in this book reflect my life work and are a mix of history, analysis, and recent case studies, including campaigns I had a hand in, or, helped lead, in the past few years.

My conviction that unions matter now more than ever is grounded in the current power structure analysis: In the United States, we are stuck with a high court that will rule against workers and the planet for another thirty to forty years. Lawsuits, legal approaches, and advocacy, the modus operandi of choice since the early 1970s for those who self-identify as progressives, simply will not work. Those strategies were shaped by the Warren Court, which can be characterized as a liberal-leaning, or at least fair-minded, court that is a reflection of the New Deal and Civil Rights era from which it sprung. If you believe that lawsuits or legal tactics are the main platforms available for a positive change, stop reading this book and go play with your kids or grandkids. Resign their future and yours to one with more extreme storms and vast unemployment. But know that it is not inevitable—not by a long shot.

Wealth inequality is the root cause of today's problems: by 2016, the richest 1 percent controlled 46 percent of all financial wealth in the United States; the next 4 percent, 29 percent; the next 5 percent, 11 percent; and the remaining 90 percent share a meager just 14 percent. In fact, the bottom 60 percent of America not only doesn't have any financial wealth; they are, on average, in debt. But 2016 is now ancient history. By 2017, a new study on inequality showed that just three people—Jeff Bezos, Bill Gates, and Warren Buffett— "have more wealth than the bottom half of the country combined." Bezos's wealth increases by $13 million per hour. In 2018, half of all people in the world experienced an 11 percent drop in their wealth; the billionaire class increased their riches by $2.5 billion each day.

Income inequality is directly linked to political inequality. According to a highly detailed study coproduced by political scientists at Princeton and Northwestern universities, the relative amount of influence over public policy that the super-rich, rich, and corporate elite have compared with the rest of the people in the United States tracks closely to the disparities in financial wealth. According to the authors, "Contrary to what decades of political science research might lead you to believe, ordinary citizens have virtually no influence over what their government does in the United States. And economic elites and interest groups, especially those representing business, have a substantial degree of influence. Government policy-making over the last few decades reflects the preferences of those groups—of economic elites and of organized interests."

The impact of economic, political, and social inequality in America is real and dangerous, and not up for debate. We are, however, in a hot debate about how to reverse course. Ironically, the billionaire class now dominates and frames the national discussion on inequality. With its wealth and influence towering above all other potential players in today's think-and-do tanks, as well as its outright ownership of key news media outlets—Fox, the *Washington Post,* and Facebook, to name only three—it has captured the narrative in policy circles, functioning as an informal horizontal national political party with equal influence on the Democrats and Republicans: what I call the "Party of Inequality." Billionaires and the corporations that undergird their 1 percent superpower status have so skewed the discussion that we no longer debate a worker's right to strike or even their freedom to assemble in their workplace through a union. With the rise of Silicon Valley, we now argue over whether a worker is even a worker.

As detailed in the Princeton-Northwestern study of our democracy being replaced by an oligarchy, the billionaire class is again advancing the tired argument of trickle-down economics. The legacy power players long associated with the Republican side of the aisle, such as the U.S. Chamber of Commerce and the Business Roundtable, argue without proof that further slashing taxes on themselves will create more jobs because they will invest their savings in job creation. The data wildly contradicts their assertions. The 2017 tax cuts have not resulted in durable or good job creation but funded stock buybacks and bulked up the already-bulging pockets of the super-rich.

In the lead-up to the passage of the 2017 tax bill, the Business Roundtable alone—under its chairperson, JPMorgan Chase & Company's Jamie Dimon—quadrupled its spending. It dumped $17 million into pushing for the tax cut bill in just the final three months of 2017. That bested how much the Chamber of Commerce doled out in the same three-month period, but not by much: $16.83 million, out of a grand total in the institution's 2017 lobbying budget of $59 million.

And that's just lobbying; it doesn't account for spending on political races. When it comes to political spending, the Party of Inequality leaves every other institution in the dust. To get a sense of this, consider that by the 2016 election cycle, the ratio of big business versus union donations to political candidates and the two main parties was 16:1. Is it any wonder that a massive tax cut for the super-rich and corporations passed? In the same period, when Republicans had majorities in both chambers of Congress and the White House, not one pro-worker piece of legislation passed, let alone was legitimately entertained.

But the Party of Inequality, seeking to hem in the parameters of any debate when it comes to protecting its wealth, spends lavishly on candidates and lobbying directed at the Democrats, too. Starting with Bill Clinton's presidency and the creation of the Democratic Leadership Council, in addition to legacy corporate money, the then-fledgling, now full-grown billionaire donors of Silicon Valley have been given a red carpet by major Democratic Party leaders because they host successful fund-raisers, refilling the money coffers that unions once raised. The big-tech elite cleverly disguises their right-wing, anti-worker politics with Democratic-backed social positions, like support for gay marriage and trans rights (rich ones only, please), pro-choice legislation (for wealthy women), ethnic diversity (but for unicorns of color), and immigration.

The big-tech, pro-immigration aspect is especially cynical. So big tech doesn't have to pay taxes for public schools, it favors immigration for self-serving, specific needs: for the least-paid laborers (nannies and gardeners, for example) and the high-income earners (big tech uses the H1 visas to import engineering talent needed because of Silicon Valley's "disruption" of public education, covered in chapter 6). And while they talk a pro-immigration line in public, they are quietly aiding mass deportation schemes by the Immigration and Customs Enforcement agency by developing and selling high-tech facial recognition and tracking technology.

Innovative my ass. Silicon Valley's delegation inside the Party of Inequality is the new face of greed, but on steroids. Disrupting the concept of a worker isn't any better than disrupting democracy, and it has had a big hand in both, thanks to its creation of antisocial media. To try to keep some actual facts in perspective: the so-called platform economy is not nearly as big as was being projected even just one year ago. There are many *nonunion* workers in "regular" jobs, not hopping around between TaskRabbit gigs. In 2018, major economists began trying to explain how wrong they were about the size and scale of the platform, or gig, economy. By January 2019, even the *Wall Street Journal* began running such headlines as "How Estimates of the Gig Economy Went Wrong: Rise in Nontraditional Work Arrangements Was More Modest Than Originally Estimated, a New Paper Says." Turns out, talking about the gig economy is a bit of a red herring; it avoids dealing with the vast majority of workers whose work is merely dull and doesn't pay enough to live, let alone live well.

Big-tech influence can also be seen in the vast sums it has poured into the California movement to privatize public education. In 2017, top donor Reed Hastings—the Netflix founder and current Facebook director and Democrat—raised a full-blown war chest against the teachers' unions, helping oust pro-public-education members from the Los Angeles Unified School Board and replacing them with financiers and a pro-charter-school majority.

In 2018, he helped make the election for the state superintendent of schools one of the most expensive statewide races in California history. (His pro-privatization candidate was narrowly defeated, the teachers and parents having learned a lesson about the power of money in the 2017 school board races.) Apparently the teachers' desires for reasonable class sizes, trained nurses in their schools, art classes, recess with play time on green space, textbooks that no longer refer to the Soviet Union as a country, and a sufficient number of guidance counselors so poor kids can have a shot at attending colleges that their parents can't buy them into amount to demands that deserve a battle by the elite of Silicon Valley.

Democrats have been smashing teachers' unions—the largest single segment of unionized workers remaining in America—as they zealously drive their corporate-backed, pro-charter-school agenda. It's the equivalent of Mitch McConnell and the Koch brothers playing football, getting really bad concussions, and waking up so confused they set out to destroy the National Rifle Association or the evangelical church in Texas, Arizona, Iowa, Georgia, and Pennsylvania heading into 2020.

Silicon Valley faux libertarianism—it lobbies for massive federal tax dollars for research, for example, but muses that big government is not needed—has so taken over the battle of ideas inside the Democratic Party that even the concept of a national minimum wage is being kicked aside for some faux-enlightened program called the Guaranteed Basic Income. The GBI is an airy idea that somehow people will be "guaranteed" an "income" when their jobs are destroyed by robots. A phalanx of Silicon Valley–oriented foundations, hedge fund donors, magazines, and consultants—including the Aspen Institute, Open Society, Rockefeller, *Wired, Fast Company,* McKinsey, Deloitte, Accenture, and the World Economic Forum (think Davos)—obsess about what they call the Future of Work, which is chiefly defined by the integration of artificial intelligence and automation into the workplace and by the rise of the "gig" or "platform" economy. Unsurprisingly, they are the ones moving this idea forward.

Under GBI, the guaranteed income would be—get this—$1,000 per month. Because it's impossible to rent a room in a group house, let alone an apartment or house, in the Bay Area or Seattle for that amount, you have to imagine a vast number of unemployed and unhoused who can allegedly have new leisure time to develop a start-up company and become rich. The GBI is as much distraction and fantasy as the language Silicon Valley innovators used to get people hooked on Uber, Lyft, and Airbnb. Their quaint notion of the sharing economy was quickly replaced with the platform economy and public stock offerings that filled their pockets while leaving workers in the lurch. These innovators are now selling the idea that we don't need wages, or even workers. But the answer is clear: the most obvious solution to the income crisis is to forgo the robots and stop the automation, which is also way better for the planet, not just the humans who are still among its inhabitants.

Despite the weakened state of most unions, workers today who are either forming new ones or reforming older ones point us in the direction of how to solve the crisis engulfing our society and our politics. In the midterm elections in 2018—dubbed the year of the woman—the misogyny oozing from the White House was somewhat rebuked at the polls. Yet the year before, working women scored a series of thoroughly impressive wins, just after Donald Trump lost the popular vote but eked out a win from the Electoral College. Many of those victories received far less media attention. As in the midterm elections, men contributed to these wins, certainly, but the central characters were women—often women of color—who waged tireless campaigns of which the outcomes would have drastic consequences. Chapter 1 discusses three such examples of women winning big.

The arena for these battles was the workplace, in the mostly female sectors of the economy such as health care, education, and hospitality, but also in the tech sector, where sexual harassment and the gender pay gap serve as a stark reminder that, despite the tech elite's rhetoric of building a new society, nothing much has changed, unless you count the creation of the new generation of Silicon Valley billionaires as progress. Women worker-led policy changes included people wresting control of their schedules away from tone-deaf managers, most of whom have never had to pick up their kids at the bus stop; securing fair and meaningful pay raises; achieving bold new safeguards from sexual predators; and ending racism and other discriminatory practices in their salary structure. The mechanism for securing these victories was the collective bargaining process, and each involved strikes—the key leveraging mechanism of unions.

Strikes are uniquely powerful under the capitalist system because employers need one thing, and one thing only, from workers: show up and make the employer money. When it comes to forcing the top executives to rethink their pay, benefits, or other policies, there's no form of regulation more powerful than a serious strike. The strikes that work the best and win the most are the ones in which at least 90 percent of all the workers walk out, having first forged unity among themselves and with their broader community. To gain the trust and support of those whose lives may be affected, smart unions work diligently to erase the line separating the workplace from society.

The methods organizers use to achieve these kinds of all-out strikes require the discipline and focus of devoting almost all of their time and effort reaching out to the workers who don't initially agree, or even may think they are opposed to the strike, if not the entire idea of the union. This commitment to consensus building is exactly what's needed to save democracy. To win big, we have to follow the methods of spending very little time engaging with people who already agree, and devote most of our time to the harder work of helping people who do not agree come to understand who is really to blame for the pain in their lives. Pulling off a big, successful strike means talking to everyone, working through hard conversations, over and over, until everyone agrees. All-out strikes then produce something else desperately needed today: clarity about the two sides of any issue. Big strikes are political education, bigly.

The women-powered collective bargaining wins described in chapters 1, 5, and 6 represent monumental improvements to worker and community lives that happened much faster than traditional policy changes—unless, perhaps, you are the billionaire class. It is precisely because unions can produce these kinds of gains, even in their emaciated state, that they have been the targets of sustained attacks from the corporate class. Unions' track record of redistributing *power*—and therefore wealth—and changing how workplaces are governed is what led to a war waged against them by the business class. In just twelve years in the private sector, from 1935 to 1947, with massive strikes at the core of their strategy, workers made huge breakthroughs that benefited most people and created the concept of the American Dream—that your kids will do better than you, along with home ownership for workers and a right to retire and play with those grandkids.

The breakthroughs in just those twelve years were as unimaginable then as the idea of rebuilding unions might seem today. Before workers decided to build power through collective action and form the United Auto Workers in 1935, conditions in auto plants essentially weren't different from the abysmal ones in today's average Amazon warehouse. There is abundant academic literature of how bad things were before the autoworkers launched the sit-down strikes, demanding unions. Situations that pundits and media give fancy labels today, such as *precarity,* have long been a feature of American capitalism. It's only if and when workers decide to harness their only real power—coming together in unity, as a union—that their lives will improve. One such academic report on conditions in the auto sector pre-unionization states,

> . . . in the early years of the Depression, autoworkers were fortunate to work irregularly; and when they were employed, they were coerced into operating at increasingly fast rates for declining rates of pay. The alternative, suffered by an enormous number of workers, was unemployment with little to no public assistance.

WORKERS WHO FOUGHT TO BUILD STRONG UNIONS turned horrible jobs in the auto factories into the kind of employment that became the backbone of the American Dream. Liberals yearn nostalgically for a time when corporate leaders seemed more responsible, for an era when CEOs seemed to understand that employees, the people who make the profits, were considered more important than, if not equal to, the shareholders. Elite thinkers today seem to think the CEOs of the inter- and post-war period actually cared about "their" workers. The "leadership role" CEOs once played, like the corporate culture liberals yearn for, was produced by the power of workers on strike. *It's workers, through their unions, who played the leadership role.*

By 1947, just twelve short years into many American workers having the freedom to wage effective strikes, the Northern big business elite chose to ally with Jim Crow racists in Congress, and pooled their money and power into eviscerating those freedoms—outlawing the most effective strike weapon, the solidarity strike—when they passed the Taft–Hartley Act or the Labor Management Relations Act of 1947. (The law is discussed in detail in chapter 2.) Even so, the gains made in just twelve years were so strong that they lasted until the early 1970s, when the employers began a second major offensive, increasing tenfold the number of union-busting firms and weaponizing trade and "globalization"—taking direct aim at the 56 percent unionization rate in American factories.

For another forty years, until the 2010 midterm elections (when Scott Walker passed a series of sweeping laws to systematically dismantle public-sector unions in Wisconsin), public-sector unionization—which also kicked off with a decade of strikes from the late 1960s through the late 1970s—was enough to sustain a decent standard of living for public servants. But we often glance over how public-sector unionization helped *all* workers because, even as workers in the private sector were being hammered overall, union financial contributions in elections continued to help balance the power of corporate wealth. Even though 1978 was the final year that workers, through their unions, matched big-business donations in national congressional elections, pro-worker Democrats were still receiving sizable union contributions and winning elections. To the Koch brothers and their ilk, this meant that corporations had to find a strategy that could attack the legal system outlined by "states' rights," because—unlike private-sector unions—public-sector unions are governed by state, not federal, laws.

Those rights are something in which the Kochs and the right wing believe, except when they don't: "states' rights" is the rhetoric first devised by segregationists in the South in defense of slavery, and it's trotted out whenever convenient, such as in debates about gun rights. But public-sector unions are governed by state laws, not a single national law like the one that controls the private sector. Big corporate interests had to hatch a different strategy, based on a different power analysis.

Thus the Koch brothers and other billionaires launched a plan to maneuver a union attack in states in which the Koch brothers and the right can't win the kind of slash-and-burn state legislative assault Scott Walker got away with in Wisconsin. A December 2018 article from the right-wing Heritage Foundation read, "Assuming that an average union member pays $600 in annual dues or agency fees, public-sector unions collect around $3 billion a year from the 5 million unionized employees in the 22 states where agency fees were legally permissible. Ninety percent of those employees are located in 11 states—California, Connecticut, Illinois, Maryland, Massachusetts, Minnesota, New Jersey, New York, Ohio, Pennsylvania and Washington," and Oregon, Illinois, and other states where public-sector unions were strong. Clearly, these billionaires have been scheming to take down today's public-sector unions.

Taking advantage of the changing Supreme Court, they engineered three successive legal cases, each one nibbling at public-sector union law, each laying the foundation case by case for the coup de grâce, the *Janus* decision in June 2018. *Janus* determined that workers in government-sector unions can't determine, even by majority vote, that their coworkers shall have to contribute either dues or a lesser fee, called agency fees, to their union, fabricating an argument that contributing to the union constrains free speech, as outlined in the First Amendment. Corporations had to manipulate the process to attack the public sector in similarly clever but different ways from when they set out to destroy the private-sector unions. They sought to offshore the most heavily unionized jobs in the 1970s as they increased spending to fight unions workplace by workplace. Today, driven by Silicon Valley, they are weaponizing technology, using AI and robots not only to help rid the country of the remaining unions but—hell—to eliminate the need for workers at all.

The conventional narrative about union decline places most blame on globalization and technological changes. These two forces of change are presented as facts of life and are considered somehow neutral, structural, inevitable. But humans—mostly white, wealthy men who can buy their access to decision makers—are behind every decision regarding robots, trade, workers, and unions (and the planet, too). Like the decision made by executives in Silicon Valley icon Apple, who began the assembly of iPhones in factories in China, where most iPhones are still made and where real unions—that's independent unions—are forbidden.

A big innovation that's not pictured in Apple's slick-hip-cool ads with people dancing with their iPhones is the suicide net. Yes, in China, in the Foxconn factories where one million workers assemble iPhones cheaply so that Apple executives and top shareholders can live like kings, so many distraught workers try to jump to their deaths that the company had to strategically hang nets throughout the plants to prevent suicide. Uber and Lyft can also be dinged with the iSuicide claim: eight taxicab drivers in New York City killed themselves because their once-profitable taxicab medallions are now valued at $200,000, down from $1 million. This kind of despair is the real outcome of the disruptor-billionaire Party of Inequality.

There's nothing neutral about suicide nets; there's nothing inevitable about creating a greater climate crisis by offshoring jobs so ships bigger than small towns cross oceans, killing the ecosystem and creating a need for more fuel; there's nothing comforting about creating millions of close-to-slavery working conditions in faraway lands that Americans can't see when they happily upgrade to the latest phone. We don't need robots to care for the aging population. We need the rich to pay their taxes. We need unions to level the power of corporations.

As the Parkland youth say, I call bullshit.

_____

CHAPTER 1

Workers Can Still Win Big

AS A YOUNG TRADE UNION ORGANIZER, ONE OF THE FIRST THINGS I had to prove to higher-ups was that I could recite our definition of a union at the drop of a hat. The definition came from Bernie Minter, a rank-and-file worker leader from the union that taught me the most important lessons not just about unions, but also about how people can win against stiff odds. From its founding in the 1940s until a merger in 1989, the union where I trained and developed my organizing skills was national and independent. It was referred to simply as District 1199, composed of health care workers. This, from Bernie Minter's typed notes, is its entire definition.

What is a union?

A collective effort by all employees who work for an employer

To stop the boss from doing what you don't want him to do. Discharge, unfair layoff, promotion, speed up, etc.

To make the boss do what you want him to do. More pay, vacation, holidays, health coverage, pensions, etc.

And, to be used in any other way the members see fit.

That's it. It really is that simple.

Unions had been around as long as the United States, but their popularity skyrocketed in 1935, during the Great Depression—incidentally, the last time the American billionaire class forced most Americans into a massive crisis. To course-correct for bankrupting the American worker, Congress passed the National Labor Relations Act (NLRA), which guaranteed workers the right to collective bargaining—the right to negotiate wages and other terms of employment—and created one national legal framework for unions in the private sector. Under the law, workers were given the right to unionize by holding elections in their workplaces, which were governed by a board called the National Labor Relations Board (NLRB).

A union basically functions like a government, whether a town board, a city council, or a rural grange. In the case of a union, however, the primary—but importantly not sole—focus is on worker-related issues. (If your workplace is a school, or a hospital, or any similar institution, however, these same issues are also community issues.) Unlike corporations, faith-based institutions, and non-profits, both governments and unions rely on democratic traditions like open meetings and elections. Some unions do live up to the pejorative labels given to them by corporate media, but most do not. People are flawed, and unions are made up of people, so unions, too, can be flawed.

That said, it's helpful to think of a union as a mechanism: nothing makes it inherently good or bad, although its internal rules heavily influence its effectiveness. As is also the case with a government, a union can be good or bad based on the rules governing its respective elections, including campaign financing, whether the bargaining unit of the workers is fairly constructed or gerrymandered, and whether the people it represents have open access to decision-making processes. If the governance systems encourage participation by the best and most diverse workers, the union will reflect the best and most diverse workers' values. Conversely, if the organization is a do-nothing union, it will reflect the least-good values among the workforce, just like elected politicians and their constituents. Unions often differ based on the culture of the employer and on the type of workforce, no different from states, which differ based on the types of people that make up its population. (Think Texas versus Massachusetts.) Unions, then, are far from monolithic.

There is significant variation among the different branches of the same union. That's true worldwide in unions, and they're commonly called locals in the United States (and "branches" in many other countries). Let's take one example and break it down: Local 1107 of the Service Employees International Union. The only international aspect of SEIU is a small number of members in Canada (125,000 out of 2.1 million) and a few in Puerto Rico (depending on how particular Puerto Ricans self-identify, this can be suspect, and certainly flows from the movement for Puerto Rican independence). The numbers 1-1-0-7 mean nothing in particular, or at least nothing relevant. Members simply say, "I am a member of Local 1107." It leaves outsiders with no idea what union or what workers they are talking about. Local 1107 is the local branch of SEIU in Nevada, and the numbers in its name were picked because someone liked them when playing the card game blackjack. The number could just as well refer to someone's birthday or a winning lotto number. To add to the confusion, one union might have dozens of different locals within the same state.

Locals can be as different and varied as the national unions are. Locals generally distinguish either types of workers or specific employers, but again, there's no rule—just guidelines. Many unions will have an entity in between the locals and the national, either a statewide or perhaps multistate but regional council, that unites the various local unions in the same state for political endorsements and statewide lobbying on issues relevant to all the union's members. Some will also have national councils of the same types of workers across their union, in addition to the region-based councils. These councils typically represent the same types of workers, and so they are usually referred to as *sectoral councils*. Staying with SEIU as an example, it has three national councils: one for health care; one for building and property-related workers, such as janitors and security guards; and one for public service workers. These councils meet to focus on issues facing workers across those specific industries.

Generally, all of these different substructures—locals, regional, or statewide, and national councils—elect rank-and-file workers to hold official positions, meaning that there are thousands of elected officials with titles in just about every union. The main commonality that binds all workers and their various substructures is to which union they pay dues, meaning their per-paycheck taxes. (Workers in many unions even get to decide how much they'll pay in dues.)

Though unions and government bodies share mechanisms like representative elections and open, deliberative meetings, two unique tools make unions very different than a government: collective bargaining and strikes. Collective bargaining is a process through which workers, united through their union, sit down with management and hammer out the terms of their employment at a particular workplace, including pay, benefits, hours, shifts, schedules, promotions, vacation and time-off policies, uniform and dress code policies, discipline and appeal procedures, and so much more. Now is a good time to mention that the "so much more," along with what and how much workers win in the collective bargaining process, has everything to do with how much power they bring to the negotiations process. If workers can build 90 percent or greater unity among all themselves, develop a tight mobilization structure (which I'll discuss more in a later chapter), and win over the broader community in which they work and live, they can vote to authorize a strike. A strike is a worker-led action in which all the workers walk off the job, united, with purpose, and shutter production or seriously hamper the employer's ability to get much of anything done, including to make money.

So: unions are conduits for worker demands and fairness in the workplace. They are structured and function in much the same way as democratic governmental bodies, and though they might have complicated structures, they are often aligned across specific sectors of the economy. When they work well, unions are the voices of all of the workers in negotiations with management and can leverage worker solidarity to not only prevent management from treating workers poorly, but to force management to create a safer, equitable, and more joyous workplace.

To illustrate how unions actually make these changes happen, I've outlined three case studies in the remainder of this chapter. Set in the time after Donald Trump took office and before the 2018 midterm elections, each of these case studies highlights a worker who decided enough was enough, and brought her fellow workers' brains and power together in order to secure a more democratic and decent workplace. It's telling that each of these examples is pulled from growth sectors in today's economy—health care, education, and hospitality—led chiefly by women. These workers are taking on a range of issues both in the workplace and in their communities, and they're winning big and changing lives. Though unions have seen their ups and downs, the 1930s system can still work ninety years later—and these stories are proof.

Health Care

Jamie Rhodes, Pennsylvania

IN JUNE 2017, I walk into a nondescript chain restaurant across from the hospital, a place that specializes in breakfast twenty-four hours a day. Years of spilled pancake syrup gives the table a permanently sticky feeling, and I try in vain to rub off some of the residue on the table. It's the 3 P.M. shift change and I'm supposed to meet Jamie Rhodes, an interventional radiology tech (IR) at Delaware County Memorial Hospital (DelCo, in local parlance), in the suburbs of Philadelphia. But because most skilled hospital workers are often late to clock out because they're tending to patient-care needs, Jamie and I have a tacit understanding that there's not a fixed time for this meeting. Forty minutes after we were scheduled to meet, just past the cheaply framed poster on the faint yellow walls announcing "Tuesday, kids eat free"—which explains why it's so noisy inside— the door opens, and in walks a bedraggled young blond woman in well-worn scrubs. Although we'd been in many rooms together in 2016, we'd never had the chance to talk without hundreds of her coworkers around us or without the pressure to speed through important agenda items in a big meeting. Rhodes smiles and sits down, happy to get off her feet.

Rhodes is from a poor family, typical of much of today's swing state Pennsylvania. She's the second oldest of five kids, born and raised in Delaware County, just outside the Philadelphia city limits. Her mother was a homemaker—Rhodes's word—and also worked part time at a fast-food restaurant. Her father couldn't read or write and was a janitor for Sunoco. When she was a girl, her father was laid off for a time; she remembers when they really had no money at all. It was from this period—she can't remember how long it actually lasted because she was so young—that she clearly recalls a thought: "When I get older, I have to get a job where I can make money to support a family."

She's thirty-four years old with a husband and two kids. She's earned every penny in her working life at DelCo, a career that began when she was seventeen as part of a high school job training program through which the company paid her to help with administrative tasks, like filing and filling out paperwork. Throughout her senior year, she wasn't fretting about SAT scores or college admissions; every day, she went from school directly to the hospital. Before she graduated from high school, the human resources director at the hospital gave her some advice: she could earn more money, faster, if she went to the local community college, Delaware County Community College, for a two-year associate's degree in one of the medical technical fields.

The message was clear: forget about the idea of spending four years obtaining a well-rounded education at a liberal arts college, despite the numerous great universities all around Philadelphia. There was no way she could afford to attend those schools, and after her childhood experience of watching her father get laid off, there was no way she'd take on the kind of debt to make it possible. Plus, the hospital human resources director turned guidance counselor explained that Rhodes could continue working while she pursued a technical degree—a degree that would allow her to move into a job that would pay her considerably more in just two years. Rhodes took that advice, kept working, earned a two-year IR degree, and finally went full time at DelCo. She married young and had two kids, Nicholas and Brian. Life was full by her early twenties. Rhodes describes it in ways familiar to many working parents today, saying, "With each kid in a different school, plus my husband and I working, it keeps us really busy."

A few years into her new life as an IR tech, she first heard about the union when a catheter lab tech returned from a nurses' meeting about starting one. Cath lab techs, like all health care workers, are people you hope are well taken care of by their employer, since your life depends on their ability and alertness as they maneuver tiny, complex instruments into and around the heart. (Spoiler alert: they aren't well taken care of!) The cath lab tech crashed the nurses' meeting and asked them whether the techs could join too. When the nurse leading the meeting said they could, Rhodes says, "We all thought, heck, if the nurses can do this, we can, too." She had no idea how much time "we can, too" was about to occupy in a life that didn't have one extra minute to spare.

Word about the union made the rounds at the hospital. The next thing Rhodes knew, one supervisor cautioned, "'The union is only for the nurses; they won't look out for you,' and the next day, the same person suddenly handed us all raises!" Looking back on that moment, Rhodes laughs. The next few months were a whirlwind: workers received sporadic raises, which were often followed by threats to cut hours or fire workers. Rhodes often thought that they'd lose. As the effort to unionize rolled out, she also needed to attend many meetings, something she couldn't have predicted because she'd never heard about unions or understood how they worked. There were several per week, some long and some short. Rumors that a for-profit vulture—er, venture—capital firm known for making pet food and blue jeans rather than caring for patients wanted to buy DelCo, which was a locally run community hospital, were giving the campaign a fierce sense of urgency.

By the day of the union election on February 19, 2016—a day Rhodes will never forget—she was petrified. She had signed up to serve as a witness for the union during the last voting shift during the NLRB election, from 6 P.M. to 8 P.M. "I wanted to see who was coming in and to know who didn't make it to vote," Rhodes says. "And there were a lot of people I didn't know."

At precisely 8 P.M., the voting closed. The government staff who work NLRB elections have always been instructed to be meticulous in every part of the process. This is because more often than not, when workers attempt to form unions—especially if the workers win—the union-busting consultants (whom I'll discuss in greater detail in the next chapter) will almost invariably urge the employer to fabricate a claim of misconduct and kick off a legal proceeding designed to examine—and so delay—every second of the process. Additionally, the law dictates that representatives from management and the union serve as official legal observers of every count. "As soon as the officials closed everything, our union organizer . . . came over to say, 'Okay, Jamie, you need to be the union observer for the count,' and I wasn't sure what that meant," Rhodes recalls. "But within minutes, I was sitting with the government agents and the hospital managers, and examining each ballot as the officials counted yes, no, and contested votes. They read each one out loud."

By then a dozen or so union supporters had come into the room and everyone was tallying the yesses and nos as the count proceeded. "As soon as we reached the exact number, when we knew we won, I felt like I was at my wedding," Rhodes says. "I remember that at my wedding, I had a mysterious, sudden, nervous quiver: my lips quivered and I couldn't stop it. I had never had it before. I wanted it so passionately, my wedding. I had been in love with my husband for ten years, and we were finally getting married. And at that union election vote count, I had a quiver in my lips! There's only two times in my life that happened: when we won the union and during my wedding."

Not everyone gets that chance.

As soon as they won their union election, Rhodes and her coworkers began phase two of forming a union: negotiations. This involves finding out what everyone wants in their first union contract, drawing up proposals that reflect top priorities, ratifying the proposals, electing the workers who will represent them, and starting negotiations with management. Good union contracts reflect the workforce and are tailored to whatever the workers themselves want, provided they can muster the power required to win those demands.

But it takes a lot of personal and professional time and effort to get to that point. The DelCo workers were several months into their contract talks when, Rhodes says, "My husband began freaking out, complaining about how much time I was spending on negotiations and all my union work. I'd go out to a meeting, and when I was at the door, he'd say, 'We have young kids, and you need to be a mom.' Every time he used those words, it'd hurt. But I'd explain, 'I really have to go,' and leave him with the boys." Unlike the lightning-fast election process, the negotiations dragged on, with even more drag than usual because the owners of PetCo and Lucky Brand Jeans, Prospect Holdings, purchased the longtime community hospital shortly after the election. That's right: suddenly decisions about patient care would be dictated by people who pored over quarterly numbers of whether sales of dry kibble versus wet food or skinny jeans versus bell-bottoms made more money, and for whom the bottom line—and not how quickly your aunt is recovering from a heart attack or cancer—is paramount. The sale of the hospital interrupted the negotiations, and management continued to trip up the collective bargaining process with well-known tactics, such as canceling pre-agreed meeting dates at the last minute or making itself unavailable for long periods of time.

After one year of more than two dozen negotiation sessions, and after swing-state Pennsylvania voted for Donald Trump over Hillary Clinton, Rhodes knew: "I knew we had to have a strike, because the other side wasn't moving. I had to just hope my coworkers would trust me and support me when I said we have to go on strike." Rhodes had been elected by her peers to serve on the union negotiations team. She was sure management didn't think the workers would, or could, really pull off a strike. It's a rare moment when bosses' unacceptably low expectations of their workers actually help the working class.

The workers voted overwhelmingly to hold a two-day strike, understanding full well their pet-food-making bosses at Prospect would likely lock them out for an additional three days, making it a one-week work stoppage, with no pay. They knew this because hospital employers routinely lock their workers out—they literally prevent workers from clocking in—once there's a strike. In the employers' minds, this is a way to punish workers. The spin doctors in the health care industry say this is because, unlike a factory or a school, the facility doesn't close when workers vote to strike in a health care setting. Patients still need care. Health care employers use the excuse that the agencies that specialize in recruiting scab labor (strikebreaker workers, usually hired from Southern states) require them to sign contracts that schedule this replacement labor for a minimum of five days. The scab agencies say it's worth it only if they can charge for at least five days because they have to pay strikebreakers top dollar (often twice as much as the regular staff), put them in premium hotels, give them equally premium meal per diems, fly them last minute, and generally spend a ton of money— all to defeat mostly women workers demanding an end to income inequality and fighting for fair work rules.

Since 1974, when health care workers were added to the list of workers covered under the National Labor Relations Act (which I'll discuss more in a later chapter), these workers have to legally give ten days' notice before they strike to allow the hospital to schedule replacement workers. One of the purposes of this ten-day period is to force the negotiating parties to come to an agreement while the clock is ticking. It would be cheaper—and way better for the patients, of course—for management to decide to respect the people doing the work and just settle a contract with the hospital workers. Just like it'd be cheaper if the United States had a single-payer health care system. Both options fly in the face of a few people at the top making a lot of money.

By the time of the DelCo strike, which began March 6, 2017, workers decided that they wouldn't picket overnight because they wanted patients to sleep. Instead, they'd raise hell from morning to evening, and everyone had to sign up for four-hour picketing shifts. Rhodes signed up for the first four-hour shift, which began at 6 A.M. on a Monday. She quickly found she didn't want to ever leave the picket line, in which, despite rain and cold, the workers were building the kind of unbreakable solidarity that terrifies employers.

Keep in mind that these are workers who generally don't have time for bathroom breaks, let alone getting to know their coworkers from other parts of the same facility. Rhodes says, "My husband called to ask, 'You did your four hours, why are you still there?' And I said, 'I want to be here, I need to be here,' but I started to worry if all this went on much longer, he'd divorce me. But it felt awesome to walk around the hospital picketing and take ownership of it and be like, 'This is our hospital.' A lot of times I'd be looking at my Fitbit and realize I got way more steps than on a normal day!" By the second day, she persuaded her husband and the kids to join her. Her sons cobbled together some picket signs that read, JAMIE'S OUR MOM AND SHE DESERVES MORE.

The strike line stretched the length of half a football field, a suburban block. One hundred percent of the nurses were out on the line, and of the techs like Rhodes, only seven workers ever crossed the picket line, meaning that they worked when everyone else was outside picketing: seven people from the lab who apparently received extra-sweet raises. Anyone who has ever been on strike before—and plenty of hospital workers in Rhodes's new union had—understood that the dynamic on a picket line is crucial. And so union organizers brought big speakers and made song lists—more like dance mixes—selected by the workers in the days leading up to the walkout. People who were total strangers, often from the neighborhood, were coming to the line each day, picking up signs and marching with the workers. Folks were playing games like mannequin on the line: when the line stopped dancing, everyone would freeze and pose and make crazy faces, and someone would take photos so they could later vote who had the best pose, then start again. The nuns in the Catholic church adjacent to the hospital opened their doors for the workers, and often their kids, to use the restrooms throughout the day.

Management, who had set up a viewing station safe from the weather behind the glass on the second floor, constantly watched every interaction and asked the nuns to stop letting the strikers use the church. When the nuns explained they supported the workers, the story went viral on the picket line. Workers from other union-ized hospitals showed up with barbecue grills to cook and serve food. Passing cars and trucks were blaring their horns, disturbing the quiet of the neighborhood. The workers were impossible to ig-nore.

Five days and a public relations disaster for management later, negotiations were back on. Only this time, it was clear the employer decided to get a contract over with quickly to avoid any more bad news coverage. By early April, despite the behemoth out-of-state multinational corporation the workers were fighting, the strike produced the level of worker power needed to win their first con-tract.

At the sticky diner table, as I listened to Rhodes finish her story, the sounds of the even-more-crowded restaurant were magically drowned out by the intensity of her smile and stare. "We got what we wanted: we got management to listen," she tells me. "We got what we needed, a union contract. And I got a fifteen-thousand-dollar annual raise in the first year alone. It's so interesting now, those in charge actually listen to us, which they never did before. We never had labor-management meetings, and now we do. We could never discuss when things were unsafe; now we do. My manager never used to get back to me about anything, but now she responds right away. Not only that, but she seeks out my opinion because she knows I know more about what's happening on the floors than she does. Even now, I find myself at home in the kitchen and the chants from that strike are stuck in my head! I am still trying to get used to it all."

When I asked how things are with her husband, Rhodes told me with relief, "He felt so much better about it all once I got the raise."

Not every worker can take on a multinational vulture capital firm and succeed, but skilled hospital workers can and in this case did, using the same grit and determination they use when they save patients' lives. There are nearly 5.95 million hospital workers in the United States, and 5.6 million don't yet have a union. If you add in nursing homes, not including home care, there's another 1.6 million, and 1.29 million are nonunion. Unless the baby boomers relocate to China, these jobs aren't moving. This is an incredibly powerful bloc.

Education

Wendy Peters, West Virginia

IT WAS EARLY EVENING ON TUESDAY, February 27, 2018, when Wendy Peters answered her cell phone. The distinctly poor quality of a voice-via-Bluetooth-in-the-car didn't disguise her thick Southern accent, her exhaustion, or her exhilaration. When I asked her where she was and if she was able to talk, Peters replied that she was thirty minutes from the site of the Battle of Blair Mountain—a 1921 strike that became the country's largest armed conflict since the end of the Civil War. One hundred workers were killed when over one million rounds of ammunition were unleashed against the strikers over several days by private mercenaries hired by the coal companies. The symbolism wasn't lost on either of us.

Wendy Peters is a fifth-grade teacher at Daniels Elementary School, in Raleigh County, West Virginia. She grew up in the coal fields of McDowell County, an area with the distinction in 2016 of ranking sixth out of 3,007 counties nationwide when the category is "poorest household family income": $24,707. Peters had told me, "This level of poverty is exactly what the big coal companies have always left behind after taking everything they wanted out of our communities." Her father works for the Mine Safety and Health Administration (MSHA). Her grandfather on her mother's side was a quiet man, proud, and a fiercely loyal member of the United Mine

Workers of America (UMWA). Peters will quickly tell you that the only reason her family had health care when she was growing up was the union. Continuing the tradition of men and the mines, her older brother, Dennis, is a coal miner. Her mother is, in Peters's words, a "great" teacher who went on to be an elementary school principal.

Seeking to escape the destiny of doing the same type of job her mother (and many women of a certain era) did, Peters earned a degree in travel administration. But no sooner had she completed her studies than she realized, "I always loved school and education, loved it," she says. "I don't know what I was thinking, trying to avoid it, because I understand my teaching as a kind of calling, as something I have to do. So it didn't take long to drop tourism and get directly to teaching. I honestly can't imagine doing anything else." Peters is forty years old and has been teaching for sixteen years, making her a little too young for the last time teachers in West Virginia did what she had just done: walk out of every school in the state, demanding that all kids have a right to a high-quality education and the educators have a right to a decent life. However, when the teachers went on strike in 1990, there wasn't 100 percent participation. It wasn't a statewide walkout, nor had the schools actually closed, because the service personnel hadn't walked out with them. That means school buses picked up kids, cafeteria workers cooked food, and administrators spent long days not teaching but keeping all the kids in strike schools in the gym, playing kickball and such, because there were too many kids of too varying ages to try to teach. The 1990 strike ended with a whimper as legal injunctions mandated that the teachers return to work.

For Wendy Peters, the stakes in the 2018 strike were clear. She said, "I have a five-year-old, Matthew. When he's in middle school or high school, I want him to have a good education. This is about whether he will have a qualified teacher. Ultimately the strike is about the idea of a good education being the great equalizer. As a teacher myself, I will always advocate for my own child, but there are many kids who have no one to advocate for them. We can be that voice." Advocating for kids is precisely the reason Peters had become the locally elected chapter leader of the Raleigh County Education Association, her county's branch of the statewide West Virginia Education Association, one of two teachers' unions in a state so hostile to organized labor it routinely gunned down coal miners for taking the kind of strong stand she suddenly found herself leading.

Automation of the mines has long since gutted the industry of its workers and hobbled the once-mighty UMWA. By the time the granddaughters of the workers in struggles like Blair Mountain walked off the job in all fifty-five counties in West Virginia, education was the leading employer in thirty counties and the second-largest employer in the next twenty. This makes the teachers, 75 percent of whom are women, the most strategic workforce today when it comes to wrestling with a power structure still controlled by the fossil-fuel industry and still acting like the entire state is a one-way piggy bank, taking everything out and leaving nothing for the residents.

As is almost always the case, the media that actually did cover the story spun the strike about money for the workers. The propaganda war against unions has long portrayed them as greedy and purely self-interested. But better pay was only one part of what the teachers were fighting for. "Wages and health benefits are almost a distraction," she says. "They were important, but there were five major stances we took before walking out." One issue that was most important to her was legislation to expand charter schools. Devised by right-wing think tanks like ALEC, the American Legislative Exchange Council, it was a particularly noxious scheme in which the state would create cash value vouchers that could be used to fund homeschooling. In a state of fairly dire poverty, it's not hard to imagine that if parents could suddenly get money to homeschool a kid, many children wouldn't be left in public schools. The second most important issue that drove Peters to the picket lines would have eliminated seniority—one of the few ways that schools retained good teachers. The legislative bills advancing each proposal were quickly working their way through the law-making process.

For at least twenty years, well-funded operations backed by corporate billionaires have pushed for the end—literally—of brick-and-mortar schools by any means necessary. They've also tried to make seniority the cause of school failure, rather than, say, the steady withdrawal of public school funding, which has accompanied the great transfer of wealth from the working class to the 1 percent. According to Peters, "I have a master's degree and years of being a good teacher. I am highly qualified, and their bill on seniority would have let them replace me with someone way less expensive, unqualified, and incapable of actually giving a good education to our kids. Seniority done well has everything to do with quality education because it keeps skilled educators in the classroom."

The third of the five issues was a basic worker-rights issue. It was a piece of legislation, cynically dubbed paycheck protection, that was drummed up by the billionaires' lobby and was snaking its way through states like West Virginia, where Republicans were in control of all three branches of government. This attack on workers freedoms was also the brainchild of ALEC and aimed to weaken unions by taking away workers' choice to deduct union dues through the payroll system. Even though workers could still use payroll deductions to, say, choose to donate to charities like the United Way via the employer payroll system, the proposed law would prevent them from doing the same for union dues. And on top of that, they hadn't gotten a raise in eight years, meaning the mostly male legislators refused to give them any money, but at the same time, wanted to control what the mostly women educators could choose to do with a measly paycheck!

West Virginia in 2018 was already a right-to-work state, where workers have no right to collective bargaining, where union membership is voluntary, and where the entire apparatus of the state is aimed at preventing exactly what wound up happening: an explosion of worker power. To Peters and other raise-denied workers listening to the conservative legislators testifying in hearings about controlling what they could and could not do with their own paycheck, this piece of legislation was a pure, unmitigated insult to their intelligence.

The final two issues of the strike were financial: the rising cost of health insurance coupled with eight years with no raise. The proposals for their health care went beyond merely raising the employees' share of the cost. The health insurance plan changes for 2018 also included a provision called Go 365, a phone app that required workers to wear devices like a Fitbit to transmit their personal data to offset some of the proposed copay increases. "It was a complete, total invasion of our privacy," Peters pointed out. In addition, the health insurance would have been using a new calculation that based the charges on total family income, not the individual employee's. "By adding my husband, I was facing a two-hundred-dollar-a-month increase," Peters says. "So when the governor offered a one percent pay raise in January, people had had enough."

When I was on the phone, talking with Wendy as she drove home, it was Tuesday, February 27, and it was the fourth day of a strike with 34,000 employees out. The strike shut down every school in the state. A steady stream of 10,000 people a day protested in the state capitol while others staffed picket lines around their schools. The parents of 279,899 kids simultaneously supported the strikers and scrambled to find places for their kids to stay. That day, West Virginia governor Jim Justice sat down and hammered out an agreement with the executives of the unions. By midafternoon, the news media reported the strike was over. And this was the reason for my cold call to Wendy Peters.

It was a huge victory. The proposed contract included a publicly declared commitment by the governor to veto all the anti-union legislation and a 5 percent raise for all the education workers, not just the 20,000 teachers but also the 14,000 service personnel who had never won what the teachers won until deciding to go on strike with them. There was a freeze on the proposed premium and co-pay increases in the plan for at least one full year, a reversal on the invade-employees'-privacy app requirement, and the creation of a task force on health care that guaranteed organized labor seats at the table—each of the three striking unions would get to appoint a member. It was a breathtaking win by any standards, not just the ones in conservative West Virginia. According to Peters, who had been standing on the steps of the state capitol listening to the details of the offer from the governor, "We won on all five stances—everything, which is pretty incredible." She got in her car and started driving home. But it wasn't over yet.

Within hours of the proposed settlement being announced, the right-wing members of the West Virginia legislature set out to upend the agreement. Governor Justice is a coal baron. According to media reports, he's the wealthiest individual in West Virginia. He ran for office in 2016 as a Democrat and won, but later switched parties and became a Republican after Trump took office. This meant exactly no one trusted the governor: not the unions, who had all endorsed him as a Democrat; nor the senate leadership, the most ideologically right-wing body in the state.

As Peters was triumphantly driving home, the senate president, Mitch Carmichael, announced on the radio that the senate didn't plan to approve the settlement. West Virginia radio station WSAZ reported that "Senate President Mitch Carmichael speculated that as many as twenty-two Republicans in the thirty-four-member senate will oppose Governor Justice's plan." Wednesday was supposed to be a cooling-off day, with everyone getting ready to return to their classrooms on Thursday, March 1. Instead of a cooling off, rolling strike votes began spreading across the state. Within hours, in all fifty-five counties, workers voted to defy their leaders and continue the strike until both the house and the senate voted on the settlement and it was signed into law by the governor. Given the comments from the senate president, that choice to strike was nothing shy of brilliant.

True to their word, the state senate voted down the deal. For the next seven days, five of which were school days, the right-wing legislators held up the deal, playing divide-and-conquer games, voting to give teachers more and the other personnel less, and then voting to add state police to the 5 percent raise but keeping everyone else at 3 percent. At every turn, Peters and her coworkers stood their ground, saying there would be no schools opening in West Virginia until the senate approved the deal the governor offered. Every day, the strikers held firm and fought hard, surrounding the capitol and holding hands, taking turns going inside the capitol to chant and protest and prevent legislators from getting anything done.

On March 6, 2018, the right-wing senate folded. Not only did they cave, but because they had initially started adding workers such as state police into the mix as a way to foment division between other workers, and, basically, to spite the education strikers, the educators wound up lifting *every* West Virginian state employee to a 5 percent raise, not only the education workers. That's right, the educators got the state police, roads workers, and everyone else on the state payroll a raise those workers could not have won because they did not strike. They achieved this in a right-to-work state entirely controlled by Republicans in all three branches of government. They understood that to win, to not go down in the record books as another huge defeat, they had to stay on strike and escalate the crisis.

REMARKABLY, ONE YEAR LATER, in March 2019, the West Virginia legislature launched a stealth attack on the teachers and tried to push through their Republican school privatization bill *again*. The same cabal of right-wing state senators introduced a version of the voucher bill and were steering it as fast as they legally could to passage, assuming that they could move faster than the time it would take for 34,000 educators to prepare to strike. The senate took up the voucher bill on a Monday, discharged it out of committee, and voted to approve it in the full senate, sending it to the house for a vote the next day.

But within hours, by that same Monday evening, the workers called for a strike the next morning. As proof that strikes are like a muscle—the more workers use them the stronger they get—the educators didn't flinch, and on Tuesday, February 19, 2019, a massive strike shut down schools in all fifty-five counties. Like the year before, even when given an assurance that they won—that the house wouldn't take up the bill—the educators remained in the state capitol for a second day to be sure they had ironclad agreements with elected leaders that the school privatization bill was dead. The nearly two weeks walking the picket lines less than one year earlier resulted in a deafening victory through a strike, for a second year in a row. This time, the media couldn't get confused that the strike had one purpose—saving public education and opening up a future for the youth of West Virginia. There was no other issue but a Koch brothers–backed scheme to eliminate public schools. Mostly women educators defeated billionaires, again.

That's the power of an all-out strike.

Hospitality

Irma Perez, California

IT'S OCTOBER 20, 2018, and it's louder than an orchestra or rock concert on the 2200 block of Broadway in downtown Oakland,

California. Irma Perez is working her bullhorn like a trumpet virtuoso. She's standing in the middle of hundreds of people who've made plastic buckets into drums, their hands holding perfect rhythm as they harmonize their chant: "Hey hey, ho ho—Mar-i-ott has got to go!" She has the kind of energy that can motivate everyone on the picket line for days on end, dancing as she's chanting to remind the workers and their supporters that they are fighting for a better life, for the freedom from having to work two full-time jobs. Every picket sign has the strike slogan and the worker's demand, ONE JOB SHOULD BE ENOUGH!

Perez was born and raised in Guanajuato, Mexico. She's a mother of three. Her daughter, Carolina, is thirty years old. Her second child, Abraham, is twenty-eight. David is the youngest; he's twenty-six. But Perez was so youthful that you'd never guess that she's fifty-two. I sat down with her in a café a block away from the picket line at the Oakland Marriott. With a deep smile, she reached for her phone to show me pictures of her children and started talking about her four grandchildren. Two live in Mexico, and two live near her in the East Bay, in California. "Near her" changed recently, because Perez—like so many other workers—lost the first house she owned during the housing crisis brought on by the unregulated financial industry in 2008. She was forced out of a nice neighborhood in Berkeley and now lives with her brother, sister-in-law, and their two kids near the towering Oakland Coliseum, where schools, access to public transit, and all available services drop precipitously in quality.

Perez's day job is at the Marriott-owned Courtyard hotel in Oakland. She's been working there for seventeen years. Because she's such a natural leader among her peers, her union, UNITE-HERE, the primary hotel and hospitality workers' union in the United States, leveraged a provision they had negotiated for in their previous collective bargaining—one that generally takes substantial worker power to win in a union contract—known as union leave.

This type of leave provision allows unions to bring people like Perez to work with the union for a specified period, generally with the union reimbursing the employer so the worker will stay on the company payroll—accruing seniority and hours toward their benefits (especially retirement)—but having a chance to develop their leadership capacity by doing hands-on full-time union activities. Perez has been serving as the lead union spokesperson for a campaign launched by her and her coworkers to win safeguards from sexual harassment.

The campaign she's working on, a collaboration between her union, UNITE-HERE, and a local community-based organization, the East Bay Alliance for a Sustainable Economy, EBASE, secured enough signatures to get a ballot initiative—in California and some other states, a ballot initiative is a law that residents petition to place on the ballot—qualified for the November 6, 2018, election in the city of Oakland. The initiative, known as Measure Z, is part of a broader campaign run by her national union, called Hands Off, Pants On, or HOPO. "I think that we have to put a face on the abuse that we deal with," Perez explains. "There is a lot of abuse of the women who clean hotel rooms. We want people to understand what is behind the scenes when they walk into their hotel room and they see it all clean, pretty, and perfumed. Behind that, there is something hidden, which is the sexual harassment of the workers who make the rooms so nice for the guests."

The numbers are shocking: more than half the hotel employees in her city, and all cities surveyed, experience sexual harassment routinely. Long before the Harvey Weinstein hotel scandal put the wind in the sails of the #MeToo movement, the hotel workers' union was tackling sexual harassment in the workplace. In a twelve-page detailed report dated July 2016, titled simply, "Hands Off Pants On, Sexual Harassment in Chicago's Hospitality Industry," UNITE-HERE documented that 49 percent of housekeepers report having experienced men exposing themselves, and 58 percent of hotel workers and 77 percent of casino workers report having been sexually harassed by a guest.

As a result, women hotel workers who were union members worked with their union to come up with solutions to the crisis of sexual harassment of hotel workers. In their biggest victory, in the nation's third-largest city, Chicago, the union won a new citywide ordinance in 2017 mandating that every city hotel provide hotel workers a GPS-connected emergency (or panic) button that they could wear on their uniforms. By the time Perez and her colleagues in Oakland began to demand the same law, but to be placed on the 2018 ballot as a voter initiative, called Measure Z, they wanted even more than their mostly women colleagues had achieved in Chicago: the creation of a registry of hotel guests who sexually harass workers in order to ban offending customers from making reservations and thereby hopefully shaming those offenders by refusing them a room. Measure Z would also create a new city department with whom hotel employees can file complaints and from whom they can expect enforcement when hotel operators aren't listening or following the law. This is smart legislating, as many laws that are passed don't have any enforcement mechanism. But the hotel workers' union has learned how to bolster the implementation of each law they've won.

"The harassment is very common. You even start to see it as normal, because it's happening all the time," Perez says. "You're always seeing men who are naked or masturbating when you come in to clean the rooms. It happens in hotels every single day. When we complain to management, they don't do anything. The managers are men, and they usually just laugh. They'll tell us, 'Don't worry about it, nothing will happen, go get one of your coworkers and have her come in to the room with you to finish cleaning.' They always tell us that the guests come first."

But workers get penalized by management for failing to meet

their grueling per shift room cleaning quota. In nonunion hotels, the mostly women-of-color workers are expected to clean on average thirty rooms per shift; in a union hotel with a good contract, the maximum allowable is fifteen. The idea that one hotel worker who feels threatened by an aggressive guest is going to go find another coworker, and ask her to stop cleaning her room—and miss her quota—so she can chaperone is ludicrous. Perez is proud that her union is leading a campaign that will help union and nonunion hotel workers alike. "Since I have a union and a contract, we have some standards already, and the boss has to respect them," she says. "But there are lots of hotels that don't have any standards. And the saddest part about this is that the bosses will make them go and punch out and then finish doing their work so that they don't get paid."

On the picket line, Perez is also fighting to save her high-quality, low-cost health insurance plan, for which the largest chain in the world and über-profitable Marriott hotel company wants to make the workers' pay considerably more each month. To Perez, these two fights—against sexual harassment and for the right to good health care—are two sides of the same coin. "This strike is important because, first of all, it is historic," she says. "In the past, the company has negotiated with us in good faith. But this time, they refused to. So we have been forced to go on strike in what is Marriott's first strike ever. We are very strong right now. At this hotel, only three union members crossed the picket line."

Supermajority participation strikes work. Perez and her colleagues won their fight against Marriott and ratified their new contract on November 2, 2018. Four days later, Perez won again when voters in Oakland overwhelmingly passed the union-backed hotel worker safety law, 76.29 percent yes to 22.71 percent no. Apparently, ordinary Americans are more sympathetic to mostly female housekeepers walking empty hotel hallways and entering hotel rooms alone than the mostly male hotel managers. The Hands Off, Pants On campaign began before the Weinstein scandal and continues today, moving to new cities and new states. To date, Perez's national union, UNITE-HERE, has passed versions of these laws protecting workers in Chicago, Seattle, Oakland, and Long Beach, California.

* * *

I can tell these three stories about three women in three distinct states, spanning three industries, all relying on the same mechanisms—strikes and the unions behind them—to make huge gains in 2017 and 2018 because of a law written in 1935. The strike, and the unions behind the strike, remains the most effective path to economic, and therefore political, freedom for the working and middle classes.

In addition to the wins I've already listed, the three unions in the case studies here have secured the right to affordable, high-quality health care; equitable pay; pay policies that eliminate gender and racial disparities, and favoritism; the right to keep control over your own schedule; improvements in safety on the job, for the workers as well as the patients, students, or guests; effective tools to combat sexual harassment; advances in paid time off, whether to have and get to love a baby, to take vacation, or get sick and avoid getting everyone else sick by going to work. Part of what makes unions and collective bargaining so effective is that workers themselves pull up to the negotiation table to decide how to redistribute the profits they make for others and design rules that actually solve their immediate problems. No other mechanisms engage the ingenuity of workers themselves.

There's something else that is fundamental to and instructive about these stories, something bigger and more important than any one issue: in order to unionize and win big, workers need to build and rebuild deep solidarity. People can choose their friends, but they can't choose their comrades. Strikes, and good union campaigns to win big on issues, are the best political education because they unite all kinds of different people, encouraging and enabling people to get beyond the self-segregation and prejudices people hold about one another (and that antisocial media reinforce). In unions, most workers decide to vote to unionize not because someone tells them to—that's never worked. No, they vote because the experience of a well-executed union campaign helps workers understand, on their own, that their employer's effect on their lives goes beyond assigning them to an overtime shift and preventing them from getting time with their family; that their employer is part of a bigger system that is contributing to the failure of their kids' schools, the rollback of anti-pollution and anti-gentrification laws, the gross inequities of the tax system, and more. It's no accident that the states, cities, and counties with the strongest union presence have consistently voted in favor of progressive policies. This is the crucial reason the corporate right wing has been relentlessly attacking unions. A well-unionized worker is a woke worker, and woke workers can change the direction of this country.

CHAPTER 2

Who Killed the Unions?

> The enemy was the collective spirit. I got a hold of that spirit and while
> it was a seedling; I poisoned it, choked it, bludgeoned it if I had to,
> anything to be sure it would never blossom into a united workforce. . . .
> Likewise, as the consultants go about the business of destroying
> unions, they invade people's lives, demolish their friendships, crush
> their will, and shatter families.

> —Martin Jay Levitt, *Confessions of a Union Buster*

BY MANY MEASURES, THE NATIONAL POLITICAL STAGE OVER THE
past fifteen years—culminating in the 2016 and 2018 elections—
has showcased a flagrant disregard for democracy. A brief survey
of the brash, out-in-the-open, unapologetic, outrageous, take-no-
prisoners behavior of Republican operatives includes former Wisconsin governor Scott Walker dismembering worker rights weeks
into his first term in 2011 through his final days in office in 2019,
when he changed state laws to hamstring and weaken the power
of the incoming Democratic governor; the recently minted governor Brian Kemp's handling of his own seriously tainted election in
Georgia in 2018; the spring 2019 actions of the Florida legislature

and new governor (who himself might not have won had the Florida election been free and fair) to thwart the citizen ballot initiative passed with a 2:1 approval in November 2018 and that was intended to reenfranchise 1.4 million African American voters by 2020; and the explicit efforts by current or former high-level presidential administration players, such as Stephen Miller and Steve Bannon, to gin up resentment between different sections of the American public. Donald Trump himself has stated that he won the election through a combination of targeted voter suppression and dividing the working class.

The power of unions has nosedived over the past forty years because workers in the United States have been regularly subjected to *precisely* the kind of polarizing political processes America experienced in 2016. By the time I became a union organizer in 1997, there were two sets of players that American workers routinely faced if they tried to form a union: the official union-busting consultants, whose specialty is just what it sounds like, and the legions of law firms, or big divisions within even bigger firms, which try hard to distinguish themselves from the union busters but do similar work. They call themselves union-avoidance firms and the difference between union busters and union-avoidance lawyers is the same as between the Ku Klux Klan and the White Citizens' Councils.

You could say that Republicans have taken a page of out of union busters' playbooks. Long before Donald Trump entered the presidential race, employers have been weaponizing many key elements of his campaign strategy against workers who attempt to unionize. I can count as high as exactly zero the number of NLRB elections I've been involved in where the hired union busters didn't stoke racial and/or ethnic divisions early, often, and throughout the campaign; where gerrymandering hasn't been routine (entire units of workers carved out of the list just before the NLRB election); and when voter suppression hasn't been a central part of their strategy.

The primary reason for the decline of unions—and the standard of living of most Americans—rests with the extensive union-busting industry that is almost entirely unregulated, absolutely vicious, and unique to the United States. Before diving into a granular discussion of what union busters do, however, it's important to understand *why* the billionaire class developed an entire sector called the union-avoidance industry. Just as any honest history of the United States begins with genocide against its indigenous people, the real history of what became contemporary union busting starts with slavery. Both slavery and union busting are uniquely American in violence, in virulence, and in their existence as fully legally sanctioned. It's indisputable that from the time of colonization up to the Civil War, the largest workforces in the United States were slaves. They had no rights, no wages, and lived under an official regime of terror.

It's equally indisputable that corporations' efforts to divide the working class by using race, class, and sex as a cudgel isn't just a bygone of our history, nor is effective voter suppression in union or civic elections. Rather, these tactics remain the core strategy for the ultrawealthy. Although this country's history is one of intense worker oppression, the formalization of the union-avoidance industry took place when inequality was easing and when American workers were making real gains. What was happening when giant corporations decided they needed an army of private special forces whose sole purpose was undoing the core human traits of compassion, solidarity, and collective action by way of psychological and physical warfare?

The American Dream Is Born

In October 1929, the stock market crash announced the beginning of the worldwide Great Depression. During the Depression, one out of every four people who wanted work was unemployed in the United States. In some other countries, it was one in three. Socialist movements around the world had been in existence for decades, and they grew stronger as the Depression discredited the capital-ist system. The Soviet Union was building its industrial economy during the Depression; to millions of people, it looked as if it was succeeding whereas capitalism was failing. The Soviet Union also gave rhetorical and even material support to communist parties worldwide that were organizing workers to end the private own-ership of the economy altogether. In socialism, the employer class saw a threat to its property, and many of its constituents resorted to even greater violence to stop the threat. In Germany, big busi-ness funded Hitler's rise to power in 1933 because they saw him as the only way to protect themselves from Russian communism.

Employers in the United States were not an exception to this trend. Many, like General Motors, Goodyear Tire, and Ford, hired thugs and stockpiled guns and other munitions left over from World War I. But another faction of employers, consisting mainly of small business and corporate leaders with Catholic or Jewish backgrounds, as well as major retail beverage companies, saw a different way to save capitalism. They would support policies that would improve workers' conditions and agree to a new legal frame-work that would contain the employers' violence, which threatened to destabilize society. This faction of employers supported the suc-cessful 1932 presidential campaign of Franklin Delano Roosevelt despite the opposition of other employers who hated him, even be-fore the emergence of his New Deal policies, because they were fine with the brute force repression strategy.

In the twentieth century, prior to FDR's election, there was one main national labor federation, the American Federation of Labor. The AFL unions, most of them founded in the latter part of the 1800s, focused nearly exclusively on unionizing only skilled workers, even in factory settings. The obvious weakness of their approach was that most workers were considered unskilled. The unskilled workers were black, brown, immigrants, and women, and by avoiding organizing them, the AFL was also avoiding drawing the added ire of racist employers. Even though their growth was stultified by their focus on highly skilled workers, this blind spot in their strategy was masked by the mobilization of the U.S. workforce for World War I, which created exceptionally tight labor markets. A special War Labor Board was established that temporarily mitigated virulent employer opposition to unions in exchange for wartime labor peace—meaning workers wouldn't strike or protest as long as management gave them what they wanted in terms of wages and benefits. Outside the World War I wartime increase in unionization rates, the only unions that were making progress were those whose workers were considered moderately skilled, such as bakers, brewers, cigar makers, seamstresses, and other women in the needle trades; to win, they helped build and relied on a strong pro-union consumer movement that used consumer boycotts of products lacking a union label to back their demands.

In the first several years after Roosevelt was sworn into office in 1933, he faced not only marches and other unrest among the unemployed, but also strikes by millions of workers who still had jobs: longshoremen closing West Coast ports, a general strike in Seattle, a strike in Minneapolis by transport workers that was close to a general strike, a massive strike in Ohio, and a textile strike in North Carolina, to name only a few. Workers were sick and tired of watching their employers' profits increasing while they and their families were suffering mightily. The strikes were creating a crisis for employers and government alike.

The result was sweeping, pro-working-class change. In 1935, in a span of just three months, Franklin D. Roosevelt won approval for the Works Progress Administration (hiring the unemployed masses for important purposes, such as building the national parks), the Social Security Act (essentially old-age insurance), and the National Labor Relations Act. The NLRA, sometimes referred to as the Wagner Act (named after Robert F. Wagner, the New York senator who introduced it), was signed into law on July 5, 1935, and created the legal architecture that legitimated unions, transforming them from organizations the employers could ignore without penalty into legally binding mechanisms that could practice collective bargaining.

The NLRA radically changed the power equation in the United States by extending the freedoms of a democracy from the rather limited sphere of civil society into the heart of market capitalism: the economy and the workplace. Since the founding of the country, the United States had held elections for government officials, based on the idea that government derived its legitimacy only from "the consent of the governed." Of course, many workers were excluded from the franchise for most of our history, and some still are. But by the late 1800s, with the advent of huge megacorporations, it became crystal clear that the major decisions that affected people's lives—economic decisions about where to build, where to invest, what to make, whom to hire and fire, how much workers were paid, and the conditions of their work—were not made by elected officials but by private dictatorships: the owners of landed property and capital.

Allowing only 1 percent of the population—CEOs, executives, and big shareholders—to determine the rules of the economy had nearly destroyed the nation when the stock market crashed. Unions, to the people who came to identify as New Dealers, would be a key societal mechanism to tame and balance the reckless behavior of the billionaire class, whose total disregard for everyone but itself had led to the Great Depression. New Dealers understood that workers could not realistically compete with owners—including shareholders—in a "free market system" without the freedom to withhold their labor, that is, to strike. The NLRA gave individual workers the freedom to choose to collectively make demands inside the market economy and at the level where workers could have the most effect: in their workplaces.

The aspects of the law that mattered most were those that prohibited employers from campaigning against unions. These provisions declared acts of violence and other forms of harassment and intimidation—rampant at the time—to be "unfair practices" that would be punishable by federal law. Employers were also not permitted to refuse to negotiate with workers in the collective bargaining process. This meant that collective bargaining was now a sanctioned, legitimate practice. There is no question the NLRA represented unprecedented progress for most Americans. It was the most radical worker rights law to date, though it contained a damning compromise.

That compromise was codifying the racial and sexual stratification of the working class. This division had begun hundreds of years before, when the largest segment of workers in the United States weren't fully considered people: black slaves. In 1935, the racist Southern delegation in Congress, fiercely committed to keeping Jim Crow laws in place, correctly viewed unions as a threatening force that could, and often did, demand integrated workplaces. These racists combined their votes with Northern members of Congress who were beholden to the billionaire class (names that now have a philanthropic ring to them and are commonly found on libraries and museums, including Carnegie, Rockefeller, and Pew).

This coalition held enough votes to block the law. To win passage of the New Deal, President Franklin D. Roosevelt compromised by exempting two occupations dominated by African Americans— agricultural and domestic labor—from the provisions of the NLRA. This effectively condemned many African Americans to a second-class status under the first *national* labor law covering workers across the private sector. (This provision is still the law of the land, and today also represses many Latinx and other people of color.) Government workers were also excluded. It would take almost thirty years until another round of worker pressure, stemming from the civil rights movement, and a 1962 executive order by John F. Kennedy, to begin to soften the path for public-sector unionization, which I'll discuss later in this chapter.

Even with racist restrictions on black-dominated industries, unions grew exponentially after the passage of the NLRA. Factory workers—which did include African Americans—led massive unionization drives and won. Previously hard-fought defeats in auto, steel, coal, and transport turned into hard-fought victories. But it wasn't just the law that changed. A new federation of labor was formed as the ink was drying on the NLRA: the Committee for Industrial Organization, later renamed the Congress of Industrial Organizations. The CIO, established four months after the NLRA was signed into law in November 1935, was founded on the idea that all laborers—skilled and unskilled—working for the same employer needed to be unionized as one force in order to have maximum leverage when bargaining collectively with management.

Before the NLRA had passed, union-led strikes were met with extreme force by employers, including mass violence, murder, and threat of jail time. The unions in 1934 understood they had to create a crisis to stand a chance to win the ability to live a decent life up against the titans of the corporate class. Remember, under capitalism, employers need workers to do one thing only: make profits for their bosses. The CIO understood that the only way to change workers' lives for the better was to take huge risks by walking off the job and stopping production, therefore creating an untenable situation for their employers. Thus, to the CIO, even though the NLRA was passed, to actually make the law come to life would require forcing the employer class to share the profits. That meant the likelihood of bringing production to a standstill, again. This change in approach by the CIO marked a huge strategic shift for unions.

Once the NLRA passed, the CIO led most of the hardest, and largest, campaigns—and secured the biggest breakthroughs for American workers. The organizers, for the most part, took jobs inside the factories so they could help workers overcome management's tactical warfare. Many of the most successful organizers in the CIO came from the various socialist and communist parties that proliferated in the era. They were driven by an ideological passion for justice every bit as strong as the employers' ideological passion for total domination and exploitation. It was the left wing of the labor movements' commitment to justice *for all* that provided the winning strategy: that hypergreedy employers could be overcome only by uniting the skilled and the unskilled into one organization. In the core industries of the CIO, large factories including auto and steel, this meant uniting whites, blacks, native, and immigrants, as well as women, not just white men.

The CIO organizers who won game-changing union campaigns had boundless determination, but they also had clear-sighted methods. They became highly effective teachers and coaches, helping workers themselves learn which organizing approaches were most successful. For instance, the International Ladies' Garment Workers' Union—a union that had experienced massive growth despite determined employer resistance before the NLRA—knew that engaging the entire community in the fight, by prioritizing working with ethnic, immigrant, and women's groups and media to highlight the brutality of the employers against the mostly teenage girls, was a key strategy. Having the backing of their community, for instance, made it much harder for employers who used violent union-busting tactics—like teargassing, clubbing, and shooting innocent bystanders, not just ordinary workers demanding their rights—to manage the fallout in news coverage and in the community.

At the same time, the CIO understood that even with the federal law in place that in theory protected workers' freedom to assemble and prevented federal troops from being called out against them in strikes, the employers had also relied on state and local law enforcement to back their union-busting efforts. This was the 1930s: a time when mass lynching was in full force to keep black workers from rebelling in the South. In company towns in the North, the local authorities and the company itself were indistinguishable. The very origin of the police in some places was in private and semi-private militias created by the employers intended to attack workers in industrial disputes. Keeping the new federal law in place, and stopping the repression of the state and local police, became a key motivation for the growing union movement's entrance into politics in a big way.

Passing the NLRA was one step in the right direction for American unions. But for many American workers, it was equally, if not more, important that the federal government, starting with President Roosevelt, would aggressively tilt the scales of justice toward most American workers. After FDR signed the NLRA into law, along with other bold New Deal ideas, the few members of the employer class who backed him in 1932 abandoned him by the time his first reelection campaign came along in 1936. Not only that, but the American Liberty League, the equivalent back then of the conservative Americans for Prosperity today, was raising huge sums of money for his Republican opponent. Unions understood, really for the first time, that to keep their new rights, they would have to work hard and work smart to get him elected for a second term.

The industries the unions were targeting to make major gains for all workers included steel and automotive industries, where the employer class was making the biggest profits. The unions knew that the governors controlled the state-based National Guard units. Unions went all out, raising more money for the campaign in 1936 than all previous union donations *combined* for the elections from 1906 through 1935. They also put record numbers of boots on the ground, not only for FDR, but also for the governorships in Pennsylvania and Michigan, the two states that housed the biggest workforces in the targeted industries. After FDR's reelection and the election of progressive governors in both of those states, unions started to build the foundation of the American Dream and chip away at inequality. When General Motors workers in Flint, Michigan, held a sit-down strike—they stopped working but stayed in the plants—they prevented any potential replacement scab workers from coming in to replace them. If Michigan's governor had called out law enforcement to forcefully remove the striking workers, GM

Union Membership and Share of Income Going to the Top 10 Percent 1917–2015

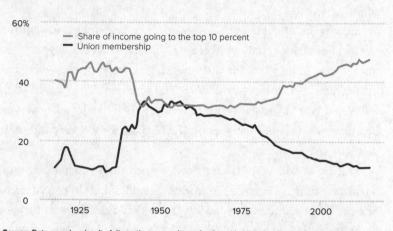

Source: Data on union density follows the composite series found in Historical Statistics of the United States; updated to 2015 from unionstats.com Income inequality (share of income to top 10 percent) data are from Thomas Piketty and Emmanuel Saez, "Income Inequality in the United States, 1913–1998," *Quarterly Journal of Economics* 118, no. 1 (2003) and updated data from the Top Income Database, updated June 2016.

management would have won—but because unions had worked hard to help elect a governor they could better control, they worried less about the threat of law enforcement. Similar dynamics played out in the big steel strikes in Pennsylvania. After much effort on the part of unions, the federal government occasionally sent those forces first to defend unionizing workers, and, later, African Americans during the civil rights movement. Shifting the federal government's apparatuses toward defending the rights of workers to unionize and strike, and later the rights of African Americans to vote and challenge discrimination, was all it took to build massive, decades-lasting structural achievements.

Throughout the late 1930s and through the 1940s, workers continued to form unions in record numbers and income inequality steadily fell. In just four years, from 1934 to 1938, the percentage of nonagricultural workers in unions jumped from 11.5 percent to

26.6 percent. This would have been unimaginable in 1932. The gap between the billionaires and workers declined because the *power equation* shifted. The workers made that shift by making strong organizations of their own, bargaining collectively, and holding the kind of strikes that could create a crisis when employers were unreasonable. Big gains for the whole of the working class were being extracted in key profit sectors of the economy. The mobilization for World War II and the tight labor markets it produced, however, overshadowed serious dangers on the horizon for workers and their new unions.

During World War II, another huge group of uncompensated laborers—women—entered the workforce and unions in record numbers, filling vacancies created by troop deployments and forever changing many women's ideas of what kind of work they could or might choose to do. Women's entrance into the workforce also then created an expectation of equal pay for equal work. Government contracts in defense-related industries greased the wheels for rapid union growth in all war-related production sectors by demanding that employers negotiate with unions. Production demands helped tame worker-on-worker issues—such as men fighting the inclusion of women and white workers resisting the increased numbers of black workers—because everyone had to be all in to fight fascism.

A War Labor Board operated throughout the conflict. Smart unions took advantage of the need for labor peace, winning breakthroughs in collective bargaining on the right to grievance and arbitration, seniority, paid vacation and meal times, differentials for night and evening work, and clauses that guaranteed maintenance of union membership. Maintenance of membership meant no worker could drop his or her union membership and all new workers would have to join the union, in exchange for pledges by the presidents of both the AFL and the CIO that the unions would not go on strike. Despite this pledge, between the start of the war and its conclusion, nearly seven million workers thumbed their nose at the no-strike pledge and their union officialdom and held more than 14,471 strikes during the forty-four months of the war. It made little sense to most workers that in the perfect climate to make improvements in wages and working conditions (that is, a tight labor market), they were prohibited from using their most effective weapon: the strike. Many rank-and-file workers began to distrust their union officials because they cooperated with management in doling out discipline when workers violated the no-strike pledge.

The end of World War II meant millions of American troops returned home with a newfound sense of self-worth and identity: they were *heroes*. While showers of confetti, lavish parades, and heartfelt welcome-home banners greeted them in their communities, they would soon return to dangerous and stultifying jobs in which employers decided to decrease wages in the name of the postwar "reconversion"—their word for downsizing production. Companies began to downsize employee counts and the number of hours of overtime to which millions had become accustomed. This resulted in an immediate postwar decrease in wages of 31 percent in war-related industries and 10 percent in non-war-related employment.

For millions of newly empowered workers, the reduction of hours was untenable. Corporations had made enormous profits on the war. It didn't take long before this more confident class of workers rightfully demanded dignity on the job and in their paychecks. These demands led to the nation's biggest, most sustained strikes: in 1945 and 1946, five million workers went on strike. General strikes broke out in several cities, along with national strikes by industry. These did even more to redistribute wealth from the elite corporate few to the mass of the Americans, radically reducing income and wealth inequality and giving rise to a new middle class. The middle class and the American Dream so commonly referred to was won by strikers, whose numbers included many war veterans who understood the discipline required to win and who possessed uniquely important experiences, including troop formation and holding solidarity through exhaustion, just honed in the fight against fascism. By the end of 1945, union membership among non-agricultural workers stood at 34.2 percent.

BY THE EARLY 1940S, life was slowly, steadily, and, of course, un-evenly getting better for most people. But the billionaire class that watched the guns, government, and laws switch from defending their side of the class war to that of the American worker set out to undo all the good. To be clear, a subset of the employer class had worked to destroy the NLRA from the day it passed. That group of employers began a legal offensive in 1935, challenging the entirety of the law itself. It took until 1937 before the overall challenge to the NLRA made its way to the Supreme Court. On this big case, the court affirmed the NLRA as the law of the land. But because the em-ployer class hadn't put all its eggs in one basket, knowing if the court upheld the law overall, it needed a plan B: attack the law bit by bit, in smaller pieces, in related cases. And in one such case, the Supreme Court did the opposite.

Even though the Supreme Court upheld the NLRA in 1937, it also issued perhaps the most serious blow to American workers, one not well recognized at the time as the *key* weapon that would slowly undo workers' ability to fundamentally redistribute power and therefore wealth: the *Mackay Radio & Telegraph* decision. In *Mackay,* the same justices who upheld the NLRA ruled that strik-ing workers could be permanently replaced by strikebreakers. Labor scholars have pointed out the uniquely schizophrenic nature of the court's rulings that year—one decision affirming that workers have the right to strike and can't be fired for doing so, but on the other hand, another legal decision that gave employers the right to per-manently replace them if they did—which had the effect of firing workers for striking.

Mackay wasn't well understood at the time as a knockout punch to unions. In just a few short years of serious organizing and real gains via strikes, the societal norms constructed under the New Deal had effectively made it culturally unacceptable to replace striking workers. Another forty-four years would pass and two more rounds of the employer offensive would be launched before President Ronald Reagan weaponized the *Mackay* decision and replaced 100 percent of the nation's 12,000 highly skilled air traffic control workers during a strike in 1981. The "societal norms" and "culture" that prevented employers from using *Mackay* were created because of the brilliant strategy of the early years of the CIO, and by the agency of workers fully engaging the entire community in labor fights.

Imagine the frustration of the billionaires. They had legally secured the right to replace strikers via *Mackay,* but in effect they had their hands tied by smart worker-organizing strategy. The employer class was experiencing sustained worker power and a real redistribution of wealth. Rather than continuing to share their enormous profits, as World War II drew to a close, corporations launched a war at home: a renewed class war against their workers. Not surprisingly, racism was a key motivation and weapon to undo worker gains. Millions of African Americans had valiantly served the country in World War II. Their demands for the equality at home that many had fought and died for abroad, along with key CIO unions that believed all workers deserved equal treatment, seriously threatened Jim Crow. This energized the Southern corporate class to do something it generally resisted: for a second time it joined forces with Northern industrialists who were concerned about the threat unions posed to their wealth and created an ideological fervor to launch a unified political offensive to gut the power of the National Labor Relations Act. In their minds, Roosevelt and the war had held them back for far too long, and their pent-up fury would no longer be contained.

THE EMPLOYER OFFENSIVE ROUND 1:

Gut the NLRA, Demobilize the Best Organizers, Contain Existing Private-Sector Unions

The end of World War II abruptly upended the relationship between the United States and the Soviet Union in 1945. While the two were close allies in defeating Hitler, with the war over, each country began a race to extend the reach of their ideologies. This Cold War, as it came to be called, marked the beginning of an anticommunist frenzy in the United States. Just as the Great Depression served as important context for the passage of the NLRA, the fear that the red menace—communism—would spread and take over the country served as an important backdrop to the next attack launched against America's workers.

For the first time in sixteen years, in 1946, the Republicans took control of Congress, winning majorities in both the House and the Senate. And for the second time in twelve years, the threat of a genuinely united American working class forged a tactical alliance between big corporations in the North and their racist pro–Jim Crow Southern allies. It didn't take long after the new Congress was sworn into power in 1947 to gut the NLRA. Congress passed the Labor-Management Relations Act (commonly referred to as Taft–Hartley for the bill's lead sponsors, Ohio Republican Robert Taft in the Senate and New Jersey Republican Fred Hartley in the House), a sweeping amendment to the NLRA that was so extreme it was vetoed by President Harry Truman. But the racist, anti-worker, pro-corporate majorities in Congress had enough power at that point to override Truman's veto.

The list of changes was significant. It included making it permissible, once again, for employers to use paid work time to actively campaign against unionization; a ban on sympathy strikes and boycotts; an end to wildcat strikes (where workers simply walk off the job with no notice, sometimes in defiance of their unions, not just their employer); an end to the closed shop (whereby employers could hire only people who were union members); the creation of so-called right-to-work laws, which gave states the option to make union membership voluntary; and a clause mandating that union leaders and members had to sign affidavits stating they had not been a member of the Communist Party or socialist parties. With the zeal of Senator Joseph McCarthy's inquisitions, the practical impact of this last provision was that thousands of the most successful rank-and-file organizers were purged from the unions, regardless of whether they had ever been official members of any party.

The ban on sympathy strikes and boycotts meant that truck drivers could no longer refuse to deliver goods to a factory where the workers were on strike. Food-service workers would have to break through a picket line to prepare food for replacement workers or risk being fired if they didn't. That didn't just weaken strikes in obvious ways. There was a more nefarious psychological objective aimed at undermining human solidarity, which is an instinct that emerges when one group of people sees another in profound duress or under attack, as in a hurricane or flood. Strikes build the same kind of bonds that events like natural disasters produce. Banning "sympathy" for the idea of "the collective good" was part of a broader long-term effort to rewire humans from acting collectively to acting individually. In think tanks such as the Mont Pelerin Society, discussions were underway about the need to resocialize worker behavior to better fit conservative economists' views that people should act only out of self-interest. But forcing workers into reeducation camps was too blunt an instrument in the United States. It was more acceptable to slowly stoke individualism by making the default acts of human sympathy illegal and so punishable by termination.

The aspect of Taft–Hartley that restored the legal right of employers to *actively* campaign against unionization essentially removed the leash employers felt restrained by from 1935 to 1947. In his book *Confessions of a Union Buster,* Martin Jay Levitt—a former union buster himself—explained how the NLRA created fair union elections for those brief twelve years: "The primary labor component of Franklin D. Roosevelt's New Deal, the Wagner Act, also outlawed many employer tactics then commonly used to break unions—most notoriously, spying on and intimidating union activists, provoking violence, and enticing unions into management-controlled 'company unions' in order to stifle their call for independent labor organizations." Restoring the employers' right to fight unionization with Taft–Hartley morphed quickly into demonstrations of egregious intimidation. Employers routinely fired highly productive workers who dared to lead union efforts, spied, gerrymandered worker voting lists, manipulated eligibility requirements for unionization votes, and used other mechanisms to rig unionization election rules that resemble the 2000 Florida recount or the most outrageous voter-suppression tactics in the 2018 U.S. midterm elections. We can draw an especially apt comparison between the 2018 Georgia gubernatorial race, in which one of the candidates was also the person who made the election rules and enforced them, and union elections, where only the employer can call mandatory meetings on paid work time to propagandize against the other.

Taft–Hartley's creation of "right-to-work" laws also chipped away at solidarity. In a right-to-work state, a majority of workers can vote to unionize but are prohibited from negotiating clauses in their own contracts stipulating that all workers need to join and pay dues. Considering how much money unions need in order to try to compete with the millions and millions of dollars corporations freely spend against them, this compromises the effectiveness of unions in those states. Within the first two years of the passage of Taft–Hartley, the legislatures in most former slave states voted to become right-to-work, once again tightly yoking institutionalized racism and labor law. As unions moved into the South during the twelve years of worker freedom, Jim Crow was under attack by left-led unions. To save Jim Crow, these states had to destroy unions. Few Americans understand that Taft–Hartley was the beginning of a never-ending bipartisan attack on American workers' freedom and power in the private sector.

With the undoing of the NLRA in place, the employers set out to construct a postwar system of "labor relations." This meant that with a few exceptions, industrial disputes were less violent than in the past, and many American workers continued to benefit from existing unions contract negotiations and the spillover impact that winning high standards had on the broader labor market. But Taft–Hartley's passage left little doubt that corporate leaders *never* conceded the right of unions to exist. Despite that, they recognized the reality that, for a time, unions would have to be tolerated in some fashion. Employer-side labor-relations experts developed ways to deal with already-existing unions and began to keep nonunion workers from forming new ones, essentially creating a containment strategy. The beginnings of modern union busting as a stand-alone industry took hold in the 1950s as a medium-term strategy to impede an institution they were determined to eventually destroy.

Two centuries of violence against those who challenged the status quo began to mutate into sophisticated psychological, cultural, and legal warfare, a tamer but no less effective tactical repertoire similar to the difference between slavery and mass incarceration. Union buster Levitt wrote, "Executives and their consultants knew that with Taft–Hartley amendments in place, employers would enjoy great freedom in combatting worker organizations. Management always had the upper hand, of course; they had never lost it.

But thanks to Taft–Hartley, the bosses could once again wage their war with near impunity."

ONE MAJOR CORPORATION STOOD OUT for its lasting contribution to the development of professional union busting: the retail giant Sears, Roebuck. Sears had always fought its workers' attempts to unionize, but the NLRA made it considerably trickier when it outlawed overt intimidation by management, like firing workers who wanted to unionize. In 1935, with the NLRA the new law of the land, Sears hired Nathan Shefferman as its human resources director with explicit instructions to fight unions tooth and nail despite the law. Shefferman turned the human resource department into a laboratory that developed cutting-edge union-avoidance strategies that remain central to the industry even now. Working with some of the top academic institutions of the era—including world-renowned behavioral psychologists at the University of Chicago, in addition to the industrial relations psychologists—they began experiments to predict which workers might be prone to join unions.

To pinpoint workers in the company who might want to unionize, management developed tools like employee-attitude surveys that allowed a human resources department to avoid violating the anti-spying provisions in the NLRA but still collect information on employee satisfaction or dissatisfaction. Employees would be fooled into believing the company was genuinely interested in their feedback, but these increasingly sophisticated surveys helped management weed out potential threats without violating the new labor laws. With the surveys, management developed a method to ascertain which workers they wanted to promote, which ones to surveil, and which to dispose of, lest the idea of workers deserving something better than wage slavery begin to spread.

Shefferman and Sears were much more successful than many of their counterparts in avoiding unionization because they used these early-warning systems to root out what they considered to be problematic employees, no matter how good or productive the worker was. None were considered too valuable to remove if they were a union threat. After just two years of Shefferman plying his trade inside Sears, the union avoidance work was occupying all his time. He eventually decided to move the operations outside Sears, although he remained largely dedicated to Sears as his primary client. Founded in 1939, his firm, Labor Relations Associates (LRA), was the preeminent union-busting operation, employing more than twenty full-time consultants working out of offices in Chicago, Detroit, and New York. With Taft–Hartley's passage, Shefferman was well positioned to sell his ideas to many more corporations than just Sears.

According to labor scholar John Logan, it was Shefferman who developed a key tactic that all labor relations firms would soon begin to use: a "vote-no worker committee" that gave the fight against workers in a union election the veneer of being led by workers, not management. It helped companies avoid legal charges when they launched well-resourced campaigns against the union. In almost any workplace, management can identify at least one worker whom it can cajole into being publicly against a union. It can sweeten the deal by, for instance, promising to promote the worker when the union is defeated. For workers who may not yet know much about unions, seeing anti-union literature and videos presented by a co-worker is far more effective than if management were putting out the same information.

It also leads to immediate division and finger-pointing among workers, and erodes trust as workers are trying to make big decisions affecting their future. This kind of divide-and-conquer approach guides every step of the union buster's playbook. It allows management's official union-busting consultants to operate in secret, in the background, meeting with only one, two, or a small group of workers, coaching them on what to say, making flyers and handouts that are written by the best advertising agency copy-writers, and putting up websites and now Facebook pages in the name of workers. This clever end run around the law was highly effective then and continues to be so now.

Shefferman hooked his clients on the idea that the unscrupulous tactics required to keep, or make, companies union-free would best be done at arm's length, so the companies would not be liable for the kind of illegal tactical warfare required to thwart a very natural human desire for their betterment. Despite LRA's successes, and because there were still some members of Congress who were sympathetic to unions, some of Shefferman's aggressive antiunion behavior, notably bribery and racketeering, was exposed by congressional investigations. By the late 1950s, LRA was forced to close. But the dozens of consultants who worked for LRA began to found their own union-avoidance firms, and those union buster names—Modern Management Methods (3M), the law firm Jackson & Lewis, and John Sheridan of John Sheridan Associates—are very familiar to organizers today.

THE EMPLOYER OFFENSIVE ROUND 2:
Eliminate Private-Sector Unions Altogether

If the postwar period of labor relations was aimed at stopping the spread of unions to contain the gains many Americans had achieved, then the era beginning in the early 1970s characterizes an offensive to actually reverse these gains, restore all power and wealth to the few at the top, and do so by eliminating unions from American soil—literally. It was a two-pronged assault consisting of the rapid expansion of the union-buster ground troops and the rise of the euphemistically termed *globalization*.

UNION BUSTING BECOMES AN INDUSTRY

The union-busting firms that took root in the 1950s exploded in size and scope in the 1970s, growing from a handful of firms to the full-fledged industry they are today. This new generation of union-avoidance experts extended their services to the financial, insurance, and hospitality sectors. According to testimony delivered by Herbert Melnick, the founder of 3M—who was compelled to testify before the House Subcommittee on Labor-Management Relations in 1979 due to mounting evidence of his own unscrupulous behavior—the number of firms increased from "100 firms in the 1960s to 10 times that number in the mid-1980s."

Martin Jay Levitt writes that when he was being trained by John Sheridan in the mid-1960s, the anti-union firms were tools of the employers. But beginning in the 1970s and certainly by Reagan's administration, he notes, "They were no longer simply responding to employers' demands for their services but were actively and aggressively creating that demand. . . . In the 1950s and 1960s, employers were hiding their campaigns behind consultants; within a couple of decades, the situation had reversed, as consultants concealed their increasingly aggressive and sophisticated activities behind management and supervisors."

These modern union busters are a cookie-cutter bunch, and the ingredients of the recipe are pure poison. They operate in total secrecy, and it's nearly impossible to get into their training sessions. They've developed complicated security checks to avoid outsiders slipping in, assuming they can pay the steep registration fees. Their training manuals are only distributed at their high-priced seminars. You won't find their books on Amazon's platform, but you will find Amazon using their services. The registration page for a 2018 union-busting seminar in Indiana, sponsored by the Chamber of Commerce, stated the following:

Program Information

Exact location in Indianapolis will be sent to you within 24 hours of your registration or the following business day. Registration is limited strictly to management personnel directly from a corporation. Please note: The discussion will be frank. The use of recording devices is strictly prohibited. Attendance is limited to representatives of business organizations only. Individuals affiliated with union organizations are not eligible for registration. The Indiana Chamber of Commerce reserves the right to refuse participation in the program to anyone other than a bonafide management representative.

One example of a manual that until recently was very hard to get is *Total Victory,* which features chapters with titles like "Management Campaign Strategy"; "Guidelines for Supervisors and Managers During a Union Organizing Effort"; "Literature Development & Distribution"; "Captive Audience Meetings"; "Job Security & Strikes—Your Future in the Union's Hands."

In the opening lines of *Confessions of a Union Buster,* Levitt tells us

Union busting is a field populated by bullies and built on deceit. A campaign against a union is an assault on individuals and a war against the truth. As such, it is a war without honor. The only way to bust a union is to lie, distort, manipulate, threaten, and always, always attack. The law does not hamper the process. Rather, it serves to suggest maneuvers and define strategies. Each "union prevention" campaign, as the wars are called, turns on a combined strategy of disinformation and personal assault.

Why is it that so little evidence exists about the despicable tactics of a vile industry? Because it is totally unregulated. Union busters are not required to fill in paperwork informing Americans what they do or how much they spend—or much else. In the last year of his final term, Barack Obama signed a too-little-too-late executive order requiring a bare minimum of information employers must submit if they hire union-avoidance firms. The order was quickly undone after Donald Trump was sworn in.

By contrast, thanks to the Labor-Management Reporting and Disclosure Act, a law Congress passed in 1959 and which is still in place, aimed at unions, not management, here's what unions must report regularly to the government, in public filings.

- Every hour of work done by every union staffer must be separately accounted for and categorized (e.g., organizing, politics, grievance handling, arbitrations, negotiations, etc.).
- Every expense must have an invoice. Invoices have to be retained for every office supply, every lunch, every day, all day.
- Every mile driven for the union must be recorded: a full record of from where, to where, how many miles, and why and how it is work-related.
- In contract negotiations, for example, if an employer provides sandwiches at lunch so both parties can continue through the meal, the union side either pays for the employer and records it, or the union must record it as a "gift from employer."

In other words, everything union staff does all day, every day, has to be recorded and tracked: where they go, what they do, and the exact amount of money they spend on what, and what they receive from who and at what exact time. If I were to add up the amount of time that I've spent itemizing minutiae, it would be apparent that months of my life have been spent writing reports so union busters can review them. Imagine writing down what you do during every hour of your workday—which always starts in the dark and ends in the dark and persists through the weekend if you want to stand a chance at defeating the union busters. By contrast, neither workers nor their unions—if the workers can defeat the consultants in the election—get to know which consultants the employers hire, let alone how they spend every hour of their day, how many of them there are, or what they charge for their high-priced services.

Talk about a stacked deck.

Since the growth of the union-busting industry in the early 1970s, pretty much every NLRB election in which workers try to form a union is even less fair than the 2018 Georgia gubernatorial election. If you understand what happened to Stacey Abrams in that contest, you can start to comprehend what happens to workers in union elections. In the Georgia governor's race, Abrams's opponent, Brian Kemp, was the existing secretary of state, which meant her opponent literally oversaw his election against her. The accusations of voter suppression and wrongdoing by Kemp include the expunging of thousands of eligible voters' ballots because their signature didn't exactly match their original registration; eligible voters who had voted previously being told their name didn't appear on the poll workers' list; the mysterious purging of thousands of voter names, with a variety of excuses, such as there was more than one person with the name (think here about how many "J Smiths" might live in a state with millions of people, and then consider the number of "J Juarez" or other "ethnic-sounding" names); hundreds of polling locations shuttered, forcing people to travel to a new voting site, perhaps father away; and people waiting in long lines for hours hoping to vote.

Shenanigans with that tone of cynicism happen routinely in NLRB elections. But ordinary workers don't get the limelight or attention of a Stacey Abrams. In any fair fight, Abrams would be Georgia's governor, and in any fair union fight, workers would win unions in droves. Union busters consistently tip the scales in their favor, and this is in large part what accounts for union decline.

GLOBALIZATION

In the next absurdly uneven power match—where all the rules are written by big global corporations for the employers and polluters and against the workers and the planet—globalization takes center stage. Globalization was the second punch in the one-two punch that crushed private-sector unions and made a few people filthy rich while everyone else stayed or became poor.

In the United States, several decades before globalization as we presently understand it, the employer class began moving factories from the heavily unionized Northeast and the Rust Belt to the Southern states. As discussed previously, the former slave states turned Jim Crow states turned right-to-work states have long prided themselves on being a union- and environmental-regulation-free zone within U.S. borders. But having to pay even a paltry national minimum wage and contribute to Social Security and Medicaid and Medicare through the employer payroll tax system demanded too much from big corporations. If the Southern states let corporations cut expenses, the global south gave the same corporations the ability to dramatically slash wages and benefits. How is it that a radical movement to drive down the cost of production—which is essentially the human cost—is not understood as union avoidance?

One of the first experiments in international free trade started in the late 1960s in Mexico, along the U.S.–Mexico border, in what became known as the Maquiladora Zone. The maquilas are factories where Mexican workers are paid pennies on the dollar per hour for work that in the United States pays a family-supporting wage. Though Mexico had unions, they were more like Chinese unions today, controlled by the state, not the workers themselves. Once enough U.S. companies made the maquilas their preferred location for opening new production facilities, the unified corporate public relations campaign began. Americans started seeing newspaper headlines like this: "American Workers Have Priced Themselves Too Far Above Reasonable Wages." Right. Well, when you start comparing what union workers in the United States earned compared to slave-like conditions, you could ironically suggest workers in the United States were overpaid. Except they never were.

In 1991, I was hired to do some preparatory work for the arrival of a delegation of interfaith leaders who were to take a tour of the U.S.–Mexico border as part of a faith-based conference on conditions in the maquiladora zone. I set up my beachhead in Tucson, renting an apartment month to month because the first part of the job required writing short briefing documents for the future tour participants. The first time I drove the sixty-eight miles through the Saguaro National Park to go south of the border to the city of Nogales, in the state of Sonora, Mexico, I got a whiff of the growing global trade problem—literally. As I drove to Nogales, I could smell the toxic exhaust emanating from U.S.-owned factories just outside the reach of much stricter laws stateside. Walking around the town, I wished I were wearing a hazmat suit, or at least hazmat shoes. The effluvium emanating from plants emblazoned with familiar American logos was so noxious that I remember wondering whether the soles of my shoes were going to melt on the sidewalk. I was not yet a union organizer and was still working full-time in the environmental movement. I began to anthropomorphize the vast stretches of saguaros on what became a regular drive. The upward-arm cacti seemed to be pissed off, shrugging their shoulders the entire way, as if to say, "Yo. Why dump on us down here?"

After just one long afternoon in the maquiladora zone, home at that point to plenty of factories with names like GM, Ford, Chrysler, Honeywell, Xerox, Zenith, and IBM—all of which had recently employed union workers in places like Ohio and Michigan—I understood that the *free* in *free trade* meant the freedom to pollute the planet, pay extremely low wages, and be exempt from all duties and obligations to society. American workers didn't stand much of a chance competing against these conditions, and neither did the planet. This was several years before a Democratic president, Bill Clinton, delivered the North American Free Trade Agreement for the corporate global elite, soon followed by the creation of the World Trade Organization, which effectively maquiladora-ized the world in one fell swoop: smashing workplace regulations, trashing environmental regulations, and decimating American unions and families. The presence of these U.S. corporations hasn't been helping the people of other nations, either.

Between overt union busting and the insidious union-busting effects of globalization, unionization rates in the private sector have plummeted over the past forty years. None of this was an accident. All of it is public policy made by the big corporations who have effectively taken control of both political parties. And—surprise!—

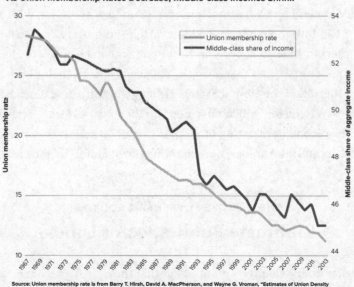

As Union Membership Rates Decrease, Middle-class Incomes Shrink

Union membership rate
Middle-class share of income

Source: Union membership rate is from Barry T. Hirsh, David A. MacPherson, and Wayne G. Vroman, "Estimates of Union Density by State," *Monthly Labor Review* 124, no. 7 (2001). Middle-class share of aggregate income is from the U.S. Census Bureau, Current Population Survey (Department of Commerce).

income inequality has skyrocketed, with neatly parallel lines showing union decline and increasing income inequality.

The governing bodies that make the rules of global trade were designed to be immune from any one country's constitution and laws, including labor and environmental laws. How is that not a direct subversion of democracy? Some people will quibble about the intent of globalization, but we are past arguing about the impact. It should be clear by now that creating trade regimes whose aim was to make it super easy to relocate American workers' best jobs—unionized jobs—out of the United States, dressed up by a powerful PR narrative about spreading democracy, didn't achieve democracy in Latin America, Myanmar, China, Cambodia, or anywhere else it promised. If anything, globalization has contributed to the downfall of our own democracy.

The creation of NAFTA was perhaps the key moment when the Democratic Party turned its back on private-sector workers. NAFTA and globalization are why Hillary Clinton couldn't win Michigan and Pennsylvania in 2016. For all the goodwill upper-middle-class and wealthy Democratic donors associate with the first Clinton who ran for president, with his intelligence and charm, workers in states that once had booming manufacturing were living in total despair, and that despair had deep roots in their plants relocating out of the United States. Hillary Clinton's defeat in a third state—Wisconsin, which cost her the Electoral College—was due to the second devastating blow that Democrats dealt to American workers and their unions: the abandonment of public-sector workers.

THE EMPLOYER OFFENSIVE ROUND 3:

Eliminate Public-Sector Unions

Earlier in this chapter, I pointed out that the NLRA, passed in 1935, excluded workers in the public sector. Before I discuss the public sector, I want to clarify a misconception. Capitalism has created a clever myth that the economy is separated into two separate sectors when, in actuality, it is one complex, integrated economic system in which shareholders and CEOs extract extraordinary sums of taxpayer money for their personal fortunes and have little to no accountability for their actions. There is no such thing as a pure private sector and with contracting out rampant in so many state and federal agencies, there isn't a pure public sector at this point, either.

For proof, look no further than the eye-popping subsidy packages doled out by state and local governments as megacorporations play them against one another in an alleged race for local job creation. Until the progressive movement fought back, New York State was going to hand Amazon CEO Jeff Bezos, the richest man on the planet, $2.8 billion to set up new company headquarters in New York City. The location would have required even more massive public subsidies to fix the taxpayer-funded transit system so workers could get to the office. Or consider the fact that Amazon and Walmart, who employ thuggish union-busting consultants every bit as brutal as Martin Jay Levitt, pay workers so little that the workers have to rely on *public assistance*—yet another massive subsidy. They pay workers so little that in essence American taxpayers make up the rest of their payroll with food stamps, Medicaid, the Earned Income Tax Credit, and more.

That said, the myth of these two separate sectors of the American economy is reflected in labor law. Starting in the 1970s, corporations set out to destroy private-sector unions first, and later (as in *today*), the remaining unions in the public sector. Generally speaking, public-sector labor laws follow the confines of private-sector law, but there can be significant differences.

One is the right of workers to strike, which varies considerably between the so-called private and public sector. It also varies greatly within the public sector, which varies by state and frequently by workforce. Public-service worker unions (labeled "government unions" by those who dislike government and unions, and black people and women) are still regulated in fifty different states, whereas federal public-service unions are governed by separate, national laws. And because states govern most public-sector worker unions, attacking them proved challenging for the billionaire right-wing forces. Unlike what they did with Taft–Hartley, they couldn't simply waltz into the halls of Congress and pass one law that would gut public-sector unions. But before turning to the present, a little more history is required on how the surge in public-sector union-ism represented a kind of *second* American Dream, chiefly benefit-ing large numbers of African Americans and women.

As with the burst of organizing in factories, workers at federal, state, and local levels began agitating to form unions in a concerted way during the Great Depression. At the state and local levels, the impetus to unionize was generated by small numbers of white-collar workers who formed employee associations to safeguard the civil service system from withering under the weight of the Great Depression. Other than postal workers, who had been unionized since the 1880s but who lacked collective bargaining rights, a push began in 1931 for other federal workers, such as shipwrights and plumbers employed by federal agencies such as defense and energy, to unionize. That created controversy among the American Fed-eration of Labor because the private-sector craft-building unions sought to claim jurisdiction over these same workers because they did the same kind of work. This is a good example of union leader egos getting in the way of worker progress. Partially because unions were in a power struggle among themselves for manufacturing and construction workers at federal facilities, few public-sector work-ers unionized in the 1930s. Mostly, however, it's because they were excluded from the NLRA in 1935.

Public-sector workers didn't secure the right to collective bar-gaining until the civil rights movement made unionization a central issue. African Americans moved into government positions in large numbers on the heels of black veterans returning from World War II. And as the civil rights movement grew, so did the demand for unions in the public sector. At the big municipality level, New York City was the first to create a legal collective bargaining framework, in 1958. At the state level, Wisconsin was the first to grant state employees the right to collectively bargain in 1959. And in 1962, President John F. Kennedy signed an executive order giving federal government workers the right to collective bargaining inside their agencies. The main federal government workers' union, the American Federation of Government Employees, grew from 71,000 members in 1961 to 301,000 by 1970.

Though there had been many threats against the Reverend Dr. Martin Luther King Jr., he was assassinated at the very moment he chose to forcefully link unionization and class issues to the black-freedom movement. He had traveled to Memphis to support a wildcat strike by black sanitation workers who walked off the job to demand the right to a union after two workers were crushed to death in the back of a garbage truck. King's assassination sparked an increased militancy among African Americans for respect and rights. For the next decade, public-sector workers at the state and local levels in addition to private-sector workers who were experiencing the early stages of globalization—kicked off another big round of strikes across the United States.

Just as private-sector workers in 1934 created a crisis so that FDR would have reason to create new accommodations for workers, resulting in the NLRA, one positive result of the strikes and disruption in the public sector was the decision in a 1977 Supreme Court case, *Abood v. Detroit Board of Education*. Because state and local public-sector unions were governed by state law, there had never been a national law that permitted public-sector unions to be effective at collecting dues. Then came the *Abood* decision. The case was brought by a worker who *didn't* want to be a member of the union or contribute to the union's political program. On one hand, the court declared that government workers' unions could not negotiate clauses whereby all workers must become members of the union even if a majority voted to form one, as is the practice in the private sector. But the ruling *did* establish the right for public-sector unions to collect an agency fee, which was an amount of dues discounted by the amount of money a union spent on political activity, that all workers would have to pay. This resulted in a substantial increase in revenues for public-sector unions. The *Abood* decision was considered "settled law" until it wasn't.

Until now, the story of the deliberate destruction of the American Dream has focused on the machinations of elite corporate forces against workers in private-sector unions. This is because the big-employer class war against workers was operating from a clear set of priorities, first taking aim at what was the largest segment of unionized workers, not to mention the ones cutting directly into profit margins: factory workers in the private sector. That successful assault resulted in a much higher rate of unionization remaining in the public sector because while their membership grew slowly or held steady, depending on the year, the private-sector unionization rate plummeted. (This is similar to recent reports that show the wage gap between men and women is closing. It sounds good, but it's mostly because men's wages are falling, not that women's pay is increasing.) In 1949, just after the Taft–Hartley attack was launched, 34.7 percent of nonagricultural workers were unionized in the private sector, compared with just 12.1 percent in the public sector. By 2017, 6.5 percent of private-sector workers remained unionized, compared with 36.1 percent in the public sector.

The asymmetry between the private-sector and public-sector unionization rates shifted corporate billionaires' sights from the earlier target, large numbers of men in manufacturing, to the new targets: the mostly women and people of color who perform public

State/local Government Has Had the Highest Union Membership Rate (36.1%) for Decades

Union membership rate, by sector, 1949–2017

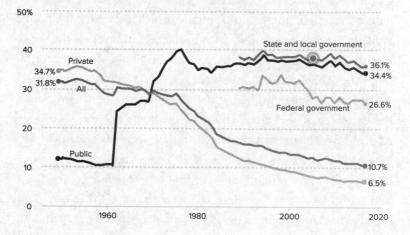

services, who still work in unionized workplaces and thus still have a decent standard of living. The largest subgroup of public-sector workers at the state and local level is teachers. It's no surprise that the attack against them has been ferocious. It doesn't hurt that they are mostly women. I'll return to this point in more detail in chapter 6, when I discuss the Los Angeles teachers' union and their 2019 strike.

The billionaire class pivoted from weaponizing globalization (moving union jobs out of the United States), which finished off what the union busters hadn't in the private sector, to creating a new fiction that's been called "austerity." Although the word *austerity* is more commonly used in Europe and the global south, it needs no translation. The shorthand definition is the deliberate creation of federal, state, and local budget deficits while corporations and the super-rich pay less and less taxes, resulting, obviously, in revenue shortfalls and manufactured budget crises. The same PR firms that created the myth that American workers were overpaid and not competitive in the global market have created the frenzy today that government workers are overpaid compared to workers in the private sector, where they spent decades destroying good jobs! The corporate PR now spins that there's absolutely no more money for public education, public parks, public health, or, really, the public. Well, that's what happens when you steadily cut taxes on the super-wealthy and corporations. There would be plenty of money for the public, provided the United States restored tax rates that existed under Ronald Reagan. There's also a dog-whistle-politics aspect to the caricatures generated about government workers. For many African Americans, working in the public sector is one of the best jobs available because it provides health care and significant retirement plans. The common message that "these workers" are "lazy" and "don't work hard enough to justify a pension" is obviously racist: what they mean to say is that black people are lazy and undeserving of decent lives.

ENTER THE KOCH BROTHERS

According to recent scholarly research into the Koch brothers' main organization, Americans for Prosperity, its recent laserlike focus on anti-union legislation is driven by the Kochs' libertarian embrace of free markets and limited government. But that focus reflects the Kochs' strategic objectives for their companies, like maximizing profit and undoing regulations. The academic research backs up what those of us in the trenches have known for decades: right-wing corporate leaders understood the power-structure analysis of the United States far better than liberals, social do-gooders, and the Democratic Party. To take down government regulation, control the electoral system, and destroy the earth with impunity, they had to first destroy the most important corporate power-balancing force this country ever had: unions. The two Koch brothers, whose net wealth exceeds $50 billion each, set out to destroy the labor movement so they could keep destroying the planet—er, making money off it—free from regulation. The moneymaking industries in the conglomerate they inherited from their father include paper production, ranching, energy production, and chemical manufacturing—all of which contribute greatly to climate change. (Like Donald Trump, the Koch brothers didn't build their companies.)

Initially the Kochs put serious, unprecedented resources into state races so that they could weaken public-sector labor law, thus unions, state by state. Wisconsin under Scott Walker—who eliminated the right to collective bargaining in the public sector, leading to a 60 percent drop in union membership in the first full year his law took effect—is a case in point. The Koch brothers have also enjoyed success in Florida, Iowa, Michigan, and Indiana (to name a few) as a bevy of laws tightening restrictions on unions have rolled across the United States since the turn of the new millennium. Their efforts were stymied by many big states, however, that are traditionally Democratic Party strongholds, such as California, Illinois, and New York. Unions are still strong in these states, which is why they remain blue states. The right-wing desire to undo labor (and progressive) laws fell flat in these states. This led to right-wing billionaires' Plan B: concoct a national legal challenge that could land at the Supreme Court and finally wipe the remaining big donations from unions out of the electoral arena.

The Koch brothers had a staunch ally in the National Right to Work Legal Defense Foundation, a conservative group dedicated to ending unions and collective bargaining. They sought out workers who would file cases to press a First Amendment challenge to the agency fees the Supreme Court had deemed legal in 1977 with *Abood*. A number of major right-wing billionaires, including the Ed Uihlein Family Foundation, Harry Bradley, the Walton family (of Walmart), and the Donors Trust and Donors Capital foundations, funneled huge contributions to the organization. The NRTWLDF understood they would need to mount a lot of cases and work their way through the lower courts until one landed at the Supreme Court.

That case was *Harris v. Quinn*. The "Harris" in the case is Pamela Harris, one of the rare white women in a workforce that is overwhelmingly women of color. She was a personal-care assistant who was paid by the state of Illinois. Pamela Harris was not a union member, nor was her agency represented by any union. Yet we are led to believe she somehow found a national right-wing organization, National Right to Work Legal Defense Foundation, that has been devoted to destroying unions for the past seventy years to assist her—not the other way around.

Up until 2003, Illinois, like most states, excluded home-care workers from the right to collective bargaining. In 1983, two hundred home care workers voted to form a union. With the backing of SEIU, a national union, they began to plot a path to collective bargaining rights. It would take the Illinois workers until 2003 to pass legislation allowing them to collectively bargain. But all along the way, they were winning steady improvements in pay and benefits by acting in solidarity with each other, much like workers in a union.

In 1990, SEIU in Illinois won a big breakthrough toward collective bargaining rights for home-care workers when it secured workers' rights to "meet and confer," which obligates the employer to meet and discuss demands with workers, but not bargain with them. In 1994 they were granted union recognition, winning an actual first contract with fair share fees, which was another name for agency fees. SEIU would next begin to heavily invest in helping home-care workers in California, followed by Oregon, making similar breakthroughs in a campaign called Invisible No More. The state of Illinois became an official joint employer in 2003, and the process of formal collective bargaining began. AFSCME and other unions jumped on the home-care organizing bandwagon. In terms of sheer numbers of workers forming new unions, home-care workers became the biggest expansion of workers unionizing, with roughly 500,000 mostly women of color across a handful of big, Democrat-leaning states unionizing in the first decade of the new century. But to the right wing, this huge new union membership was the exact opposite of what they wanted: no unions. Thus they set out to undo the fastest-growing union sector: home-care workers.

The conservative-leaning court ruled in favor of Harris, and the decision hinged on a spurious argument: that the mostly women of color workforce paid by the state were only "partial public employees" because they worked in people's homes and not in an institutional setting. And because the court deemed millions of mostly women of color partial public employees, they were therefore exempt from rules and protections covering public employee unionization in Illinois.

It's important to dwell on the racial implications of the *Harris* ruling. In *Harris,* the court created something eerily reminiscent of the 1857 *Dred Scott* decision, when African Americans were deemed to count as only "three-fifths" people. Recall that when the NLRA passed, it omitted job classifications dominated by people of color—agriculture and domestic workers. In one fell swoop, *Harris v. Quinn* in 2014 essentially renewed and doubled down on the Jim Crow–era NLRA by once again foreclosing a path for women of color performing essential home-based, state-funded work to form strong unions by instead deeming these workers "partial employees."

SOME OF THE SAME CORPORATE BACKERS of today's *Harris v. Quinn* decision—and the 2012 case *Knox v. SEIU,* which set up *Harris v. Quinn,* which then set up the slam dunk *Janus v. AFSCME*—were funders of the 1947 political offensive to pass the Taft–Hartley Act. Yes, you read that right. And yes, that's been missing from most mass media headlines. But the anti-worker, anti-union crusade is one long string of tactical warfare in a strategy to return the riches of workers' labor back to the 1 percent. *Harris* is less well known than 2018's *Janus v. AFSCME* (the American Federation of State, County and Municipal Employees union), but it is understood as a direct precursor. In fact, it's in *Harris* that Justice Samuel Alito had to fabricate legal rationale that he could refer back to as a way to justify his decision in *Janus*.

The throughput of systemic racial violence in the early agricultural and domestic workforce—to the post–Civil War creation of lynch mobs in the South to armed militias and company armies and police forces South and North—continues through to the creation of the modern union-avoidance industry, which takes its current form beginning in the 1950s. It is abundantly clear that union decline is primarily the result of a multi-decade sustained war waged by the wealthy against the working class.

CHAPTER 3

Everything You Thought You Knew About Unions Is (Mostly) Wrong

FOUR DECADES INTO THE CURRENT WAVE OF ATTACKS ON UNIONS, I find myself in conversations that reveal how successful the propaganda campaign against unions has been and how deeply its messages have penetrated the public consensus. Liberal acquaintances of mine say that union members are spoiled, that unions protect incompetent workers, charge too much in dues, and preclude business innovation. Liberals also see unions through a dusty historical lens: they appear to be corrupt, racist, and sexist; they seem to be blocking global economic progress; they are tools of U.S. imperialism and are in cahoots with the mafia. Friends who wouldn't dream of eating nonorganic food, who drive electric vehicles, send money to save Tibet, and marched wearing pink pussy hats complain that the teachers' union is the reason public schools are deteriorating, or that striking transit workers ruined their commute, or that unions are the reason they can't get an appointment this decade with their HMO.

For several generations, the idea of a union has been intentionally twisted, maligned, defamed, attacked, and systematically equated with the "last century." In this era of big tech and globalization, the idea that unions are "anti-innovation" and "irrelevant" has gained new traction. Of course, these ideas aren't based in any sensible reality. The best Madison Avenue advertisers can make nearly anyone tear up when they use images of a mother who is a breast cancer patient needing an overpriced drug that a profit-driven pharmaceutical company is pushing. So it isn't hard to figure out why one of corporate America's most persistent marketing efforts, one that unifies all kinds of different sectors of employers—the marketing that attacks unions and continuously tars worker power—has the public suspicious, if not downright confused, about unions. It's important to debunk these ideas, one by one.

ASSUMPTION 1:

Union Membership and Union Dues Are Compulsory

While *mandatory* was once the fashionable word for the union-avoidance industry, in the past couple of decades a pollster must have discovered that *compulsory* has more traction. Just about everywhere you see a defamatory article about unions these days, you see the word *compulsory*. It's usually repeated for emphasis, as in: "We object to compulsory union membership and compulsory dues and fines." Like other concepts spun by the right wing, the terminology has little to do with the truth. During the twelve years between 1935 and 1947—the era when workers built unions strong enough to rapidly reduce income inequality—it was possible for unions to have a closed shop, which meant that everyone in the workplace had to be a member of a particular union *before* being hired by a certain employer. Closed shops were, it's worth noting, the product of workers first deciding, by democratic majority votes, to form a union. Once workers in a given workplace had voted to unionize, they then negotiated a clause stating that any future workers had to be union members. (In order to do this, workers had to find the union hall and sign up before applying for a job at a closed shop employer.) These clauses were not merely provided for by the law; a majority of workers had to vote in a union and then negotiate for a closed shop.

The Taft–Hartley Act, discussed in chapter 2, made the closed shop illegal in 1947. After Taft–Hartley, private-sector workers (but only in states that were not or are not right-to-work) can still negotiate what's called a "union security clause" into their own union contracts with management. A union security clause can stipulate that once a worker is hired, he or she has a designated period, typically thirty days, to join the union and begin paying dues. But even still, these clauses are negotiated *contract by contract,* workplace by workplace; weak unions don't generally have the ability to win this kind of clause in their agreements. For those workers who develop the kind of union strength it takes to win a union security clause, they then have the right to vote their proposed contracts up or down—meaning vote yes or no to ratification. Because of this, even workers who weren't working at a particular employer when the union was first formed get the opportunity every few years to vote on whether or not they still want to have a union security clause in their contract. Since all workers do have the right to vote on this more often than they get to vote for their mayor or the president of the United States, it seems obvious that when billionaire-funded right-wing organizations such as the National Right to Work Committee or the Mackinac Center or the Heritage Foundation call this "compulsory," they are lying.

In 1977 in *Abood v. Detroit Board of Education,* the Supreme

Court decided that workers in the public sector—employed by a government entity—could not be compelled by the majority actions of their coworkers to join the union, unlike their private-sector counterparts. Invoking the First Amendment on the grounds that the employer was the government, the court ruled that if an individual worker chose not to become a member of a union that a majority of their coworkers voted to form, then they could pay a lesser amount than union dues, called an agency fee. The Supreme Court recognized that because every worker in a unionized setting benefits from the union, it would be fair that all workers contribute to the nonpolitical aspects of the union's work. Since 1977, then, each union in the government or public sector has calculated a lesser fee for those who objected to becoming a member. The fee covered the cost of collective bargaining and representational assistance to nonunion workers in a unionized workplace and excluded any donations to political causes or elections. Part of the rationale for the fee is that each union in the United States has what's called "exclusive representation" for whatever groups of workers vote to unionize with a union in their workplace, which means that the union is the sole entity that represents all unionized employees within a given workplace.

Exclusive representation developed as an important strategy for unions after the passage of the National Labor Relations Act. Prior to the passage of the NLRA in the United States, employers often broke up unions by establishing "company unions," which were distinct from independent trade unions because they were most often tools of management. Even if employers denied they had a hand in it, they would intimidate, offer preferential treatment to, and otherwise "encourage" the workers to set up an organization that they would claim was independent of the employer. The NLRA explicitly banned company unions, but to safeguard against softer versions of company unions—say, a situation in which management cajoled a few workers into forming "an independent union" in exchange for a raise—unions demanded exclusive representation. The courts said fine, but in exchange for securing the right to keep out competition from a weaker, invisible-hand-of-the-employer-type union, then *all* workers had to be represented by the union. This concept, "exclusive representation," carried over from the private sector to the public sector.

For forty-one years, *Abood* was considered settled law. Then, rather suddenly, Justice Samuel Alito began to signal that he was inviting challenges to *Abood*. In 2016, the court deadlocked in a related case, *Friedrichs v. the California Teachers Association,* but only because Justice Antonin Scalia died before the decision. That case litigated the exact same question as the case that came one year later, in 2018, called *Janus v. AFSCME.* The newly appointed conservative justice Neil Gorsuch provided the fifth vote in a 5–4 decision that overturned *Abood* and abolished the agency shop, which meant no one has to pay a dime for the benefits of collective bargaining.

The 1977 *Abood* case endured for forty-one years because previous challenges failed. It's well worth reading the dissent by Justice Elena Kagan in the *Janus* case for a deeper understanding of just how blatantly politically motived the *Janus* decision was. For example, she wrote,

There is no sugarcoating today's opinion. The majority overthrows a decision entrenched in this Nation's law—and in its economic life—for over 40 years. As a result, it prevents the American people, acting through their state and local officials, from making important choices about workplace governance. . . . And it threatens not to be the last. Speech is everywhere—a part of every human activity (employment, health care, securities trading, you name it). For that reason, almost all economic and regulatory policy affects or touches speech. So the majority's road runs long. And at every stop are black-robed rulers overriding citizens' choices. The First Amendment was meant for better things. It was meant not to undermine but to protect democratic governance—including over the role of public-sector unions.

In addition, just weeks after the 2018 *Janus* decision, Mark Janus himself quit his job with the state of Illinois and went to work for the National Right to Work Committee. Enough said.

To be crystal clear, since 1977, no worker employed by the government *had* to be a union member, not Pamela Harris of *Harris v. Quinn,* not Mark Janus of *Janus.* They did not have to join or pay dues. The system was not broken. It was absurdly fair, in fact. In sum, then, no one is forced to join a union. Every few years, when workers renegotiate their contracts, they have a chance to vote on whether or not they have a union security clause when they vote to reject or ratify their contracts. That's only in the private sector, in states that are not right-to-work states. The only thing that strong union security clauses, voted on by members, "forced" was a steady decline in income inequality, because when everyone has to contribute to their union, unions have more money and can better compete with the bosses at work and the billionaires in politics.

Now, in the public sector, any worker can join a union or not, pay dues or not, pay a fee or not. The public sector is the Wild West for employer-bribery schemes and employer favoritism. To weaken or destroy a union all managers have to do is invite workers into their offices one by one and promise workers a special raise, or a better shift, or their preferred vacation schedule, if they drop their union membership. It's simple, and it's corrosive.

As of this writing, in the private sector, if workers are not in a right-to-work state, they still have the ability to negotiate a union security clause if they choose. There's a bevy of cases making their way now to the high court—all intended to overturn other key aspects of labor law, including undoing exclusive representation.

Given the conservative bent of the current Supreme Court, it won't be surprising if they soon outlaw membership and dues in the private sector, too, and for that matter, collective bargaining. Nothing will be too extreme coming from today's Supreme Court, which is why organizing and strikes are the only real solution.

ASSUMPTION 2:

Unions Are Only for Blue-Collar Workers

Employers frequently say that professionals don't need unions and imply that less-skilled workers (which itself is a loaded judgment) might need them. This has never been true, and interestingly, white-collar workers—*white collar* typically referring to professionals who have some kind of college degree or special certification—have been organizing in droves the past few years. The National Education Association, the largest union of teachers in the United States, was founded in 1857; the American Nurses Association, in 1897; the International Federation of Professional and Technical Engineers, 1918—there are countless other examples. In fact, with many factories intentionally sent out of the United States to foreign shores to avoid unionization at home, the past decade has seen an explosion of union formation in the "white-collar" professions.

Gabriel Winant, a historian finishing his doctorate at Yale, points out in a 2018 article:

> Professionals are not wholly unique. After all, all workers exercise judgement; every job requires skill, recognized or not. But autonomy from management has traditionally been an explicit part of the job description only for the credentialed. The reason, in fact, professionals are such rule-followers is exactly because they must behave reliably to be trusted with this autonomy. Yet in recent years, this

white-collar autonomy has been eroded. The testing regime imposed on public schools has routinized teaching. Nurses do paperwork rather than spend time bedside . . . the rise of contingent academic employment has eroded scholarly control over teaching and research—gutting the academic freedom once at the ethical core of the profession.

In the past several years, two types of white-collar professionals in particular have been unionizing in record numbers: journalists and college professors. On college campuses, after three decades of austerity—of corporations and the rich paying less taxes and thus draining public university budgets—administrators have slashed the number of full-time tenure track professors. This has led to huge downward mobility for new Ph.D.'s who are coming into teaching positions on college and university campuses. Many of these new young professors who teach a full workload are now adjuncts, which means they don't have any job security, have low wages, poor to no benefits, no academic freedom, and no path to tenure or permanency. In 1995, 75 percent of all teaching positions on college campuses were full-time and tenure track, with only 25 percent of all positions as adjuncts. The concept of the adjunct professor decades back was to have a few positions on campus that enabled outside experts to come into the university and, for a semester, and for compensation that amounted to something more like an honorarium for their labor because they were employed elsewhere, offer their expertise from the field to students. Twenty years later, by 2015, the reverse was true: 75 percent of all teaching positions are now temporary or adjunct positions.

In June 2018, the *Chronicle of Higher Education* published an analysis of unionization and teaching contracts between 2010 and 2016 at thirty-five colleges and universities and reported, "Adjunct faculty won salary increases at every institution we looked at," and that salary increases for the unionized full-time faculty were significantly above the average. Further, they found that unionizing improved working conditions across the board, from increased access to professional development to increased teaching resources to greater academic freedom.

Likewise, a surge of organizing among journalists has been taking place among digital media. What began in 2015 with a union drive at Gawker, which owned Deadspin, Gizmodo, Jalopnik, and Jezebel, has mushroomed into a movement, spreading to *New York* magazine, BuzzFeed, Salon, *Jacobin,* ThinkProgress, and Law360, to name a few. This unionization movement has even reached longtime major newspapers, including successful organizing drives at the *Los Angeles Times* and the *Chicago Tribune.* Union busters were hired in some of these campaigns, most egregiously at Gothamist and DNAinfo, where, despite the union busters, the journalists voted to form a union. The next day, journalists woke up to the insanity that many other types of workers experience: the employer shut down the otherwise excellent websites because, in his own words in a published letter, he doesn't believe in unions!

Like most workers pushed to the brink, white-collar workers realize they don't have much ability to make changes when up against a CEO or shareholders. One highly skilled registered nurse with whom I worked in contract negotiations—Alfredo Serrano—is a perfect example of the reasons white-collar workers form unions: in the case of nurses, it's generally to force management to hire more nurses in order to maintain a more balanced nurse-to-patient ratio, or safe staffing ratios, so that nurses can actually care for their patients. Serrano is an operating room nurse who works for the single largest hospital corporation in the United States and the world, the Healthcare Corporation of America, now HCA Healthcare, which owns more than two hundred *for-profit* hospitals in the United States.

Serrano and his colleagues work at Sunrise, a sprawling HCA hospital complex in the heart of Las Vegas. It includes a children's hospital with specialized pediatric care, a level III trauma unit, and outpatient clinics. To Serrano, "The mentality of a nurse is to care for those in need—at least it should be—and most of us are doing this work because we want to care for those in need, meaning everyone, our entire team, and our community, not just our patient. Some nurses do come into the field with an elite professional attitude; until someone shits all over them and they realize they are just a nurse in a big, moneymaking system."

Nearly all HCA facilities are in right-to-work states, where unions exist on a purely voluntary basis. This isn't an accident: it's part of HCA's strategic plan to operate in states with weaker union laws in order to profit off cheaper labor. This might be a good time to mention that the founding family, and current major shareholders of HCA, a family from Tennessee named Frist, practiced a similar profit maximization strategy to grossly underpay workers and to control their income stream. Senator Bill Frist was elected as the majority leader of the U.S. Senate from 2003 to 2007 and decided how much his family business would be reimbursed by Medicare and Medicaid payments, which is the largest income stream to so-called private-sector hospitals. Stacked deck?

As I discussed in chapter 2, professionals can choose to unionize with other professionals or to be part of a union with all other workers employed by the same company. While a lot of professionals are in unions with professionals in similar fields, from a strict analysis of power standpoint—as well as from the standpoints of social justice and solidarity building—that is a less effective option than unionizing with workers in the same sector who work for the same employer across all workers. The CIO understood this weakness back in 1935 and built stronger unions by uniting all types of workers who work for the same employer together under a single union. Winning a good union contract is about power and strategy. The more workers, the more leverage, the more power.

Serrano's experience illustrates the brilliance of the CIO's approach even today. During negotiations HCA routinely sets out to bust or at least weaken the workers by dividing and conquering them. HCA successfully pit nurses against non-nurses in their first union contract by offering the nurses considerably bigger raises in exchange for the nurses vocally supporting management's decision that the non-nurses would win far smaller raises and inferior benefits. It worked, and there was huge resentment between the workers for the next four years, which was the life of the collective agreement. This wasn't just bad for the workers: this affected patient care, too, since caring for patients requires seamless cooperation of all the workers. You don't want to be a patient in a hospital where, say, the anesthesia tech hates the nurse or vice versa. You want high levels of communication and cooperation and respect between all staff.

But when an organizer was hired and helped the workers understand that they could win more by standing together, the nurses built solidarity with the rest of the workers and won even bigger raises! And so did everyone else. The cooperation between all the workers at HCA improved dramatically. As I discussed in chapter 1, this importance of solidarity-building played out in the West Virginia education strike, where teachers won a 5 percent raise because nonteachers, such as bus drivers and cooks, walked out with them. The unity results in everyone getting even better contracts. In the case of Seranno and his colleagues and the teachers and their colleagues, they secured their biggest raises in decades by working with the nonprofessional staff.

ASSUMPTION 3:

Unions Are Racist

Some unions in the United States have a long, storied history of racism. Because unions are composed of people—and the United

States has a deep history of racializing its workforce, beginning with slaves—racism is a significant issue in many unions. As labor activist and author Bill Fletcher wrote, "White workers are taught to prioritize their racial identity as white over their reality as part of the laboring classes and later as part of the working class." That's not an excuse: unions, as institutions of the working class for the working class, should be held to a higher standard.

Racism can be most apparent in construction-related unions, some of which are also plagued by rampant sexism—which I'll address more directly in another section. Overt racism was (and can still be) more transparent in the construction trades primarily because of the structure of labor relations with employers. Unionized construction contractors need a big mix of skilled labor to erect, say, a big building. In the construction field, strong unions have the power and ability to win contracts where they stipulate that the workers who build or renovate a building, or road, or bridge, etc., shall be selected by the union for each construction job, not by the human resource department at a company. These provisions create what's known as union hiring halls—functionally a casting call for jobs that typically takes place in physical union halls. When done well, hiring halls are the most powerful form of solidarity and relationship building possible because workers engage with their own organization face-to-face by going to the union hall to get a new gig. Workers understand that their good wages and benefits flow from their unity and commitment to one another. The flip side, which might already be obvious, is that when racists and sexists are added to this scenario, racism and sexism in the unions become immediately transparent. For instance, if there's an all-white and Italian workforce on a construction site in a highly diverse region, the union made the choice to hire those workers, not management.

For much of my life in the labor movement, because I place such a premium on seeing the broader community as an extension of the power of the workers, I've listened to numerous African

American ministers explain how their community was excluded from the union. Indeed it was. But there's an equally powerful history of unions challenging racism and actively supporting the civil rights movement. There are also plenty of enlightened leaders in the construction field, and I've personally watched as the union becomes the primary mechanism in the workers' lives to help them to overcome racism. In the United Brotherhood of Carpenters, in their Southwest and Northeast Regional District Councils in this century—to name just two large unions in the midst of construction booms—the transformation from racist to anti-racist was extraordinary. Classes of Latinos and African Americans graduated from the all-important apprenticeship programs in high numbers, were placed on big jobs together with white workers, and forged solidarity in the union halls and work site by work site, helping overcome racism.

In addition, some unions played very important roles in the civil rights movement. The national health care workers union District 1199 was birthed in the civil rights movement; labor rights and civil rights were inextricable from each other. Malcolm X and Martin Luther King Jr. themselves were frequently on union picket lines. As I mentioned in the last chapter, King was assassinated when he traveled to Memphis, where he went to support a strike by African American sanitation workers. The United Auto Workers, at the national level, was one of the biggest financial backers of the civil rights movement, although it has been criticized for not directly challenging racism on the shop floor.

Although 1199, AFSCME, and the UAW were key players in the civil rights movement, perhaps the single best example of a union directly challenging racism from its earliest founding and among many white working-class people in the era of the Jim Crow South was the mighty United Packinghouse Workers of America. (The UPWA later merged into the United Food and Commercial Workers Union, UFCW). There is an excellent book on this by Roger

Horowitz, titled *Negro and White, Unite and Fight: A Social History of Industrial Unionism in Meatpacking,* in which the author details the lengths to which the UPWA directly and consistently tackled racism in its ranks and in its community. Headquartered in Chicago, the UPWA, like most anti-racist unions, was headed by left-wing leaders who understood that no division of the working class could be tolerated if workers were to overcome the deep and violent anti-worker, anti-union tradition in the United States.

In 1952, the union surveyed their members in the South to understand issues workers wanted addressed in upcoming contract negotiations. The survey results revealed that nearly all Southern whites didn't want to work with blacks or share eating facilities. Dismayed by the results but determined to use the union as a social tool for undoing racism, according to Horowitz, the union committed to a radical, bold anti-discrimination project. It established a new department, with substantial financial resources, dedicated to ending discrimination, and put a top vice president of the union, who was African American, in charge of this effort. Horowitz writes:

> The UPWA's expanded anti-discrimination program had three broad areas. First, unionists identified discriminatory practices in their own plants and tried to correct them. This included integrating lily-white departments and dressing rooms and ending hiring discrimination against black workers. Second, locals attacked discriminatory practices in their communities, primarily restrictions on black access to bars, restaurants, and public facilities and also employment restrictions by local businesses. Finally, packing house workers consciously worked with and influenced community-based institutions, especially the NAACP.

This last point matters because integrating class and race is a two-way effort. Back then, the NAACP and the Urban League were focused on what historian Erik Gellman calls the "talented tenth," which was a strategy of advancing the most elite African Americans through politeness and friendly negotiation. This wasn't an effective tactic. Gellman's historical research highlights the work of the National Negro Congress, a black liberation movement associated with the Communist Party and founded in early 1936, on the heels of the passage of the NLRA. The NNC set out to build a bottom-up working-class civil rights movement by partnering with the CIO and placing black organizers in key CIO unions so that as they built factory power, they were tackling racism and economic exploitation as one struggle.

The Packinghouse union even addressed specific actions to support black women—not only black men—in the workforce. In the Chicago locals, they began to use the nondiscrimination clauses in contracts to force plants to hire black women, not just white women. Given their effectiveness, UPWA—along with all left-led unions that were addressing racism—was singled out as a target by McCarthyism's ideological witch hunts. The very unions that did address structural racism were attacked by elite power racists using other structures—the Cold War, Congress and the Taft–Hartley Act—to eradicate leaders who understood unions as a social force for ending discrimination.

There are plenty of examples like this that are less well known, perhaps because corporate media covers businesses more than they cover unions, thus helping erase the rich and radical traditions of unions as a force for challenging racism. Given that the motivation for the Taft–Hartley Act was primarily about Southern whites understanding unions as the biggest threat to Jim Crow, it seems rather evident that unions were, in fact, challenging racism in profound ways.

As political scientist, community organizer, and former MSNBC host Dorian Warren points out, "Organizations shape political identity and behavior. For white men in America (across class), the difference between whether they vote Democratic or Republican, conservative or progressive, can be summed up by whether they belong to a union or a church. This has always been true, but in our current context of the rise of a nativist, racist, white identity politics, the crucial role of unions in shaping political interests and voting behavior for white Americans and especially white men is more important than ever."

ASSUMPTION 4:

Unions Are Sexist

Of course, some unions are sexist for the same reasons that they are racist: union formation is a product of a sexist society. The reality, however, is that women have long done significantly better by having a union than by not having a union.

Because of the intentional strategic offshoring and thus dismantling of the unionized domestic private sector discussed in chapter 2, there's a huge and growing asymmetry in the percentage of unionized workers in the public sector, which is now a sector that is chiefly staffed by women, versus the private sector. This means that the once-male-dominated union movement is about to be a female-dominated union movement. According to one new report by the National Bureau of Economic Research, "Currently, 47% of all unionized employees in the U.S., and 53% in Canada, are women. A typical union worker today is more likely to be a female teacher or nurse with a university degree than a male factory worker with only a high school education."

If you look at the differential pay and benefits for women who are unionized—and for that matter, people of color as well as women of color—everyone in a union is better compensated. (According to the most recent data, the comparison of union to nonunion wages across all people in the United States is $1,041 to $829 weekly.)

When it comes to family-supporting health care coverage, 76.6 percent of unionized women are covered versus only 51.4 percent for nonunion women. The weekly wages of unionized women are $942 compared to $723 for their nonunion counterparts. Latinas within unions take home on average $739 per week compared with those who don't, whose paycheck is considerably less: $520 a week, a 42.1 percent improvement with a union.

Many factors contribute to the disparity, including education levels, sectors of the economy, and geography. But the simple fact is that unions create real economic advantages for all categories of workers. Pay and compensation transparency are greatly improved when workers are unionized because most union contracts have full pay transparency.

Here's an example that illustrates how a good union is the best way to tackle both racism and sexism head-on.

On April 10, 2018, during the morning news on New York City's NPR station, there was a story about Equal Pay Day, the day each year when women finally catch up to the amount of pay that men doing the same work had received on December 31 of the year before. In 2018, for white women, that date was April 10. For black women, that day didn't come until August. Reporter Shumita Basu interviewed Joi Chaney, executive director of the Equal Pay Today! campaign. Chaney argued that one solution to the problem, the solution they were making their focus in 2018, is "pay transparency"—encouraging workers and employers to be open about how much they are paid. In closing, Basu appealed to listeners: "If you work somewhere where you and your coworkers know at least roughly what each other makes, call and tell us how you learned that information. Is it a company policy? Did you figure it out through informal channels? Leave us a voicemail."

There was no mention of the word *union* during the broadcast. Or even a hint that Basu had an inkling that pay transparency is a part of every good union contract.

Here's the reality: under the National Labor Relations Act, every unionized worker with collective bargaining rights may submit, through their union, what's called an information request as they prepare for negotiations. Anything involving "pay and working conditions" can be requested and the employer must answer in a timely fashion. Failure on the part of the employer to respond to a union information request can result in legal charges and fines, as it would constitute what's called an unfair labor practice, or a ULP, in union lingo. Plenty of employers stall, resist, and more in actually turning over the information, but eventually they must.

The results can be shocking and can reveal long-standing patterns of racism, sexism, favoritism, and retaliation.

I witnessed this personally in late August 2016 in Philadelphia, where I was serving as the chief negotiator in contract talks between a thousand nurses and their employer. I was negotiating alongside Marie Celestine, a quiet and demure four-foot, ten-inch black nurse who worked in pre-admission testing. Celestine had been working at her hospital for forty years. She was among the most tenured nurses in the hospital, and she commanded the respect of her colleagues for her decades of dedication to her patients. Pre-admission testing nurses are calm by training, if not by nature, because they are the nurse a patient sees as they prepare for an operation. The patients are often scared, and the pre-admit nurse isn't just performing a litany of tests to assess physical readiness; she's also holding her patients' hands and carefully explaining that everything will be fine.

We had developed a quick Excel spreadsheet tool using data supplied by the hospital that allowed each worker to type in their name to see their pay compared with that of all other workers in their shift, their unit, by years of service, by years of experience. When Celestine saw her pay rate compared with those of one thousand other nurses—almost all were considerably younger and more recently hired—she finally broke. She was making thousands of dollars less annually than her mostly white juniors. Forty years of acting as a well-behaved woman, the social conditioning she learned in life as a young black woman raised in the era of Jim Crow and in nursing school, where the creed "service above self" is administered to nursing students as steadily as an IV drips medicine, unraveled as she stared at my computer screen, shocked by the disparity.

Finally, she looked up from the spreadsheet. "Under our merit pay system, you get rewarded based on how your managers rate your attitude," she told me. "I've been denied the merit raises for most of my entire lifetime at this hospital." Celestine is highly skilled and has the patience of a saint, so it seems her being black was the only possible explanation for why she had been denied merit pay increases. Over the course of the next six months of weekly negotiations, which took up to twelve hours a day, she never missed a session. Her mission from that point forward was to wrest control of her life away from the management team.

At the fourth negotiation session, on September 28, 2016, Celestine stood up tall and made a presentation to the management team about the racist nature of the merit-pay system. By the end of the collective bargaining process, Celestine won a fair and equal wage scale, eliminated the abusive merit-pay system, and ended racial disparities, securing 100 percent parity between men and women.

When people can easily see that a black woman—such as Marie Celestine—is making far less than a white woman, or a white woman is earning less than a male colleague with comparable education and even less experience doing the same work, but whom the employer hired many years later, there's immediate grounds for a unionized woman, and in this case, a unionized woman of color, to take action. Nonunion nurses, who are unaware of how their employer is playing favorites or merely paying according to the managers' mood the day the person walked in to negotiate an individual versus collective hire agreement, is at a serious disadvantage. Even if a national mandatory pay transparency act passed Congress (don't hold your breath!), that wouldn't give women the right to sit united at the negotiations table and demand equal and fair pay the way union negotiators can and do.

A union contract creates the vehicle for women to be armed with knowledge and the ability to do something about generally lousy conditions at work, including child care, dependent coverage in health care, maternity leave, and the ability to control their own schedules. The Hands Off, Pants On campaign discussed in chapter 1 is another example of how unions create the terrain for women to engage in immediate problem solving—in the case of the Hands Off campaign, by effectively challenging sexual harassment. In 2018, unionized graduate workers fought for and won pathbreaking anti-sexual-harassment language, including at the University of California and the University of Connecticut, to name just two.

You can find shelves lined with books about gender; class; gender and class; gender, class, and race; and their relationship to unions and vice versa. On the subject of women and labor, there's probably no author who has handled it more comprehensively than Dorothy Sue Cobble. She's written volumes on the complicated history of women fighting for their own needs through their unions in the 1930s up to the beginning of Second Wave feminism, when mostly white and middle-class women began what they called the women's movement. The result was huge tension in upper-class women making proclamations that were often amazingly tone deaf to working-class women.

In her seminal book *The Other Women's Movement: Workplace Justice and Social Rights in Modern America,* Cobble lifts the history of working-class women fighting for gender justice inside and through their unions and gives it a name: labor feminism. She outlines the many achievements won by women in unions, including more recent ones, such as John F. Kennedy's 1961 establishment of the President's Commission on the Status of Women, which contributed to the passage of the Equal Pay Act, Title VII of the Civil Rights Act, and amendments to the Fair Labor Standards Act (FLSA).

More privileged women, like those who wrote the still-unpassed Equal Rights Amendment, failed to seriously consider the needs of working-class women who had spent decades winning specific union-negotiated protections that the ERA would have abolished, creating an unnecessary and damning class division in the women's movement. This is also covered well in a more academic book, Jane Mansbridge's *Why We Lost the ERA*. Unfortunately, some of this same tension was on display in the largest protest in national history, the Women's March in Washington, D.C., on January 21, 2017, one day after Trump's inauguration. One week before the march, I was interviewed on an NPR-affiliated radio station, along with one of the national march organizers. When the radio show's host asked about whether the demands of the march would include the right to unionize, the representative of the march replied, "I don't know a thing about that. Unions aren't my department." I wanted to scream or cry, or both. But in any case, I did point out that the reaction was a serious problem.

Today, with women-dominated fields growing, including societally urgent ones such as home health care, the future of the union movement is even more so the future of the women's movement. If only women will unite, together.

ASSUMPTION 5:

Unions Are Anti-Environment

In the polarized United States, recent discussions about the climate crisis have fixated on the Green New Deal proposed by Congressmember Alexandria Ocasio-Cortez and Senator Ed Markey. Headlines have alternated between descriptions of the resolution's clear vision and more skeptical assessments of its prospects—including from important potential backers: "AFL-CIO criticizes Green New Deal, calling it 'not achievable or realistic.'" The backdrop to the debates raging in the first quarter of 2019 have been a catastrophic series of extreme storms predicted by climate scientists since the 1980s. So-called bomb cyclones hit the Midwest, massive rainstorms battered California after a devastating wildfire season, and killer tornadoes hit the South, wiping out crops. Tragically, people are dying because of the lack of preparation in dealing with the crisis. And although a letter from the AFL-CIO criticizing the GND may seem like a willful refusal to face the scale of the crisis, we need considerably more than a bold vision to get labor to come out swinging for the Green New Deal. It simply doesn't matter that well-intentioned progressive environmentalists reject the divisive frame of jobs-versus-environment—the progressive environmentalists have yet to prove they can move from rhetoric to reality about good, unionized green jobs.

There have always been union leaders who care deeply about ecological issues and who put safeguarding the natural environment on equal footing with allowing workers to win a decent, if not great, quality of life. Likewise, there have always been unions that ally with environmentalists. The best example from the 1970s through the early 1990s was, amazingly, the Oil, Chemical and Atomic Workers union. The OCAW leadership, particularly its longtime president, Tony Mazzocchi, understood perhaps more than most that their industries were killing their members and the planet. They worked hard to fight for a "Just Transition," which was a 1970s forerunner of the Green New Deal. OCAW was arguably the most important organization in the fight to pass the Occupational Safety and Health Act (OSHA) in 1970. It remains a key lever in efforts to prevent, understand, and fix issues relating to environmental hazards and contamination. OCAW was also a significant player in the fight to win the federal Superfund law, an accountability program that requires corporations to fund the cleanups of their environmental contamination.

In 1986, OCAW and other unions worked with community-based

organizations to get Congress to amend the Superfund act with a provision that most billionaires fought tooth and nail, the right-to-know amendment. That law revolutionized people's understanding of what chemical poisons are being used by companies in their communities. Up until the law's passage, major corporations avoided responsibility for their actions by claiming they weren't responsible for massive fish die-offs, children and adult cancer clusters, and other illnesses. Workers, with and through the union in the polluting industries themselves, provided essential information that helped the coalition finally win the law's passage. The amendment is credited with sparking the environmental justice movement; for the first time, activists could prove the correlation between polluting industries and their proximity to communities of color.

Demands for real climate justice got a welcome boost in the spring of 2019 when youth walked out of schools worldwide on March 15, urged to go "on strike" by sixteen-year-old Greta Thunberg, from Sweden. Images in mainstream and social media were constellated with pictures of young people marching into plazas across the world, confronting intransigent elected officials and speaking truth to power. Youth has always brought two essential ingredients to social movements: moral compass and an exciting, unique form of energy. Their goals are brilliant, and they are uncompromising. But to halt and reverse the carbon economy, save the planet, and create a future with jobs that youth will look forward to requires far more power and a serious strategy.

To win, we must heed the advice from union organizer Nato Green. In a March 2019 article about how public service unions like the one he works for, local SEIU 1021 in California, can—and must—negotiate for climate justice, he wrote, "Any seasoned union campaigner worth her salt loves a contract fight because it has a hard deadline that focuses everyone's attention—expiration and a strike threat. Climate science gives us a new deadline and an opportunity to show that we're up to the task. We have 12 years."

Green is certainly right that good union organizers love a contract fight. If we take the twelve years outlined in the recent Intergovernmental Panel on Climate Change report as our deadline for drastically cutting carbon emissions, what's a *credible* plan to win by 2030?

For people serious about winning really hard fights—and there are virtually none more difficult than tackling the fossil fuel industry—making a plan starts by conducting comprehensive power structure analysis and building a real war room. The fight to save the planet is indeed a war, one that so far has been won by the Koch brothers and their ilk. Our side needs to get used to militaristic language because what we've been doing—being polite and attending big, orderly marches—isn't saving the planet or creating a fair and just economy; it's wishful thinking to imagine otherwise.

During the past forty years, environmental groups have relied on advocacy, mobilizing, and legal strategies instead of doing the much harder, more powerful work of building a mass movement. The result has been an environmental movement with little in the way of a popular base, easily scapegoated as elitist and thus lacking the power needed to win.

One recent important example of unions tackling the climate crisis started when unions in New York sat down in 2014 to do something serious about climate change. According to Vincent Alvarez, the president of the New York City Central Labor Council, the official body of the largest regional organization of the AFL-CIO in the country, "We took a look at the frustrating discourse and inaction on climate issues that was taking place in Washington, D.C., and decided that we wanted to get something done on the ground that tackled the climate and inequality crises. We wanted to build a program that could start actually making measurable improvements in building a more resilient climate, addressing the dual crisis of climate change and inequality."

Alvarez explains that rather than focusing on the 10 percent of the issues that are divisive—such as the Keystone pipeline and fracking, the issues that have garnered the most media attention in the climate fight thus far—it makes more sense to start with the 90 percent of the issues that environmentalists and unions can easily agree on, including infrastructure, public transportation, and energy production. But before we can address the 10 percent that divides unions from environmentalists, environmentalists need to demonstrate, with real actions, that they can help win high-quality union jobs in these three sectors. In the absence of concrete evidence that we can actually produce realistic alternatives to pipelines, the fossil fuel lobby will continue to drive division.

Lara Skinner, the executive director of the Worker Institute, who has been driving the New York State union climate jobs initiative, says that establishing a union-only working group on climate was central to making progress. Skinner, like many unionists who care deeply about climate change, spent several years racking her brain trying to bring environmentalists and unionists together. The fight to block the construction of the Keystone XL pipeline in the late Obama years made headlines but led to tensions and fissures in a budding blue-green movement. The fossil fuel lobby dug into the protests against the Keystone pipeline, using it as a wedge issue to turn workers against environmentalists by making it seem as if the environmentalists were trying to take away jobs. Environmentalists played into the fossil fuel lobby's messaging by arguing in lengthy diatribes that there were fewer jobs at stake in the KXL fight than the industry claimed.

But that wasn't the point. Coming out of a massive recession that had hammered the working class—wiping out savings, pensions, 401(k)s, and the value of houses, and bringing new construction to a standstill—high-paying unions jobs were hard to come by. Debating exactly how many workers would lose those jobs played right into the bosses' hands: environmentalists seemed willing to accept job loss as collateral damage. Instead of nitpicking how many workers would keep suffering the effects of the recession, the environmental movement should have doubled down on lifting up the many infrastructure projects in states along the pipeline route and pushed back with shovel-ready jobs as a real alternative. But as some doors were closing because of the divisive nature of the fight, others opened.

A few months after the height of Keystone dissent, Hurricane Sandy hit. According to Skinner, Sandy "drove home to union members in New York City how serious the issue was. And Irene had hit upstate New York, and everyone was realizing how unprepared we were for what's coming." The storms created an opening for what Skinner and her team realized had to be a union-only discussion about climate change. Environmentalists pay lip service to green jobs but consistently underestimate how seriously unions take high-quality, really good union jobs. So in 2014, a group of New York unions, whose members were hit hard up and down state by Sandy, decided to start a process to educate themselves about the climate crisis. They formed a working group that included unions key to the solutions: in the energy, transport, and infrastructure sectors, as well as the public service unions. They committed to meet once per quarter and to start by educating themselves by bringing in climate scientists to better understand the threats.

As part of their self-education, the unions took a delegation from New York to Denmark, hosted by Danish unions. According to Alvarez, "It was really important to get beyond the discussion and witness first-hand and meet with unionized Danish workers in the manufacturing plants, to see how the transition to wind power was experienced by and embraced by the Danish union workers."

In just three years, the working group produced a groundbreaking report coauthored by Skinner, titled "Reversing Inequality, Combatting Climate Change: A Climate Jobs Program for New York State." The report—comprehensive, smart, with buy-in from all key unions—should serve as a blueprint for what ought to happen state by state and nationally. The unions quickly transitioned from the report to action, using union power to secure a huge victory: New York will get *half* its total energy needs met by renewable offshore wind power by 2035. Worth $50 billion so far, the agreement they won contains a union-jobs guarantee known as a Project Labor Agreement, or PLA. There's no other state, let alone a big one, that has a concrete plan to reduce by half its reliance on fossil fuels that fast. It happened because, as Skinner says, "Unions educated themselves and got really clear on what we need to seriously get to scale on green jobs." Green jobs plans must be driven by the people who will do the work.

A real war room to win the Green New Deal must start with unions doing what unions did in New York: take initiative, be dead serious about the issue, educate themselves, and use their own knowledge and power to scale up and make a credible plan to win. Unions in New York did not sit around complaining, waiting to be invited to some half-ass policy table where everyone talks past one another and nothing much gets done while opponents continue to drive wedges that leave lasting wounds. The deal for the most radical conversion from fossil fuels in the United States to date happened in New York precisely because the unions had the *power* to shift public subsidies—that's taxes—into a deal that enabled them to meet both scientific standards for emissions reduction and the good unionized wage and benefit standards that members expect and are willing to fight for. Both are key to shifting the economy at the pace and scale needed.

There's plenty of money to make a Green New Deal happen. Investigative journalist Christian Parenti has recently pointed out that corporations are currently sitting on $4.8 trillion in cash—a subset of $22.1 trillion they hoard. That money could be used to quickly transition the economy to a robust unionized green economy, one that can reproduce a dignified quality of life for workers of the future and end the destructive jobs-versus-the-environment debate. But to access that money, it takes real power and know-how—the kind of authority that unions in New York still have, along with a few other major states. To rebuild union power elsewhere, the environmental movement will have to stand up and fight alongside them—really fight, not just talk about green jobs. That means actively throwing their support behind workers' right to strike and actively backing workers. That kind of organizing and the power it builds will be necessary to raise taxes on the rich (versus just talking about it) and make progress on shifting federal subsidies away from fossil fuels and toward a safe, resilient economy that works for humans and our planet. And it will be necessary to quickly rebuild the environmental movement by shifting away from what's now clearly a losing strategy of litigation and advocacy, toward building a real base of mass support and the power that comes with it.

To actually institute a Green New Deal means rebuilding a robust public sector. A robust public sector means a future filled with good jobs for women and people of color. But the right-wing attacks on what's left of the public sector and its unions will continue. It's not too late for environmentalists and all progressive allies to forcefully stand with workers and their unions—but there's no time to waste. Asking workers to save the planet by killing the few remaining high-quality jobs is a losing strategy. So too is asking people to blindly support the corporate class's agenda of creating jobs that kill the planet and line the pockets of the 1 percent. The sooner greens and unionists realize this, the better for both of them—and all of us.

ASSUMPTION 6:
Unions Are Corrupt

So, who was responsible for the crash of the global economy in 2008, who plundered decades of savings of an entire generation by playing fast and loose with others' money and never went to jail for it? Which CEOs are gutting the pension funds of coal miners, stealing money that the workers actually earned for decades as they made profits for their employers? Not labor leaders.

When the image of a corrupt union pops into your head, it's usually because there's a corrupt employer in predictable sectors such as trucking, cargo shipping, and construction. Corrupt employers seek to create corrupt unions, and sometimes it works. Most people can conjure an image of Jimmy Hoffa but can't name one corrupt corporate CEO from the waste hauling or transport and logistics business.

Though some union members and bosses are corrupt, of the many issues confronting unions, corruption plays a bit part at best. Corporations prefer to have no unions. But if there has to be one, it seems that on the whole, corporations prefer to have corrupt ones for at least two reasons: One, they are easier to deal with than confronting a democratic union where tens, hundreds, or thousands of workers actually have the power to make real demands. Two, they are convenient punching bags to drag out in public for the media whenever actually good unions are making progress when confronting employers.

Two excellent books that deal with this topic with nuance and finesse are *Reds or Rackets: The Making of Radical and Conservative Unions on the Waterfront* and *Left Out: Reds in America's Industrial Unions*. In each, the authors outline that corruption in unions, where it exists, generally starts with corrupt employers that find willing partners in their generally more conservative unions. (Conservative unions, by nature, aren't particularly democratic.) The kind of union that can accept bribes and sign contracts that are bad for workers, their families, and communities are by definition unions that don't engage in broad, democratic decision making that involves transparent and open processes. In a highly democratic organization, getting away with corruption would be hard. That's yet another reason why all workers should insist that their own unions operate in the open.

I've long said most unions are decent if not good (and some are great), but when it comes to accusations of corruption—which is rare, in the scheme of things—it's more often that unions are what I describe not as corrupt but as morally or ethically bankrupt. To be clear, big corporations have way more issues with corruption and being morally and ethically bankrupt than unions. But there certainly are unions that collect worker money and do nothing much with it but ring up fancy restaurant tabs, pay exorbitant salaries to the top echelon of staff, and create a family business where those pulling in the big money are the sons, daughters, siblings, and in-laws of the person in charge. These folks hire lawyers who might even do a good job defending a fired worker here and there, and maybe even win contracts with decent wages, but not much else.

In *Reds or Rackets,* author Howard Kimeldorf documents that the more radical and democratic dockworkers unions on the west coast could never be bribed because their demands weren't simple demands. They were less interested in big raises than in demanding that workers wouldn't be injured or crushed by faulty machinery. That kind of demand can't be easily satisfied by a bribe or payoff to a handful at the top. In contrast, the conservative union of dockworkers on the east coast was easy to bribe. Its officials wanted personal wealth and could control the impulses of the rank and file by getting many employers to buy labor peace with big raises. But that was it. Don't ask about trivial matters like safety, health care, or work hours and schedules.

Governance is a huge issue for all forms of democratic organizations. Good governance mechanisms can help severely constrain corrupt or bankrupt unionism, and enable the best kind of unions. That brings us to the next subject.

Unions Are Old-Fashioned

Along with liberal and progressive (and even young radical) gripes concerning unions—anti-environmentalism, sexism, and racism—the next most common complaint is that unions are old-fashioned, or last century. But it's no truer than any other common anti-union slur. There's almost nothing monolithic about unions. The singular aspect of unions that's true (except with the abjectly corrupt ones, such as the previous waste hauler example) is that without them, workers are way worse off. Accusations that unions are old-fashioned are often the by-product of the long PR war against unions, or a product of ignorance about the many good unions workers have built, which are responsible for many gains that have long been taken for granted.

It's hard to think of any human institution that doesn't run the risk of becoming inflexible, or worse. The more recent fad of "horizontalism"—organizations in which no one has authority over anyone else—might seem attractive, until you realize that demands for non-hierarchical organizations are themselves old demands. A classic article that emerged out of the 1970s Second Wave feminist movement, "The Tyranny of Structurelessness," by sociologist Jo Freeman, identified many contradictions of what is today often called "horizontalism," including that only wealthy people have time to sit through unstructured meetings that last way too long, and that people with more educational experience and more confidence often come to dominate, precisely because there is no structure. As she wrote, "We need to understand why 'structurelessness' does not work."

Within unions, there's long been a left and democratic culture and practice that emphasizes a specific kind of transparency that seems to work well. For example, in 1199, the union's constitution guarantees all workers the right to participate in collective bargaining. In addition to having the ability to partake in and bear witness to the development of their own union contract, workers know pretty much everything about their union. For example, 1199's constitution stipulates that the highest-paid people in the union have their salaries and compensation set based on the *average* pay rate of what the members make under their union contracts with the employers. This is quite different from similar wording in other union constitutions that links the full-time officials and staff to the ranks; if the language doesn't specify the average, the union position holders could be looking at the highest-paid worker on triple overtime, tying their pay to that one worker, and claim, "Our pay rates are tied to the ranks." While it would be a factually honest statement, it would be disingenuous at the same time. The latter version of tying union officials' pay to the ranks also creates odd incentives for a union official to want to stay in their higher-paying union position than return to their actual job in the ranks.

The kinds of mechanisms that exist in the constitution of 1199 or other highly democratic unions should be safeguarded within a union as strongly as unions should be safeguarded in a democracy. The most dynamic modern unions rely on very democratic mechanisms. Most important, as will be shown in chapters 5 and 6, workers are building new democratic unions and also reforming do-nothing or corrupt unions and making them great again. Unions are institutions. If the best workers run them, they are great; if the best workers take a back seat and decide to let "someone else" worry about the union, well, then the union will become a lot less than it should be, and a lot less than is needed.

For further reading see Bill Fletcher's book *"They're Bankrupting Us!" And 20 Other Myths about Unions.*

CHAPTER 4

Are Unions Still Relevant?

Press coverage of the industry was boosterish and sedulously
uninvestigative, as journalists tended to embrace Google's old "Don't
be evil" motto as a factual description of its aims. But the gap between
tech theory and tech practice has grown increasingly difficult to ignore.
Many now know the tech elite as a hive of misogynists and sociopaths,
and their companies to be indiscriminate vacuums of sensitive personal
data that they package and sell to the nation's intelligence agencies
(and the Trump campaign).

—Alex Press, 2018

SILICON VALLEY POSITIONED AND PROMOTED ITSELF AS THE VAN-
guard of a utopian future where liberated global citizens groove to
music on the very latest iPhone, and have time to rock climb, hang
glide, write poetry, paint, and tap their personal creativity. Workers
would be liberated from boring, traditional jobs, free to work whenever and for whoever they wanted. No longer would the status quo
go unchallenged: it's time to move fast and break things, as Mark
Zuckerberg says. Thus far, the biggest things they've broken include
standard social norms—like looking people in the eye when you're

commuting and, say, starting up a conversation—not to mention our democracy. But from its beginnings, the tech industry, now a key driver of today's economy and therefore politics, has engaged in union busting, facilitated a worsening climate disaster, and reproduced the centuries-old big corporate behaviors that make a few people filthy rich while impoverishing everyone else.

They've done this with some of the most sophisticated public relations campaigns and, along the way, created their own new media source, one that distracts grown-ups and kids alike with funny cat videos on little screens, or—less funny—with much less innocent posts and memes that confirm people in their worst resentments, fears, prejudices, jealousies, hatreds: *anti*social media. A significant part of their public relations strategy relies on the suggestion that unions are no longer relevant to the structure of today's workforce. These doubts are part of a larger conversation about "the future of work," which is usually characterized by two ideas: the adoption of automation in the workplace and the rise of the gig economy. Bullshit. Unions are perfectly flexible enough to adjust to different types of employment structures. Look at the difference between the building and construction trades—discussed in chapter 3—and, say, a hospital. Both workplaces are served equally well by unions. So it shouldn't be a surprise that Uber and Lyft drivers have turned to the idea of building a union, especially after an official study commissioned by the city of New York showed that 85 percent of them are earning below minimum wage. Or for twenty thousand Google workers to walk out in a giant collective action in the fall of 2018 when they realized their individual employment contracts prevented them from addressing sexual harassment and gender equity issues.

Though big tech claims to be "disrupting" the status quo and innovating ways to make our lives better, "disruption"—like its predecessors globalization and automation—is essentially synonymous with the downward harmonization of the quality of life of *all* workers. As I followed the story of one tech worker's career in Silicon Valley, I learned firsthand about the quasi-progressive rhetoric and false workplace chumminess that cloaked worker exploitation. But it isn't just the tech sphere that faces these challenges. Silicon Valley's influence is having a spillover effect: college and university professors now have the same lack of job security or fair wages as Uber drivers, fast-food workers, and the like. With the disruption of the traditional workplace, backed by strong and consistent public relations telling us so—and oodles of think tanks and foundation dollars suggesting some new something will fix the mess—many people think that unions aren't nimble enough to address the changing demands of work today. But for workers, nothing could be further from the truth.

Now these disrupted workers—adjuncts on campuses, coders, platform workers, journalists, and more—are beginning to fight back, and unions are at the heart of these responses. Though the new activist right-wing Supreme Court is backing, if not leading, every attack on worker power, one important 2018 court case that skirted under the radar crucially reinforced that today, as in the past, workers have just one choice: to reconcile differences of race, ethnicity, and gender, and create effective, unbreakable class solidarity through building the best kind of unions: democratic, bottom-up, with the power to force the billionaire class to share.

Silicon Valley Technology

Taylor Hesselgrave, California

WHEN TAYLOR HESSELGRAVE WAS IN HER TEENS, she dreamed of becoming a globe-trotting international businesswoman. Both her parents had traveled extensively before having children, and Hesselgrave inherited the need-to-explore-the-world gene. She was raised by her single mother with a lot of support from her mom's sister. At age fourteen, Hesselgrave took off to Japan for a yearlong high school exchange program. Having Japanese language skills made good business sense to her.

When, four years later, she started her undergraduate degree at the University of Washington in 2005, she majored in economics with two minors, Japanese and women's studies. The economics, to her young thinking, would set her up for a future M.B.A., and Japanese language skills would make her marketable in the workplace. Everything had a logic to Hesselgrave.

By Hesselgrave's third year in college, she traveled to India on a study-abroad program. She went to a lecture by an Indian professor who identified himself as an ecological economist. As he spoke, she felt herself reconsidering her entire academic career. Two years of academic studies, in which she had tried to reconcile business classes with her women's studies, unraveled. "The Indian economist made it really simple by just explaining that things aren't valued properly in the formal economy, and that's why there's so much trouble in the world. It was so clarifying."

She began to see the glaring omissions from her economics and business courses, including women's unpaid labor as they raised kids and managed the home, and extractive industries like coal, in which corporations cause both massive pollution and huge human health crises but don't have to pay for any of it. In traditional economics, these costs are considered "externalities," and the bills for these unaccounted big-ticket material items are left on the tab of ordinary taxpayers. She returned to the University of Washington and finished her undergraduate degree but hatched a new plan that would draw on her four years of studies: she was headed to graduate school for ecological economics.

By 2010 Hesselgrave had her master's from the University of Edinburgh and was ready to put her degree to work. She soon landed a job she loved, working as a researcher for an environmental organization called Ecotrust. It is a think-and-do-tank in Portland, Oregon, and its vision is "to be a catalyst for radical, practical change." While at Ecotrust, she researched a path to a more sustainable planet, one that valued and included the full cost of production and that could also turn a profit. Her first big assignment was contributing to a major report that backed the claim that if the Environmental Protection Agency permitted mining in the pristine Alaskan waters of Bristol Bay, in the Bering Sea, it would allow the destruction of the largest wild salmon population left in the world. It was the kind of campaign that even stalwart Republicans—such as the longest-serving Republican senator in history at the time, Alaska's Ted Stevens—could get behind because the coalition strategically included hunters, sport fisher folks, and native Alaskan tribes in its decision-making.

The data for this project was voluminous. The more she crunched the data, the more she loved working with the macros in the Excel spreadsheet and data program. The more analysis she did, the more she worked with computer programmers at Ecotrust. The programmers often told her that she was so good with macros that she was basically coding.

She asked Ecotrust to invest more in her by paying for her to attend Excel trainings, and they agreed. She then enrolled in an evening course to learn a "real coding language" called Python. "Python is beginner friendly, and there's a big learning community built around it in meetups," said Hesselgrave. "So I found a great support meetup in Portland called PyLadies, for women learning Python."

Hesselgrave, at that point in her fifth year at Ecotrust, appreciated the congeniality of the PyLadies and loved learning Python. At an annual staff retreat, she realized that most of her colleagues at Ecotrust were on their fourth or fifth or sixth job. This was her first job, and she'd been there for five solid years—which for millennials can feel like the equivalent of a century. Something clicked for

Hesselgrave: she loved her coworkers and her job, but she was ready for a new challenge. The PyLadies told her about a well-regarded coding boot camp for women called Hackbright in San Francisco. The first thing you see on Hackbright's website is an image of a smiling woman, a software engineer at Dropbox and Hackbright alumna, with text that reads, "800 women have done it. You can too." Another link declares, "A Community Is Waiting for You!"

The video on Hackbright's homepage is enthralling. It's not hard to see why a young woman like Hesselgrave would jump at the opportunity to apply. The introductory video says it's the "Bay Area's #1 All Women's Coding School," putting you right in the heart of the Silicon Valley tech scene. The scenes and background images throughout the short recruitment video feature beautiful, cheery women from different ethnic backgrounds radiating empowerment. Their mission is to "Change the ratio by removing any barriers that might stop a woman from wanting to become a software engineer." A student of the program, Olivia, looks right at the camera and says, "I am so happy to be in this program with fantastic, powerful, go-getter women. We need women in tech, and here's the place to get you the education." It's hard to *not* notice how often the video uses the words *empowering, supportive,* and *nurturing.* The application process is highly competitive and it's a steep financial commitment: tuition is $15,000 for the three-month boot camp, and there's no time for side jobs. But Hesselgrave thought, Hell, I've already basically taught myself Python. In conversations with her brother, who was also interested in tech work, the two made the decision to move to San Francisco together. After their father's death, it had become their goal to live in the same city again. They moved into an Airbnb while Hesselgrave did the intensive three-month Hackbright Academy. It was January 2015, and life was great.

A lot of the teachers and mentors at Hackbright work at sponsoring companies who lend time and contribute to the scholarship funds in exchange for getting first crack at the hiring pool of women, who are desperately needed in tech. (Hackbright's website states that by 2024, there will be 480,000 new jobs for women in tech.) Hesselgrave was determined to land one, as was everyone in her class. She loved everything about Hackbright, but as the program drew to a close, the atmosphere became more competitive as students jockeyed for the same jobs. Just after they graduated, in early April 2015, Hackbright set up a meet-and-greet between the graduates and companies seeking engineers. "It was like speed dating," Hesselgrave said. "Each of us presented our final Web development projects to show off what we can do."

Among the Hackbright corporate partners was Winmore, a customer relations software firm. Two of the mentors who had volunteered with Hesselgrave's cohort, Danny Douglass and Kyla Farrell, from Winmore, showed up for a brief recruitment session. According to Hesselgrave, Winmore announced it had two engineering positions to fill. It made offers to two students from her cohort, one of whom was her.

She snatched it up because, in her words, "Winmore doesn't do whiteboarding, which is part of the predatory practices used by a lot of Silicon Valley firms when they interview. That's where they put you on a panel of four people and give you a silly algorithm question and say, 'OK, work it out on the whiteboard in front of us and talk out loud.' It's super high pressure and high stress. Everyone hates them. In my interview, they asked me to present my final product, asked me to open the code and walk them through everything. It was great."

Hesselgrave got an offer for $110,000, plus standard benefits, including stock options, and managed to negotiate a little for moving expenses. Hackbright tracks the data on job placements and salaries for its grads. $110,000 was an above-average offer for Hackbright graduates and was more than Hesselgrave's other offers. Accepting the position meant she would be the second woman to work as an engineer at Winmore. The first and only woman engineer at that point was Kyla Farrell, who had graduated from Hackbright a few years earlier. Hesselgrave liked her immediately, but was reporting to Danny Douglass. That wasn't strange, because Winmore followed a management method from *The Lean Startup,* a book from which it gleaned that constantly changing up people on the various teams was a good idea.

According to Hesselgrave, Winmore was constantly improving and "It was kind of fun and cool. They adopted a work-style approach that was popularized by other successful start-ups. So we reorganized our teams every six months, and we reorganized the actual office about as frequently." Relative to the rest of Silicon Valley, once Winmore hired several more women engineers, it was above average in its ratio of women to men. But women were still vastly outnumbered.

Hesselgrave was asked early on to become a recruiter herself and make presentations at Hackbright and elsewhere about Winmore. She helped recruit several more women in the next year to join the team. Two years into her tenure and performing well, she decided it was an appropriate time to ask for a raise. At that point, she was working under Douglass and made the pitch. She also asked for Douglass's advice for getting onto a management track.

Douglass seemed surprised by her requests but said he'd get back to her. In a few days, he told her they had decided to give everyone a 3 percent cost-of-living adjustment. Hesselgrave said, "Danny [Douglass] told me I'd be getting the COLA. I told him that was awesome, but what about my raise? He said, 'Oh, sorry; did I say COLA? I misspoke. You are getting a three percent raise!' I wondered: What?"

While Hesselgrave was pleased that she would be getting a cost-of-living adjustment after two years, she had been expecting a real raise, a reward for her growth, her hard work, and her effort in recruiting for the company. Douglass had turned that "raise" into the across-the-board COLA for all employees. Not long after that happened, Kyla Farrell became pregnant with her first child. Because she was the first person working at Winmore to get pregnant, Farrell was asked by management to write a maternity leave policy for the company. She discussed this with the other staff, and she mentioned that part of her developing the policy they later approved involved surveying other similar Silicon Valley tech firms for how they handled parental leave.

Around this same time, one of the cofounders of the company—the only really high-ranking woman—mysteriously left. There were rumors speculating about the reasons for her departure, but it was all very hush-hush. Her number two, another woman—these two were in sales, not in engineering—was promoted. Her promotion was made in public in an all-staff meeting, which was unusual. Everyone thought it was awkward, as it seemed the promotion even caught the soon-to-be VP of sales off guard. The only thing the staff had heard was confirmation of the strangeness: the woman who was made into the new VP of sales wasn't told before the announcement and apparently wasn't given a raise. Not long after, that woman resigned.

"It's spring 2017 and we've lost the two most powerful women in our company within a couple months," Hesselgrave explained. "Everyone in engineering said not to worry, that it was something that would only affect the sales side of the company. Then the CEO brings in a high-powered woman executive from Walmart to give us a pep-talk. He asked us, 'What'd you think? I just love powerful women. Don't you?' Right on the heels of two senior women disappearing!"

About this time, with so much change happening, many Winmore engineers started discussing how bad the company's paid time off (PTO) policy was. They complained that they were being expected to work hard but were discouraged from taking any time off. The engineers decided to do something similar to what Farrell had done about maternity leave: ask other Silicon Valley companies about their PTO policies. Farrell stressed that the survey would help employees make an evidentiary case to management. If other companies had good PTO policies, why couldn't they?

After Winmore employees collected and parsed the data, they realized that Winmore was significantly behind its competitors with PTO policies. The more that the engineers discussed PTO, the more they realized everyone was given different information about how to interpret Winmore's policy. Notably, recent new hires weren't being told what more tenured staff had been promised: they shouldn't worry about the policy—if they worked hard, they could take off whatever they needed. There was a basic problem with the assurances about PTO for the most senior engineers: they could never really take advantage of this alleged "unlimited PTO" because of the constant time pressures to produce new products on rush deadlines. The staff decided to ask one of its best engineers, Mike, to approach management and present a request to improve the PTO. He agreed and met with Douglass to discuss it. Douglass said that the proposal for improved PTO was interesting and that he'd get back to them.

Before the workers received any response on PTO, Ann, the CEO's sister who functioned informally as Winmore's HR person, suddenly announced via e-mail that effective immediately, Winmore had a new referral bonus program. If an engineer recruits someone, at three months of the new hire's employment, the recruiter will get a $3,000 bonus. The wheels spun fast in Hesselgrave's mind and she realized she had recently recruited four women to the firm, all of whom were productive and still working at the company. She explained, "I replied to Ann's e-mail, saying, 'Very exciting. I was thinking about who I could refer but realized I've already referred four of my best connections. Any chance you would consider a retroactive referral bonus?'" A potential $12,000 bonus was fair, Hesselgrave believed, and would abate any bad feelings about a raise that she deserved turning into a 3 percent COLA for the entire staff. The response came to her from the CEO himself. John Golob, who went by "JG" in the office, asked her to go get coffee together. In start-up parlance, that means "have a discussion." She had barely ever spoken with him, but agreed to go regardless.

During their meeting, JG brought up both Hesselgrave's request for a referral bonus and the PTO policy. It took her by surprise. "JG flattered me and caught me really off guard," she said. "We talked about the referral bonus very briefly. He said, 'Okay, we'll see what we can do.' Then, 'I've heard that if I want great ideas about making working here really great, I should talk to you. I've heard you're *the* person to talk with. I really want all of the ideas, all of them. I don't even care what they are. Just off the top of your head, no idea is bad! So what are they?' I told him I wished that I were prepared to talk about that; he assured me that he was getting feedback and we were only brainstorming."

When Hesselgrave returned to the office, she was excited. She immediately told Douglass everything that she and JG had discussed. He was dismissive about the talk, she said, and warned her that JG was very manipulative. Douglass cautioned her that she likely wouldn't get a bonus or raise, and that even though JG said he'd set up a joint employee-management committee to hammer out a new PTO policy, there wouldn't be one. In a matter of minutes, Hesselgrave went from being enthused about the progress to being discouraged. But a few days later, JG e-mailed his sister and instructed her to give Hesselgrave a $10,000 raise.

Days after meeting with Hesselgrave, he also announced that he had established a PTO committee and that Hesselgrave would serve on it as a voice for the engineers. Things were moving start-up-caliber fast. JG met with Hesselgrave to hear the results of the information-gathering effort and agreed with their recommendations to increase PTO. He then called a full-team meeting and asked her to present the new PTO policy—which basically doubled the PTO and made it more clear how and when it could be accessed— and the CEO approved it in front of everyone.

Winmore's employees were ecstatic. A coworker, Bjorn Wester-gard, called Hesselgrave a working-class hero. Hesselgrave was next asked to lead a team that would work on a complicated coding project, which she took as another sign that she had management's confidence. These abrupt assignments and changes fell well within the standard frenzy of start-up culture. It seemed that Hesselgrave had made solid gains for the workers in the company.

A few weeks later, however, in mid-November 2017, with no notice or discussion, Danny Douglass fired her on the spot. Kyla Farrell and another manager sat stoically in the termination meeting, staring into space. When Hesselgrave asked them to explain why she was being fired, they refused to discuss it. They told her to shut down her computer and leave the office immediately.

Hesselgrave was shocked. Winmore had an open office—Silicon Valley start-up style—so people saw her ghost-white face as she left. *Fired* was never a word she imagined she'd ever hear, not to or about her. By the end of the workday, most of the engineers in the San Francisco office (Winmore also had an office in Virginia), led by the women who had come from Hackbright, were at Hesselgrave's door with copious amounts of wine in hand, furious and demanding to know what had happened. She was blubbering as she told them she had no idea, but had been fired.

The next day, some Winmore engineers were called one-on-one into management meetings in Virginia and San Francisco and asked whether they wanted to discuss anything concerning Hesselgrave. Most either said no or, when prompted, asked why she was fired. The Virginia team was less close to her, and most people assumed there had been some egregious behavior on her part or something since generally she was doing good work. Nevertheless, management refused to discuss it.

Hesselgrave showed me texts from those meetings, in which co-workers sent her expletive-filled messages wondering why management would meet with them and then refuse to say anything. What was the point? Over the next week, almost all engineers in both offices were put through the bizarre ritual. By the end of the month, the entire engineering staff had had enough. They decided to collectively write a letter to management, stating their dissatisfaction about her firing. In it, they wrote:

> We, the undersigned, are Lanetix [now Winmore] employees who have helped build a product and a company. We look back on our years of taxing effort with pride, knowing that we have pushed forward both the state of the art and the cause of a diverse, inclusive, professional software industry.
>
> Your decision to fire Taylor—with no warning, breaking with all past practice—shocked us. She was a valued co-worker whose contributions to the company were obvious, and to our knowledge there has never been cause to question her capabilities or performance. Her manifest intelligence, skill, and professionalism under trying circumstances were an inspiration to us all. But Taylor's greatest contribution to the team was her willingness to hear the grievances we shared with one another and bring them to you.
>
> Taylor was an effective advocate for all of us, especially for those women who joined her here in an attempt to build careers in an industry in which the deck is stacked against them. She spoke up, most visibly about Paid Time Off, but on many other issues as well. As such, her sudden termination—with no explanation from the company—has been a cause of alarm and concern for Taylor's co-workers. We believe women and we believe in women like Taylor. She is not only an advocate for her peers at Lanetix, but women in tech everywhere; her moral compass, empathy, and strong convictions are to be admired. In

*an industry lacking diversity, losing her at Lanetix is a blow to
our core values.*

*Lanetix engineers have enjoyed vibrant conversations about
our working lives in person and through media of our own
creation. Your decision to retaliate against us for discussing the
terms and conditions of our employment and approaching you
through representatives like Taylor, fully believing you would do
right by us, is deeply hurtful and unjust.*

*We've come to you because we believe the culture we've built
at Lanetix is worth fighting for and are eager to retain our valued
colleagues. The lack of transparency surrounding the termination
of Taylor's employment has undermined what was, until very
recently, a solid working relationship between employees and
management. We bring these concerns to management with the
aim of fostering open and serious dialogue.*

We have two simple requests for you:

Do right by Taylor.

*Recognize that we have a right to discuss work with our
coworkers and bring concerns to management as a group, and
cease trying to prevent such communication.*

Sincerely,

[redacted: a supermajority of the engineers signed this letter]

Within minutes of receiving the letter, JG offered to have a
town-hall meeting that same day. But he canceled it an hour before
it was scheduled to begin. At this point, the engineers refused to attend one-on-ones, demanding a public response to their collective
letter. Management sent e-mails to the company, demanding they
stop discussing Hesselgrave's termination. Hearing nothing but
vague threats, the group of engineers did something that most of
them had never imagined: the engineers reached out to a union.

A fellow engineer had previously been a journalist before shifting to tech, and had been a member of a union that she admired. The union sized up Winmore's actions and quickly counseled the workers to sign union authorization cards for their protection. Under the National Labor Relations Act, employees cannot be terminated for taking collective action, whether for officially attempting to form a union or taking the kind of collective action that had apparently led to Hesselgrave's firing, like coming together to discuss such things as improvements in their PTO policy.

The engineers were essentially functioning like a good union without officially being one. They came together as a team, collectively working out demands for management that mattered to them, in order to improve their quality of work life. The union they called told them if they privately signed union membership cards, it would give them better protections later if the employer tried to retaliate. Plus, they'd have the resources of the union, with its knowledgeable staff. On December 4, the majority of engineers sent a carefully written second letter, which said they had a right to organize and requested JG to honor their intention to form a union. After being uninvited to Winmore's annual staff retreat, on January 26, *every* software engineer was fired in a mass termination.

Winmore tried to frame the firing as a layoff, which was a lie. That the tech workers were stunned by the firing is an understatement. Like Hesselgrave, they were highly skilled engineers who loved their work and their specific jobs—and for the most part, they liked their employer. In their mind, they were trying to help management overcome a lack of fair or effective systems. They felt as though they were working *with* management.

The union they had turned to, the Washington-Baltimore Newspaper Guild, a local union of the national Communications Workers of America, took up the cause. Hesselgrave had retained her own lawyer before the mass firing. She was working up details for a gender discrimination case—which in Silicon Valley should be as easy as shooting fish in a barrel, but it was proving hard despite the few women in engineer posts. Even so, the National Labor Relations Board ruled that management had illegally terminated the engineers, including Hesselgrave. The labor board was involved because the workers had made a legal demand for union recognition.

On August 22, 2018, the NLRB issued a decision stating that Winmore must offer to hire back every engineer, in their same positions, with the same pay; pay them retroactive to January 16; publicly apologize in writing as well as verbally at an all-staff meeting; state publicly that employees in the United States have the right to collectively discuss work issues; and promise to never intimidate them again.

Among many details contained in the August 22, 2018, "finding of facts":

About December 18, 2017, Respondent [Winmore], by Seth Carney [a manager], by telling employees that they could organize any way they wanted to short of unionizing, and that Respondent would never be union, informed employees that it would be futile for them to select the Charging Party [the union] or any other labor organization as their bargaining representative.

Hesselgrave and her coworkers had won something humans need as much as they need a living wage: validation, a sense of their own worth and confidence in their own judgment, their understanding that what their friendly-sounding bosses had been doing to them was outrageously unjust and illegal. They won the wage, too: Winmore was forced to pay out substantial financial back-pay settlements to each fired software engineer. What they didn't win was a union. That's because the NLRB took too long to move on their firing, which is typical when handling these kinds of cases, and the bosses bank on that slowness. Under the 1935 NLRA, before it was gutted by the Taft–Hartley Act in 1947, the workers in such a case would not have had to sit through months and months of deliberations while their boss's abusive actions were being investigated by an agency starved of resources by all Republicans and even some Democrats. As long as the federal taxpayer-funded NLRB lacks funds and investigators to pursue these cases, corporations will have the advantage.

Because all the workers actually needed to keep earning salaries, they were forced to take other jobs. And by the time they were informed they'd won their case, everyone already had jobs they quite liked at other employers. Though the back-pay settlements the company was forced to pay were hefty, given that the illegally terminated employees had done highly paid work, the company simply wrote off the legal settlement as a loss, rebranded, and moved on, no doubt relieved that this forced profit-sharing amounted to a single payout, not a permanent employee benefit. This is not uncommon: workers win a case but lose the union because the pace of the investigation is so slow. My impression from my own experience of these cases is that employers always appeal a guilty verdict in the labor courts not necessarily to overturn the verdict, but simply to stall as long as they can, hoping that the workers involved get jobs elsewhere—which is what happened in the Winmore case.

I asked Hesselgrave for her reflections on leaving the nonprofit save-the-planet job at Ecotrust, rolling with giddy, bubbly enthusiasm into her "for women, to empower women" Hackbright boot camp, and then segueing into a high-paying tech job amid the glitter of San Francisco start-up land. She said, "I never thought I'd get fired from anything, anywhere, but I did. And it was really unfair. I learned life isn't fair. These companies, no matter what they say, are not our family—which they all say—they are engaging in business and we are a business transaction. Don't let them flower up the relationship. This is at-will employment, and you could get fired tomorrow with no explanation. We provide them with our time and skill, and they pay us money, that's what's happening."

Union Busting Is Integral to Tech from the Start

Despite the fierce individualist and competitive spirit among them, the first CEOs and executives in Silicon Valley were united about one innovation: being union-free. As far back as the 1970s, when Intel's founder and CEO, Robert Noyce, decided to establish his new silicon-chip processor company across the country from his alma matter, the Massachusetts Institute of Technology, and its emerging high-tech corridor along Route 128 in Boston, it was explicitly to avoid the labor-management dynamics and unions from "back east." In a 1983 *Esquire* biographical essay about Robert Noyce, author Tom Wolfe wrote, "He was the *father* of Silicon Valley!" Whether or not Noyce was "the" father, he was certainly a defining figure in the emerging world of corporate big tech, which was a direct outgrowth of the massive amounts of public taxpayer money that funded Noyce and many of his generation after the Soviet Union beat the United States into space in 1957 with the successful launch of Sputnik 1.

Noyce's entry into the engineering workforce was perfectly timed: there was an urgent need to make computers small enough to fit into a rocket. While taxpayers footed the lion's share of the research bill, Wall Street firms saw a way to make a few people extremely rich: the new technology's investment opportunities. Noyce's distaste for all things "back east" did not include Wall Street money. Backed by Wall Street capital, he helped stage a coup at his second job, where he worked for the inventor and patent holder of the transistor, Nobel laureate William Shockley. Noyce and a handful of similarly skilled men fled Shockley's shed in the fruit orchards not far from Stanford to build their own company and do faster and better what Shockley Semiconductor was already doing. Shockley would later emerge as a horrible eugenicist, but there's no evidence that's why Noyce fled his shop. Rather, Noyce created the future business model of Silicon Valley as far back as the 1960s, but the term they used back then wasn't "disruption." It had a different name: "defection capital."

By the early 1970s, Noyce, already the equivalent of today's multimillionaires, framed the narrative and set the example that companies like Winmore are still following in the second decade of the new millennium. He smashed early efforts by Intel engineers to unionize with several different labor organizations, including the International Association of Machinists and Aerospace Workers, the Teamsters, and the Stationary Engineers. According to Wolfe, "Noyce made it known, albeit quietly, that he regarded unionization as a death threat to Intel, and to the semiconductor industry generally. Labor management battles were part of the ancient terrain of the East. If Intel were divided into workers and bosses, with the implication that each side had to squeeze money out of the hides of the other, the enterprise would be finished."

But in the 1970s many of the most successful companies in the United States were unionized, with CEOs in the auto, steel, and chemical industries, and others with incomes putting them in the top 1 percent. Noyce's antipathy toward unions raises another question: Was he not content to be filthy rich and instead needed to make more than any other CEO, or was he ideologically opposed to unions and didn't believe that the company's rank and file were as valuable and crucial to its success as management? Or was it both, given that greed and the defense of inequality go together like *integrated* and *circuit*? We won't ever know for sure, since he died in 1990 at age sixty-three. But judging from the case of the fifteen high-level engineers fired illegally by Winmore in 2018, whom we do know, and who were seeking simple things like clarity about paid time off, fair work rules, and better management systems, casting unions as a "death threat to the industry" was likely as absurd then as it is now.

Not surprisingly, today's Silicon Valley disruptors have reproduced the Gilded Age—which was characterized by garish wealth and merciless business practices—by simultaneously minting small numbers of billionaires and millionaires while spreading gut-wrenching, systemic poverty. As author Jonathan Taplin describes in his book *Move Fast and Break Things: How Facebook, Google, and Amazon Cornered Culture and Undermined Democracy,* "Not since . . . Rockefeller and J. P. Morgan, has the country faced such a concentration of wealth and power" in the hands of so few. And "the fortunes created by the digital revolution may have done more to increase inequality in America than almost any other factor."

In one of his many interviews after the book was published, Taplin explained how big tech has cozied up to both political parties in order to throw off the shackles of government regulation, including labor standards that retard unions, such as whether workers are workers (who can unionize) or independent contractors (who can't): "Here's the deal. These people in Silicon Valley have been able to put a Svengali move on the Democrats just as much as they put on the Republicans," he said. "Obama was under the spell of Google more than anybody I know about. Eric Schmidt [executive chair of Alphabet, the parent company of Google] visited the White House by a factor of five more than any other CEO, and that's just the official stuff that was written down at the White House gate." The evidence speaks for itself: under all recent administrations, big tech's contractor workforce exploded in size.

Like giant corporations a century before them, Silicon Valley corporations personally wooing U.S. lawmakers paid off: based on market valuation, the five biggest companies in the world in 2018 were Apple, Amazon, Alphabet, Microsoft, and Facebook. All of these titans of new capital have cozied up to government and are involved in serious union avoidance. Why do the top executives and shareholders of these companies and throughout Silicon Valley and the high-tech sector have the same attitudes toward organized labor as CEOs and executives did one hundred years ago? Why does Tesla today rely on union-busting tactics used by the Ford Motor Company in the 1930s? Why does Amazon cast itself in the mold of every big union-busting company since capitalism emerged from the ashes of feudalism? Because they can. It's pretty simple: the CEOs and shareholders of megacorporations have always wanted the wealth for themselves. And there's no instance in the United States of major progressive changes in the division of corporate profits that required anything less than mass strikes and collective action. The tech sector may be new, but its executives' desire to increase their own profit is anything but.

The hedge fund Bridgewater, in their April 2019 report, reinforces this idea: "While changes in union activity have been smaller in recent years, *even small moves toward or away from unionization* can be linked to changes in how much firms pay their employees" (emphasis added). The most common union avoidance technique that these competitors share is straightforward: the offshoring of major production facilities to countries where the labor movement is highly repressed, if not outright forbidden. Wolfe's *Esquire* essay vividly describes how, in the early years of experiments in Silicon Valley, Intel created and maintained sweatshops inside California:

> The work bays where the transistors were produced looked like slightly sunnier versions of the garment sweatshops of San Francisco's Chinatown. Here were rows of women hunched over worktables, squinting through microscopes, doing the most tedious and frustrating sort of manual labor, cutting layers of silicon apart with diamond cutters, picking little rectangles of them up with tweezers, trying to attach

wires to them, dropping them, rummaging around on the floor to find them again, swearing, muttering, climbing back to their chairs, rubbing their eyes, squinting back through the microscopes, and driving themselves crazy some more.

Those sweatshop conditions haven't disappeared. They still exist, but now Intel and company have strategically moved them to China and other faraway countries where sweatshops thrive, thanks to decisions made by billionaires in the United States colluding with repressive regimes. Certainly, big tech wasn't the only sector of the economy to take advantage of the cheap labor and zero environmental accountability regimes being created in China, Myanmar, Bangladesh, and under the ruthlessly repressive regimes in El Salvador and Honduras—the countries that today produce so many refugees fleeing the violence that comes with the extreme inequality *U.S. companies created*. That's globalization. But what about for the jobs that can't be shipped out of the country?

We've developed a whole host of new mechanisms that enable corporations to cheat workers and communities of wages and wealth, including subcontracting, fissuring, the platform economy, the gig economy, and artificial intelligence (AI). No matter what you call it, or how you spell it, all these words amount to union avoidance. Every idea or system they represent aims to keep profits soaring high for a few by depressing wages and benefits for the many. Each new schema has worked as a distraction from the ones that came before it. Each has allowed the greedy employer class to avoid even payroll and related taxes, thereby doing serious damage to Social Security and Medicare and Medicaid, whose income streams are built into traditional payroll systems. Then, without missing a beat, their Wall Street investors produce reports saying the Social Security fund is in trouble. Just like austerity, it's a deliberately constructed "trouble" from CEOs who won't face a retirement crisis and are on the winning end of the profits and the flexibility. These various union-busting, American Dream–crushing tactical charades were created largely by and for the tech sector, but they've spilled into most domestic industries that can't easily shift jobs abroad, including transport and logistics—think about all the get-it-fast guarantees the various tech sector companies rely on—but also sectors such as health care, education, and building and construction.

Subcontracting and Fissuring

Of the new "innovative" approaches to enriching the few, subcontracting is one of the most significant union-busting tactics today. The tech industry has created a fast-growing pool of subcontractors who don't receive the same wage or traditional benefits, or most of the Silicon Valley perks like enticing stock options or lavish related benefits—such as organic salad bars, food from real chefs in high-end cafeterias, on-site gyms, and child care—as the full-time workers, although the subcontractors often do the same work. The disrupters among the elite look at a big workforce and figure out how to chop it into smaller workforces who all have different employers, even though they often work in the same buildings. And because they have different employers, these neighboring workers, doing the same tasks, can't unify to make demands.

In his book *The Fissured Workplace: Why Work Became So Bad for So Many and What Can Be Done to Improve It,* Brandeis professor David Weil calls this new union-busting technique the "fissured workplace," and creating this kind of workplace is today's go-to company strategy for silencing workers—even outside of the tech economy. When I walk the floors of American hospitals, brick-and-mortar facilities that by necessity remain tethered to the soil, I see the new "fissured workplace" even there: nurses in the same scrubs, inside the same hospital, tending to the same patient, on the same floor, and yet working for different employers! The workers don't always understand that they are on different payrolls until they try to form a union, and that's the whole point. Instead of a thousand nurses in a hospital teaming up to form one union, those thousand nurses now "work for" dozens of "separate" employers. We can think of this as the latest form of gerrymandering in union elections.

Weil's book was published in February 2014, and a few months later he was appointed by President Obama as head of the U.S. Wage and Hour Administration in the Department of Labor. In the minds of policy wonks, Weil was on the case! The nation had a rational, logical president who, for a change, knew something was wrong with workplace norms. But David Weil, like his boss, had a problem—Congress was blocking every fix-the-fissured-workplace policy that he devised. He followed Obama's intelligent lead: he wrote regulations to be implemented as mechanisms that didn't require congressional approval. He assumed that these internal departmental regulations would soon be real laws. Like his colleagues, he probably believed Hillary Clinton would be elected in 2016, and a better Congress along with her, and they'd be able to convert barely enforced departmental rules into solid legislation. And, they thought, hell, they'd have not just four years under Hillary Clinton but eight, right? They'd have a slew of Supreme Court appointments coming, so they'd get the judicial backing workers would need to end this pernicious form of modern union busting, right? Wrong.

Instead, Donald Trump became president. And unlike Democrats, who can be obsessed with process and spend too much time making sure they don't offend corporate backers as work rules are made fairer, the Trump cabinet waltzed into office and immediately hacked away at every bit of progress made by the Department of Labor in the last couple years of Obama's tenure. They weren't just undoing Obama's regulations: they launched a blitzkrieg against every regulation that protected ordinary Americans. The Trump administration aimed to undo every regulation left from the New Deal, and any rule or law that protected the environment or women or civil rights. Although the media has framed the Trump era as chaos, it's anything but: its orchestrated cacophony has drowned out the sinister buzz-saw hum of the destruction of the government and, along with it, workers' rights.

Platform and Gig

Another invention to avoid paying workers through the traditional payroll system is the so-called gig or platform economy. Think: Uber, Lyft, and Mechanical Turk. It's particularly challenging to discuss the platform economy because in addition to the fact that the mechanism itself is a union-busting technique, two things are simultaneously true: it presents a number of difficult problems to the workers who rely on a computer platform and not a traditional-looking human resources office, and, yet despite the rhetoric, this sector is not nearly as big as the media, pundits, and politicians were making it out to be.

Several recent studies, including a study by JPMorgan Chase and a major breakthrough report, were published in June 2018 by the Bureau of Labor Statistics. A BLS follow-up in September 2018 went deeper into the specifics of gig work and emphatically showed that there's much more hype than reality in the claims that the world of work has radically changed. Doug Henwood, the publisher of a decades-old newsletter called the *Left Business Observer*—a wonderful resource for ordinary people who want a clear layman's analysis of economic trends—dispelled the idea that the gig economy had a stranglehold on workers in an October 2018 report to bondholders:

> But what about what the BLS calls "electronically mediated employment," platforms like Uber and TaskRabbit? Data released by the BLS at the end of September challenges this

story. In fact, such platforms account for just 1% of total employment. And over a fifth, or 22%, of such workers are in the transportation sector, more than four times that sector's share of total employment. Take those away, and the electronically mediated account for just 0.8% of employment.

Dean Baker, of the Center for Economic and Policy Research, shares Henwood's skepticism about the dominant narrative by those obsessed with "the future of work." In response to a World Bank report containing overinflated claims about the gig economy and its implications, Baker recently wrote in a blogpost on the CEPR website, "The U.S. experience matters because it is often viewed as the model of a modern deregulated labor market. There are far fewer obstacles to gig employment in the United States than in other wealthy countries. This means that if gig employment is not as big a factor in the US economy as is widely believed, there must be greater advantages to the traditional employee–employer relationship than is generally recognized." Turns out that there are many nonunion workers in "regular" jobs, not just in gigs sponsored by companies like Uber or TaskRabbit, that need good benefits, reliable hours, and decent overtime.

This panic about a changing labor market isn't new. Precariousness has always been a central feature of capitalism. Without strong unions, capitalism fails the majority of the workforce, as it is doing today. Pay is decreasing for ride-share drivers because there are so many drivers working on the apps, and because the platforms have increased fees they charge drivers to operate on their apps. Every month, one out of six workers are new to whatever platform they're working on, and more than half will quit altogether before the end of one year. Most platform workers use employment options like Uber and Lyft only several months a year to supplement other income. This, of course, reflects the larger problem: people need to supplement their income, and so spend less time with their families because regular nonunion full-time work simply doesn't pay enough to live on anymore.

Traditional Union Busting in Tech

Despite this, traditional union busting is still high atop the list of corporate priorities. Take Amazon, incidentally a company rolling in public-taxpayer subsidies, as an example. Although the company attempts to hide it, evidence of its hostility to unions is starting to pile up. Journalist Bryan Menegus was given access to Amazon's "top secret" union-busting training video used by the conglomerate's brick-and-mortar division, Whole Foods. Its narrator states that the video is "specifically designed to give you the tools that you need for success when it comes to labor organizing," Menegus writes. The video is set in a warehouse and distribution center—something the company can't offshore. The video instructs managers to tell workers, "We do not believe unions are in the best interest of our customers, our shareholders, or most importantly, our associates. Our business model is built on speed, innovation, and customer obsession—things that are generally not associated with a union. When we lose sight of those critical focus areas we jeopardize everyone's job security: yours, mine, and the associates'."

Taylor Hesselgrave and her coworkers at Winmore—out to make things better at work but not to form a union—were engaging in several of the key tactics that Whole Foods managers are coached to identify as "union behavior," including: "associates raising concerns on behalf of their coworkers" and workers "who normally aren't connected to each other suddenly hanging out together . . . showing an unusual interest in policies, benefits, employee lists, or other company information." Talk about surveillance! Imagine how good Alexa must be at listening in at Amazon workspaces.

Tesla's Elon Musk has also taken unions to task, notably after

Tesla workers tried to organize the company's flagship plant in Fremont, California. Workers at Tesla have complained about the company's racism and abusive management culture. When Musk promised to produce the Tesla Model 3 cars back in 2018 in a seemingly record short period of time and thus was way behind schedule (now known to be habitual for him), he considered only the needs of the shareholders when he shortened the timeline, not those of the workers who would produce the cars. Although the stories that glorify the hardworking Musk for sleeping under his desk for days on end might seem charming, the forced line speed-ups imposed on his rank-and-file workers have taken a serious toll—namely, a steep increase in workplace injuries. Unlike Musk, these employees don't work around the clock for a few days, missing their kids' soccer match or failing to help them with their homework, then return to a privileged lifestyle. This *is* their life. As at Winmore, management abuses at Tesla have been so egregious that the NLRB has issued a complaint against the company. Like every twentieth-century tech company before them, Tesla has lawyered up to fight the charges and is demanding a trial. Based on years of my experience with the NLRB process and from what I glean from reading what Tesla's workers' testimony has come out so far, the company *will* be found in violation. But that won't change much. Like most CEOs today, Musk, or his replacement, will likely make the same immoral decision to relocate Tesla production to someplace where workers can't make reasonable demands to have a safe workplace and fair, just compensation. That, or he will join the ranks of executives who think human workers are a pain in the ass and instead invest an obscene amount of resources in robots.

Automation and Robots

CEOs' and shareholders' obsession with automation is another key indicator of their disdain for workers and institutionalized profit-sharing, aka, collective bargaining. In January 2019, the *New York Times* published a story by Kevin Roose about the global elite and automation: "The Hidden Automation Agenda of the Davos Elite." In the story we learn that Apple subcontractor Foxconn—the iPhone factory in China responsible for the suicides of multiple workers—has figured out that it can dispense with its suicide nets by replacing workers with robots that won't jump to their deaths after "going crazy," as Wolfe put it in his story about the women-powered sweatshops in early Silicon Valley chip plants. A key takeaway from the 2019 Davos meeting was that U.S. corporate elites know they can't say exactly what they want to, lest they enter into a public relations disaster: not only do they not care about workers, they'd like to do away with them completely and replace them with robots. As Roose notes, "For an unvarnished view of how some American leaders talk about automation in private, you have to listen to their counterparts in Asia, who often make no attempt to hide their aims."

Do you wonder why CEOs of Asian companies *can* say what they like about their workers? Because the workers in some Asian countries are so explicitly repressed: they aren't allowed to use an independent Internet search engine to read stories of workers forming unions in places where the government doesn't attack them. So, yes, if you are an executive in a non-U.S. country where most U.S. consumer products are made, there's no need to hold back predatory comments about humans when no one in your factories will ever see them. You don't need to worry that your employees will be angry if they hear that you find their human existence—needing to eat, rest, use the bathroom—to be a business problem. On the most basic level, robots solve the fundamental problem that workers pose for CEOs by removing power from the equation. Workers who don't like their conditions have the ability to create a crisis for their boss when they organize and withhold their labor—robots don't.

Like the platform economy, robots *are* a problem, but despite the blather that the robots are coming to replace us all, they still haven't. Since the days of Sputnik 1, executives have promised that robots will replace human workers. Of course, as Roose mentions in his article, when talk of robots does slip out, executives still try to peddle the idea that they will liberate people from the drudgery of work and allow us more free time. They made that same promise when they invented washing machines and dishwashers, but there's not a mother today who feels less stressed than before those two machines hit the scene.

Claims of "positive" automation today generally perpetuate similar myths about the impact of the washing machine: Leisure time will increase, fewer hours per worker will be needed, consumer prices will fall, people will consume more goods, and profits will rise. Pro-automation rhetoric posits that while automation has eliminated some jobs, don't worry! It will create others. The problem is that the jobs that have been eliminated—in fact often prioritized for automation—are the very ones that have tended to be unionized, paying people a union wage, and the "new" jobs that get created are nonunion, low wage, no- to low-benefit jobs. The only other positive argument people make about robots and automation has to do with removing workers from dangerous environments. But it's the actual environment itself, not just the workers, that can't tolerate the industries that create those jobs, from cleaning out melting-down nuke plants to deep mining to chemical manufacturing. We don't need to automate those jobs: we need to replace those industries with highly unionized clean energy.

One use-case for robots is getting a lot of traction, and that is the effort to replace elder-care workers with robots. With the aging baby boomer population and the radical shift from one breadwinner to two breadwinners with no substantial change in household income, the crisis of who will care for the aging population—once addressed by the institution formerly known as the housewife—is urgent. According to AARP, by 2025, there will be a shortage of

450,000 caregivers in the United States alone because each day 10,000 people turn sixty-five years old.

As such, personal-care and home-care health aides are among the fastest-growing occupations projected well into the future at a growth rate that's as rapid as the creation of factory jobs was at the turn of the twentieth century. There are two straightforward ways to solve this crisis within the cultural and legal tradition of the United States. Either or both would hugely benefit society: vastly improving the job of caregiving, which now pays on average just $13,000 annually with few to no benefits; and/or vastly improving all other jobs, which would make the United States once more a country where many unionized workers could raise a family and live decently with only one full-time breadwinner.

There is a third option: the kind of income supports that come with the social democratic policies found throughout much of Western Europe. This would allow greater labor-force participation by both parents, but it would require radical changes to the fabric of our economy. In Sweden, people have generous paid parental leave—two back-to-back years, one for each parent—so that each baby born has a parent as its primary full-time caregiver for the first two years of life. When this parental leave is exhausted, Swedish toddlers enter a nationalized child-care system that is essentially free: paid for with a fairer taxation system that levels the playing field for children's opportunity and success from birth forward. Letting a parent of any gender or gender-identification stay home for one or two years to raise a baby, and/or having a robust system of high-quality affordable child care, would offer gender-equitable high participation in the workforce. Many countries in Europe have similar policies, though few are that generous.

Rather than being alleviated by any of the above three pro-family, pro-society options, the crisis of care work is being hijacked by profit-oriented corporations with the narrowest possible view of a "market solution" to the problem. This "solution" involves both overt union busting (remember the *Harris v. Quinn* case discussed in chapter 2, in which 500,000 mostly women of color caregivers were stripped of key union protections) and the less obvious union avoidance tactic of automating that workforce. In an October 2018 feature in their online magazine, AARP reports that small "socially assistive" robots are all the rage in elder-care planning, and companies are investing heavily in developing and testing prototypes: "During August's [2018] World Robotics Conference in Beijing, humanoids that resembled a shorter, cuter, white C-3PO sang, danced and told stories."

With crises of underemployment, unemployment, and a preponderance of below-subsistence jobs in the United States and most of those same countries, with millions of people seeking meaningful work and a family-supporting income, the drive to create robots to replace care workers is absurd. It's even more absurd from an environmental standpoint. Robots are made of plastic, rare metals that should be left in the ground, and batteries and other toxic components. They're manufactured in toxic factories and produce the worst kind of detritus: e-waste. *E-waste* is short for "electronic waste," and it's creating profound water and soil contamination all over the world, though the chances that a rich executive lives anywhere near a waste repository of the junk they produce is slim to none. Take just one example of e-waste that's a lot smaller than socially assistive robots: cell phones. In 2012 alone, 1.6 billion cell phones containing polybrominated flame retardants, lead, and arsenic were manufactured. The average life span of these phones in the United States is 18 months. Most parts can't be recycled due to the toxic nature of them, thus 60 percent goes to landfills, where most of the poisons leach into the ground.

If you're wondering whether a certain practice should be "disrupted," a good rule of thumb is to ask yourself: Do you want, or are you willing, to work in or live next to either the factory producing the product or the landfill housing the waste? If you answer no, then seek your answers elsewhere.

A great example of technology as union busting is a story published in the *New York Times* in 2018 about Zorabots, a socially assistive robot manufacturer. In it, Tommy Deblieck, co-chief-executive of Zorabots, was quoted talking about why he founded his company. "We need to help with loneliness," he explained. The article then describes how the nurses made to use his robots are instructed to stay out of view of their elderly patients as they punch the keys of the computers that run the robots, so that the robots appear to be real. It seems like a far easier way to "help with the loneliness" would be simply letting the nurses do what they know best: touching and caring for their patients. Nathalie Racine, a nurse quoted in the story, is right: "Nothing will ever replace the human touch, the human warmth, that our patients need."

The union avoidance of this effort becomes clearer in that the setting for this particular robot story is France, where unions were strong until it elected its first union-busting president, Emmanuel Macron. In 2017, the choice in the French election was vote for him or the ultranationalist fascist Marine Le Pen. Macron, who is often aptly compared to Bill Clinton and Tony Blair politically, spent his first few months in office gutting long-standing French labor laws, belittling France's working class, and weakening unions. For nearly two years, Macron has attacked workers' rights, and this assault lies at the heart of France's new need for the robots. As the *Times* story states, "The challenge is particularly acute in France, where hospitals have been facing a national crisis, with health care professionals striking and protesting budget cuts and staff shortages. A rise in suicides of nurses and doctors has made national headlines." But in the same breath, the *New York Times* falls prey to the faulty thinking I've outlined above. "The figures point to an emerging gap," the author writes. "There simply won't be enough people for the required health care jobs. Proponents argue new technology must be created to help fill the void." Those three sentences in the paper of record are a good example of how false narratives and false choices are propagated.

There is no reason to manufacture robots to care for the elderly when the clear, preferred, nontoxic, better-for-the-planet-and-the-patient, higher-quality alternative is staring society in the face: human workers, millions of whom are in dire need of decent and purposeful jobs. This *is* technology as union avoidance, made all the clearer by the article itself, which describes the need for robots as a way to circumvent pesky, overempowered, unionized French nurses and doctors striking for decent solutions for the elderly and their needs. Caring for the elderly is not best done by a robot. It's obvious that robots don't have the same capacity for empathy, touch, and understanding as humans. So why are decision makers rushing to automate a solution despite the fact that countless independent health care workers organizations have consistently argued that robots are incapable of adequately replacing human caregivers? The answer can't be separated from the opening thesis in the introduction of this book: Decision makers are disproportionately big corporations and the super-rich who own them. Having enough people to fill health care positions is a result of policy that can be changed, not a product of unchanging nature.

Now that corporations have innovated the newest versions of very old precarity, workers are turning to strikes, collective action, and unions as the solution. Ironically, the activist anti-worker right-wing Supreme Court left them no other alternative at the end of the 2018 court session in a little-understood decision: *Epic Systems*.

Epic Systems Reinforces Unions as the Solution

Nonunion workers have long relied on lawsuits, both individual and class action, as mechanisms to challenge unfair practices in employment. Women workers at Walmart won a landmark sex discrimination class action lawsuit in 2011 in *Dukes v. Walmart,* ending unequal pay, mandatory work meetings at Hooters, male-only company social gatherings, prohibitions the company had against giving women certain types of jobs, and more. African Americans have relied on class action suits to challenge racist employment practices and won dozens of important cases. The 1993 *Haynes v. Shoney's Inc.* is a standout. The *Shoney's* decision ruled that Shoney's restaurant chain had "an overt policy of blatant racial discrimination and retaliation" that was "developed and directed by top Shoney management." Not surprisingly, both Shoney's and Walmart are headquartered in Southern right-to-work states, which both developed along the same slavery-to-Jim-Crow-to-anti-union legal framework. The outcomes of these big, high-impact cases, along with dozens if not hundreds of wage-theft cases—a popular tactic in the past ten years developed by immigrant worker centers—as well as individual cases, have now been made moot in the face of the U.S. legal system, leaving workers no alternative to tackle huge issues but to form a union. The *Epic Systems* case is a little complicated, but it's central to understanding how the American legal system, through corporate-backed lawsuits, has weakened workplace protections.

The May 21, 2018, *Epic Systems* case was a consolidation of three cases: *Epic Systems Corporation v. Jacob Lewis, Ernst & Young LLP v. Stephen Morris,* and *National Labor Relations Board v. Murphy Oil.* Each involved employees alleging they were shorted income and wages under various provisions of the Fair Labor Standards Act, which is the law that governs workplace conditions like overtime rules and meal and other breaks. The court ruled that the Federal Arbitration Act, the law governing arbitrations, superseded the Fair Labor Standards Act. Arbitrations are essentially a private court system in which corporations hire an arbitrator that serves as a judge. It might be obvious that a judicial system where one party hires the judge is a rigged system. The numbers bear this out: according to the Economic Policy Institute, when workers are subjected to forced arbitration versus state court, they win only 38 percent of the time, and, when they do, they get a fraction of the financial settlements that actual courts award.

To make a complicated case simple, the court ruled that workers can be *forced,* as a condition of employment, to sign mandatory binding arbitration agreements that preclude them from taking their employer to court. But the decision was even worse, as it essentially backs anything the employers want to put into their individual employment contracts, including stipulations that workers can't discuss issues of concern to them at work, or share attorneys in an arbitration claim. It states that each worker can be forced to individually hire an attorney even for an arbitration case, be required to pay a filing fee to take the employer to arbitration, and pay for the arbitration if he or she loses the claim decision. The ruling was so comprehensive, it left nonunion workers' rights in rubble. Think about the nonsolution women's advocacy groups have been demanding for years, pay transparency. Nope, not anymore—not unless the workers have a union.

With a union contract, workers can negotiate to eliminate all these restrictions. That's the point of a collective agreement: it replaces individual hire agreements, or at least defines the terms of hire agreements. Ironically, the only way to get out from under this sham case is to form a union and negotiate a contract with your coworkers. That this decision came down just as the #MeToo movement was revealing pervasive sexual harassment by male bosses adds a special sting: at the moment women are realizing they can stand up and fight back against sexual harassment, most can't because their employer, like Google, forces the employees to sign these very kinds of forced arbitration agreements.

The *Epic* decision also eviscerated the core strategy funded by well-intentioned philanthropists and backers of what are referred to as alt-labor—groups such as immigrant worker centers and advocacy groups. Many of these nonprofits developed class action wage-theft claims, for example, as a staple strategy for low-wage workers to combat wage theft. Women's groups had been using class action suits to win equal pay and stop sexual harassment. Now, forget it. People of color suing their bosses over racial discrimination? Nope. By making mandatory, or, using the right wing's preferred word, *compulsory* arbitration agreements legal, including those that ban class action suits, the high court gutted a long-relied-upon option for abused workers.

When twenty thousand Google employees staged a one-hour walkout on November 1, 2018—a collective action—they were demanding the removal of language in their individually negotiated hire agreements forbidding them from suing their employer for sexual harassment. They won—or so they thought. Turns out Google decided they would only permit the full-time employees to have this right, not the huge contractor workforce. So then the same Google employees pushed to end mandatory arbitration clauses altogether, seeking to reinstate workers' right to sue over any kind of egregious corporate behavior, not merely sexual harassment, and for all people Google employs, contractor or direct employee. But news reports in April 2019 allege that some of the key women leaders are facing retaliatory actions by Google. And it's starting to resemble Hesselgrave's situation at Winmore. The surest way, if not the only way, for Google employees to take control of their hire agreements, and, avoid retaliation, is to form a union, come up with democratic demands, and win a good collective bargaining agreement.

IN 1932, the most prestigious organization of the economic elite, the American Economic Association, declared unions all but dead.

The argument then sounded much like today's, delivered with an air of certainty and inevitability. The president of the AEA, George Barnett, said in his annual address to the body, "American trade unionism is slowly being limited in influence by changes which destroy the basis on which it was erected. . . . I see no reason to believe that American trade unionism will . . . become in the next decade a more potent social influence." And just after that stellar prediction, a worker's revolution broke out. Workers decided to mount a crisis for corporations by building a national strike movement across the country on the heels of FDR's election. Creating sustained, serious levels of unrest by shuttering workplaces in key economic sectors and key labor markets, they built enough power to force the passage of the National Labor Relations Act.

Unions matter more than any other option available today, because income inequality—just as in 1932—reflects a much deeper power inequality. To solve the crisis caused by 90 percent of Americans sharing only 14 percent of the total wealth of the nation, and 60 percent of Americans living in debt with no savings, we have to force a redistribution at the top. That takes enormous power, the kind of power that comes when workers act collectively, walk out of their workplaces en masse, and demand that the people for whom they are making a profit share it.

Untenable conditions in the era before Roosevelt and the Congress of Industrial Organizations were transformed by workers acting collectively in their workplaces, joined by the broader society in an all-out fight to build unions that could change workers' lives and communities. The backbone of their strategy was the supermajority, all-out strike. It worked. And there's no time like now to realize there's simply no substitute for unions or supermajority strikes.

Being nice and polite, playing by the rules, occasionally voting in elections just doesn't cut it with the billionaire class. The only way to make the richest man in the world, Jeff Bezos, give a meaning-ful percentage of his profits to the people who made him a multibil-lionaire is for the workers, all of them, to walk off the job until he does. That's what good, democratic unions do, and why they matter as much in 2020 as they did in 1932.

CHAPTER 5

How Do Workers
Get a Union?

All questions need two answers,
(1) what do we want to do
and (2) how do we do it.

—Bernie Minter, District 1199,

National Hospital Workers Union (circa 1965)

MOST WORKERS WHO ARE UNIONIZED TODAY HAVE NO IDEA HOW their workplace became unionized. They showed up, got hired, and found a union card or a horrifically outdated union membership form in triplicate, still layered with carbon paper, buried in their folder of paperwork at new employee orientation. The carbon paper alone tells most younger workers that *union* means "last century."

As discussed in chapter 2, there were two periods in the past one hundred years when U.S. workers formed unions in large numbers. The first involved a surge in private-sector unionization, just after the passage of the National Labor Relations Act, back in 1935, which made collective bargaining legal in the private sector. The second period came on the heels of the civil rights movement and affected public-sector workers. In both of these eras, labor scholars and historians have noted, broad social movements raised the expectation of large numbers of ordinary Americans that life could be better.

Today, the odds of a successful organization drive are stacked against workers in this country, in spite of the fact that a majority of Americans have favored unions for as long as pollsters have existed. In August 2018, Gallup reported that 62 percent of Americans approve of unions. And yet only 10.6 percent of Americans belong to one. If 62 percent of American workers were unionized, this country would be more like Sweden, where 67 percent of all workers are unionized, and they've created a societal standard that all workers have a right to high-quality free health care, a year each of maternity and paternity leave for a child's first two years of life, free child care after that, a national mandatory six paid weeks of annual vacation, and the right to retire and enjoy the grandkids.

It is vital to understand what kind of campaigning on the part of unions is needed to close the gap between most Americans favorably viewing unions and most Americans having unions. Union organizing, and for that matter, most organizing, is a craft, and the knowledge that wins a campaign is founded on experience. Workers who have never been through that experience—and most haven't—need an experienced, skilled union organizer. This wouldn't be true if the rules for unionization were fair, but the rules are heavily stacked in favor of employers.

How do union organizers help workers beat those odds? There are two key methods that animate two key principles behind any successful union drive and any union development. The methods are leader identification and structure tests, and the principles are democracy and participation. Leadership identification is grounded in the belief that natural leaders already exist among workers, long before organizers or activists get involved. These natural, or organic, leaders have no title, but they are people whom other workers trust, whom they turn to for help when they aren't sure how to get something done. Structure tests are mini-campaigns designed to help assess the level of worker participation by work area, be it a unit in a hospital or a shift at a fast-food restaurant.

A good organizer must be able to recognize organic leaders. Fortunately, there is a tried-and-true method for identifying these leaders, and though it's not complicated, it does require good listening skills and a lot of patience and discipline. To identify leaders effectively, an organizer has to ask most of the workers by work area variations of the same question, which is: Who is the worker you turn to when you need help understanding something? There are more questions, but they are *all* a variation of this single question. Once an organizer hears the same name over and over, they will then use a structure test to assess whether this worker really is the worker that most everyone else relies upon and trusts. If the identified informal leader can get everyone in their own work area to do something, like sign a petition to management, then it's likely they are the natural leader among their peers. Structure tests are always done by hand and face-to-face, not using online tools, because, in addition to assessing the capacity of workers to get their coworkers to do something, they also help build solidarity because they force workers to engage in face-to-face conversations. This was already important before the advent of social media, but it's even more important today because chatting late at night on social media is very different than when a worker looks another worker in the eyes and helps them work through fear, ambivalence, and all the normal things that happen when a union buster shows up.

Identifying worker leaders is one method of ensuring high participation in a collective effort, which is one of the key principles in helping workers win. High participation is defined by successful union organizers as a supermajority of 80 percent or more of any given constituency engaging with one another in a collective effort (for a strike, no less than 90 percent). The other key principle is a commitment to democracy, which means breaking down the barriers—including directly confronting racism and sexism—that divide workers and weaken them in the fight for their common good.

Given this, there are two ways the battle to unionize is fought today: in either what is called a hot shop, or as part of a strategic industrial or geographic campaign. The difference is significant.

The Winmore workers were a "hot shop." The employer did something horribly wrong, which enraged a majority of workers pretty much overnight, and they rushed into a drive to organize. Most hot shop efforts in our current climate end up similar to Winmore's: they fail, despite the agitation ("heat") for a union. Though unionization efforts in hot shops fail for various reason, there are usually a few commonalities.

The most typical reason is that because workers moved so quickly, employers simply didn't have the time to hire union busters to thwart the workers in the process. In this case, these union-busting professionals enter at the post-election, pre-first-contract phase and undo worker unity while it is still new and vulnerable. According to a 2013 Congressional Research Service report, on average, a little more than half of all workers who vote to unionize wind up getting a first contract.

Another reason is that the employer who sparks a hot shop unionization effort generally manages business poorly, including its finances. When the newly unionized employees begin negotiating a first contract, they find out the employer really doesn't have the money to pay fair wages, hire additional staff, buy new safety equipment, or do much else they are demanding. At this point, most of the good workers quit and go someplace else, leaving the skeleton of the original group, and the union itself eventually dissolves.

Finally, and unfortunately, employers aren't the only ones who are inept. Unions that are clueless about building worker unity in a tough campaign are a dime a dozen. Because workers in a hot shop situation are scrambling, they don't have much time to carefully research *which* union they should reach out to for assistance. While this is understandable, it can lead to disaster. Building unity quickly when a boss does something bad is very different from sustaining a supermajority of workers who are united, and also equipped to remain so, when the union busters show up. As I mentioned earlier, if workers want to stand a decent chance against these ruthless professionals, they need to use leader identification and structure tests in order to build a lasting supermajority of workers. Sadly, most unions couldn't tell you what these concepts mean.

It's more likely that union organizers will apply these tactics in the second type of unionization fight, strategic sectoral or geographic organizing. This involves organizing workers in a region or industry that workers, through their union or set of unions, decide to target for strategic reasons. Strategic organizing campaigns, unlike hot shop battles, tend to be fought by experienced organizers, drawing on workers already in the same union but in a different unionized facility, who have experience winning hard-to-win NLRB elections or big strikes—like the three unions described in chapter 1, and the teachers' union in Los Angeles in the next chapter. The nonunion workers in these kinds of targeted industries or specific locations are likely to be dealing with a union that is actively trying to improve collective bargaining standards in their sector or region. More workers in a collective bargaining relationship to the employer, and in relationship to the sector, means more power for those workers, and this generally suggests that the union not only has a vision for workers' futures, but also the resources and staff competencies to back that vision.

A strategic campaign usually begins with strategic research. Which industries can't be offshored to China or Mexico? Within these industries, which employers are expanding and flush with cash, so that if the workers win, they can pull up to negotiations knowing there's money to make real improvements? Which industries and employers have groups of workers who are skilled enough that their employers can't easily replace them? Do the workers have some kind of other important campaign asset—for example high public prestige, like firefighters?

Both of the multiyear strategic campaigns I was hired to direct early in my union organizing years had two equally important motivations. First, the state or region was key for emerging geopolitical reasons: the industries involved were in a red state or a red region, and the national unions I worked for had a long-term goal to shift the politics of the area to pro-worker and pro-union, that is to say, blue. Second, the industries and employers involved were making a killing financially and were not unionized at all. In each case, in southern Connecticut in the late 1990s and in Nevada in the mid-2000s, we achieved both goals: We unionized thousands of workers and shifted the regional politics from Republican to Democrat. The former victory is the truly hard one to achieve; the latter happens quite naturally after successful unionization or a great contract win. Why? As discussed earlier, good unionization or contract campaigns, and certainly strikes, help clarify whose side the employer class is on; it becomes easy to see this when your employer, like Winmore, or Google, is forced out from behind the curtains into showing their overtly antihuman worker side.

A UNION THAT CONSISTENTLY WINS CAMPAIGNS through strategic organizing is the kind of union that is more likely to build momentum in those sectors, and so is more likely to attract nonunionized workers. The best way for nonunionized workers to find out if a given union could help their workplace is to speak directly with other workers already in the union. Workers in a region that has union shops can go on the Internet to research unions that represent workers in their industry and can contact those workers. Workers based in a region that has no unions can call a national union and request that a staff member help organize their workplace. These workers

need to be smart about what they're asking these union representatives: they should ask that representative to provide them with a
list of rank-and-file workers in the union from other states, including their phone numbers, so they can contact those members. Then
they can discuss these members' experiences with the union before
moving forward. In either case, workers should ask union members meaningful questions about participation: Do the workers like
their union? Are the most important decisions in the union made
by workers themselves? Are the workers directly informed about
or, even better, directly involved in contract negotiations? Or do
they only vote to ratify an agreement in which they've had no say?
Are workers directly involved in making decisions on arbitrations
and political endorsements? Workers who are considering joining
a union should want to know if the organization values and facili-
tates their participation.

The workers at Hahnemann University Hospital in Philadelphia,
where the night shift in the emergency department was experiencing one crisis after another, did precisely this: they called another
hospital that had a union to discuss the union. In September 2015,
at four thirty in the morning, a nurse named Michael Winn cold-
called nearby unionized Temple University Hospital to ask about
the hospital's working conditions and its union.

He and his coworkers in Hahnemann's ER had just experienced a
deeply frustrating patient care crisis caused by systemic short staffing. Winn didn't know the nurses he was calling. When he reached
the switchboard, he simply asked to speak with the nurse in charge
in the emergency department. When he got through, he introduced
himself, and explained he was a nurse over at Hahnemann Hospital
and said he and his coworkers were having an incredibly bad night
shift. He told the nurse on the other end of the phone line that he
had a few, short questions for her: Do you like your union? Does your
hospital get away with substandard care and nurse abuse the way
our hospital management does? When Michael heard the response

from the unionized Temple hospital nurse, which was that she loved her union and would never tolerate the conditions Winn described to her, he knew he and his coworkers need to form a union, as fast as they could. The next day, nurses from Temple University Hospital, who are members of the Pennsylvania Association of Staff Nurses and Allied Professionals (PASNAP) union, met with Winn and their nonunion counterparts at Hahnemann Hospital.

Winn knew that the nurses at Temple had a union because they were frequently in the news, often on strike to demand what they, their patients, and their community needed, and generally won excellent contracts that empowered health care workers to do what they love most: fix and heal. In 2010, nearly two thousand nurses and technical workers at Temple walked off the job in an open-ended strike. *Open-ended* means the workers intend to stay out till they win. Such strikes require far more support from the rank and file than predeclared one-, two-, or three-day strikes, which have become more common in the past twenty years or so. Nurses like Winn, and any nurse in Philadelphia in 2010, knew about the Temple strike.

The central issue that led the Temple workers to go on strike was not wages; it hardly ever is when nurses are involved. It was a gag order on nurses proposed by hospital management during negotiations for the Temple workers' fourth contract with PASNAP as their union. The gag order was intended to silence mounting complaints about dangerous short-staffing levels, lodged by empowered union nurses through a special state of Pennsylvania reporting hotline, Project DISCLOSE. The management-proposed gag order read: "The Association [PASNAP], its officers, agents, representatives and members shall not publicly criticize, ridicule or make any statement which disparages Temple, or any of its affiliates or any of their respective management officers or medical staff members."

Adding to the fury of the nurses and technical staff, Robert Birnbrauer, a Temple human resources department director, was quoted by the media during negotiations as saying to the nurses and techs, "If you want your constitutional rights, you need to go somewhere else." Taking Birnbrauer at his word, the nurses and techs decided that "somewhere else" would be the streets of Philadelphia. They were there for twenty-eight days, until they defeated management in a public relations romp. The strike received so much press that it would be difficult even today, nine years later, to find a nurse in Philadelphia who wasn't aware of the month-long Temple strike.

Area nurses—like Winn—also knew that as a result of the strike, Temple had the best-paid nurses and best staffing safeguards in Philadelphia, won through their union strike and struggle. When Winn cold-called the nurse at Temple, he heard rave reviews. Had he reached a nurse who didn't know or care about the hospital's union, it's fair to say he wouldn't have considered forming a union as the solution to Hahnemann's problems.

PASNAP was founded in May 2000 by nurses from Temple, who were dissatisfied by two different unions they'd joined in the 1990s and who decided to break away and form a new, independent union. While the Temple strike garnered the most attention, it hasn't been PASNAP's only action. Nurses and technical workers in PASNAP have walked off the job eight times. Seven of those strikes took place after 2010. Despite right-wing blather to the contrary, no one can force a worker to engage in a high-risk action; that decision is made by the worker alone.

Being prepared to "strike to win" is the mark of a good union whose members are serious about achieving real control and a decent quality of life. Being strike-ready requires building mass participation and a resilient workplace structure. That's why another hallmark of a good union like PASNAP is that on the heels of a union election, no matter what percentage of workers voted for or against the union, organizers continue the same aggressive approach that they used during the initial organizing drive. This goes to the heart of the issues that Bernie Minter addressed in his 1199 manual in the early 1960s (previously mentioned in chapter 1), when he discussed the two directions in which a union can go: from the top down or bottom up. If the primary purpose of the union is to teach workers to win—PASNAP's core mission—strike preparation is a way of life, central to every aspect of the organization's work, including its approach to the ongoing life of the union in its governance phase.

Winn's timing couldn't have been better. PASNAP's organizing team was then being seriously strengthened by a new three-union partnership, called the Northeast Nurses Association (NENA), which included the Massachusetts Nurses Association (MNA) and a smaller nurses union in New York. Like PASNAP, MNA is independent of any national union or national federation but is a member of its local central labor council (CLC, or body of the AFL-CIO) and collaborates with other unions on local politics and other key labor-solidarity efforts. PASNAP and MNA created this new strategic cross-state organizing alliance by forming a contractual partnership to pool union-dues money and union-organizing staff to assist workers in the hardest organizing and contract fights. Days after Winn first sat down with savvy nurse leaders from Temple, who easily persuaded him and his coworkers to unionize, they then brought in the professional organizers from NENA to assist them with their effort. The NENA organizers knew exactly what it would take for Winn and his coworkers to actually win an NLRB union election.

The first person hired by the rank-and-file nurse leaders on the NENA board of directors was the head of the organizing operation, the regional director, Nela Hadzic. Hadzic, a highly skilled union organizer, got her start in California with a health care workers' union called United Healthcare Workers West, a division of the Service Employees International Union. Experienced in 1199 organizing principles, Hadzic understood workers could only win what they themselves were willing to fight for, and only if they were willing to build their workplace organizations to strike-readiness. She also understood the risk that strikes involve, given the sorry state of labor law in the United States today. And Hadzic had as much training in facing risk as she did in organizing. Hadzic had been a Bosnian war refugee, and the dangers she and her family experienced moving from safe house to safe house then shaped her lifelong belief in the rights of workers and her determination to fight for them.

When she met with Winn and the nurses from Hahnemann, after the initial meeting Winn had with the Temple nurses, she knew from the get-go that he was likely to emerge as a natural leader, though she would have to test that assumption before being sure. "You could just tell right from that first day that Michael was the kind of person who people trusted, including his former high school coach, who opened the doors to the cafeteria so we could all meet and keep it really convenient to the hospital," she recalled. "Michael also talked about his father at the first meeting. His father had been in a union and that was important to the family. And of course, most importantly, he brought key nurses from other departments in the hospital with him, showing yet another side of his leadership."

Once Hadzic began listening to the nurses talking at the table, it was clear there were many issues angering them. The hospital had promised there would be one charge nurse per unit and shift who would not have patients, so that if any of the nurses needed backup, there would be someone available. But that hadn't happened. Another problem was nurses from one unit getting pulled to another unit, one that had patients that specialized nurses from other units weren't familiar with. On top of that, the ratio of patients to nurses in the ICUs was highly imbalanced; it was three patients for one nurse, which is dangerously high for intensive care. At most, depending on the patients, there should be two patients for every one nurse.

Hadzic explained that the first step would be for workers who had attended the first meetings to talk with everyone they knew, and trusted in a confidential conversation, at the hospital, to ask each one to come to a face-to-face meeting. The organizing work was slow going at first. But once Winn understood from Hadzic and her team that he needed to literally walk the floors of the hospital in order to identify other workers from units, like maternity and critical care units, and get them to meetings, the pace of the campaign picked up quickly.

Hadzic knew that keeping the nurses at Hahnemann in touch with the unionized nurses at Temple was key in maintaining the momentum of the campaign. For much of October up until the week of Thanksgiving 2015, the organizers coordinated weekly meetings between the Temple nurses, talking with Hahnemann nurses after or before their work shift. By then, another hospital's worth of nurses had gotten wind of the Hahnemann campaign through the tight-knit Philadelphia nurses' network. Hadzic was hiring and deploying more NENA staff along with PASNAP, trying to keep up with the surge in demand.

After PASNAP and the NENA team had met with more than 50 percent of all the Hahnemann nurses face-to-face, Hadzic and the other organizers decided it was time for workers to sign union authorization cards. If organizers collect a sufficient number of cards that authorize them to do so, they can trigger an official union election. Under NLRB rules, a workplace only needs to secure 30 percent of the workers on union election authorization cards in order to file the legal paperwork to then hold a secret ballot election, conducted by the NLRB. But no smart organizer would *ever* file for an election with only 30 percent. That's because once the employer campaign begins, work by the boss and union avoidance firms will shave the numbers down by as much as 20–25 percent. Effective organizers coach the workers to get supermajorities on union authorization cards before considering filing for the election itself, so they can win despite the boss picking away at the numbers of workers who want a union.

As they were preparing to file for the NLRB election, Hadzic started to investigate a rumor that late into the second Obama term, the NLRB had ruled that workers could sign authorization cards electronically. "We designed the digital online card to be gray, to look just like the regular PASNAP membership card, and we designed it so the nurses could easily sign it on their cell phones," Hadzic says. "Workers were texting each other and demanding the link. Something about the excitement plus the speed was leading to reports of record card authorizations per shift, per day." The entire campaign happened under management's radar.

Within days, a supermajority of Hahnemann nurses had signed authorization cards. When the organizers filed for the unionization election with the NLRB, one week later, management felt ambushed. This is an ideal situation for workers: it doesn't give management much time to hire a union avoidance firm or to prevent workers from voting to form a union. The NLRB verified that the union authorization cards were valid, which took about one month of meetings with the government agents from the NLRB, who sit down with the union and the management team to review each name of each worker (all of these timelines are "about" because the union busters will do their damnedest to stall at every step). The NLRB then set the election for a little less than one month later (using "business days, not calendar days"—one of so many byzantine factors), and, by January 20, 2016, the 850 Hahnemann nurses overwhelmingly voted yes (516 to 117) to form a union through an NLRB election, and the hospital became the first hospital campaign in the country where a union used electronically signed authorization cards.

The momentum had spread fast on the nurse grapevine. Nurses at DelCo—the hospital discussed in chapter 1—had about half as many workers as Hahnemann, and they voted 164 to 130 to unionize. Then two weeks after the pro-union vote at Hahnemann Hospital, on February 8, just off Broad Street—the same street as Temple—470 nurses at St. Christopher's Hospital voted 311 to 49 to unionize. Over the next two weeks in February, two more units of outpatient and technical workers at St. Christopher's and DelCo voted to join the nurses in their hospitals. All this organizing was successful because PASNAP has so many nurses that love their union, so they had plenty of members who would volunteer to go out in teams with full-time organizers to speak with nonunion nurses about the benefits of the union.

By the time of yet another election, nearly the entire PASNAP and NENA hospital organizing teams were overwhelmed by calls from health care workers about forming a union, too. PASNAP had more than doubled in size in a matter of months. With the record pace of the unionization among different units across three medium-to-big city hospitals, PASNAP would need to work hard and work smart in order to solidify the internal structures and work-site organizations so all workers could fight to win strong first contracts. While the swirling nurse and hospital workers movement was unfolding up and down Broad Street, the nurses from an even bigger hospital, Einstein Medical Center, decided they wanted to unionize, too.

Seeing the writing on the wall from other hospitals' nurses, however, Einstein management hired one of the top union-busting firms in the United States: IRI Inc. Einstein nurses reported seeing dozens of union busters in the hospital in the weeks leading up to their election. In fact, workers had first spotted IRI consultants inside the hospital in late March 2015, when the union had leafleted outside the hospital about unionization. Nothing much had happened at that point in time, but it meant that union-busting consultants had been working for a year by the time the workers had called an election.

Despite the union busters' tactics—including a snazzy anti-union website, captive audience meetings, and one-on-ones to intimidate every nurse at Einstein—the success of the nurses at nearby hospitals helped sustain their momentum. On April 8, 2016, the nurses at Einstein, the biggest hospital in the city-wide nurses movement that year, voted to unionize. But the margin was much closer: there were 926 nurses eligible to vote, 806 of whom cast ballots. (Eighty-six percent of all nurses cast a ballot.) There were 463 yes votes, which was basically equal to the number of no votes combined with the 120 who hadn't voted (343 no votes, with 120 who didn't participate in the vote). Compared with the momentum at the other hospitals, Einstein had been a hard-fought election win. It was also the most strategically important in some ways because it was considered more prestigious that the others, and was the largest of the then-unionizing hospitals in Philadelphia.

Then it happened.

Within the NLRB-mandated period of seven days from the date of the election—the number of days that employers or workers in an election have to file objections to a union election—an urgent fax arrived at PASNAP from a law firm: It was an official objection by management's lawyers to the union election at Einstein, seeking immediate injunctive legal relief. The objection stated that the hospital refused to recognize the union election as valid and alleged malfeasance on the part of union. This was all without evidence. This is cookie-cutter union busting: if management loses at the first step, they will do everything they can to "poison and choke and bludgeon the collective spirit," in the words of union buster Levitt.

The nearly one thousand nurses at Einstein and the PASNAP leadership understood that management intended to destroy the union by stalling and tying up the election results in court for half a decade. This is very common and often does lead to workers giving up on their original dream of forming a union. The vote to form the union at Einstein was 463 to 343. If the purpose of the union is to teach workers to win—meaning having a good contract that addresses the core issues negatively affecting the workers every day—a good union should immediately make a plan to win over the 343 no votes to its cause. To build to at least 90 percent visible and mobilizable unity, which is the percentage required to make a credible strike threat, there's no possible way to achieve those numbers without directly engaging the 120 who failed to vote and the 343 who voted no.

With the overzealous legal charges filed by the biggest hospital at that point in the campaign and with even more nurses calling from yet more area hospitals, PASNAP was overstretched and overwhelmed, even with the help of the NENA team. They needed even more reinforcements. They needed someone who had handled hard boss fights and could help lead the overall city-wide negotiations campaign, not just deal with the immediate crisis at Einstein. That someone was me.

IN LATE APRIL 2016, I was brought on by PASNAP as a full-time consultant to coordinate the city-wide first contract campaign across hospitals and to win recognition of the union at Einstein. There were two things I understood from prior experience. First, we had to force the employer to *drop* its trumped-up, baseless legal charges. It simply would not work to allow the legal fight to run its course, even if the workers won the fight at every stage, because employers continue to appeal each ruling in the legal fight and can postpone the unionization for years. Second, the workers themselves would have to overcome the internal divisions and build the work-site organization strong enough to demonstrate supermajorities for the union if we were to have a credible campaign to convince the broader general public that the employer's actions were immoral and antidemocratic. The conundrum was that, in order to achieve a supermajority, we needed to convince a substantial number of workers that unions were a force for good. We needed to do this at the same time that the employer continued to tell its employees that they would never surrender to the union (standard use of what union busters call futility).

Because Einstein management had hired an A-level union avoidance firm, the full-time consultants brought in to devise and direct the management's anti-union campaign hadn't packed up shop when the election was over. The consultants remained and built their anti-union beachhead in several departments. The biggest was in the telemetry unit (Tele), where sixty-six nurses had all but shut out the union and voted no in the election. Although there were smaller pockets of scattered no votes throughout the hospital, the largest block of anti-union nurses resided in a unit that is literally walled off from other units. Tele nurses are the nurses who monitor each patient's oxygen level, heart rate, status of liquid medications, and so forth (the beeping machines in every room). From the view of winning a strong contract, 7 percent of the anti-union animus at Einstein resided in this single unit. Without the support of the Tele unit, the Einstein workers couldn't achieve a credible strike threat.

Because the Einstein's Tele nurses, inveigled by IRI, had actually led the anti-union campaign, knowing how to approach Tele was particularly challenging. They had published an anti-union Facebook page and an official website that was openly hostile to unions. When pro-union worker leaders tried to talk with Tele nurses about the campaign, the Tele nurses would walk away and refuse to engage with their colleagues from other units. This led to most of the strong union supporters getting really frustrated—and this is all the goal of the union busters, to get workers to stop talking to each other. Whenever pro-union nurses discussed Tele, they would throw up their hands. There was no way to change Tele's mind! They had tried everything, they thought. But we, the organizing team, were insistent in coaching them: you, the workers, have to win over the no votes throughout your hospital to be able to seriously win anything substantial.

My initial strategy was to step back and do a serious assessment of the leadership in Tele, who were the most respected workers among all the workers in that department. Had we correctly assessed who the real, informal, or organic leaders were among their peers? What had been the effort to move the department previously? Even though NLRB union elections are conducted by secret ballot, good organizers and strong worker committees that practice a discipline called *work-site charting* can predict how each worker will vote. Work-site charting involves teaching the workers themselves to build unit by unit charts, about the size of big flip chart paper, with all the workers' names on the charts, and to then track each worker's response to each structure test. Using big wall charts, organizers and nurses discussed what the heck was happening in Tele over and over. We agreed that our assessment of Tele's most respected workers might have been off-base because the union avoidance firm had instructed the workers not to talk to anyone about their unit or the union.

We re-reviewed the anti-union effort in Tele, and the names of several key nurses bubbled up. Out of sixty-six workers in Tele, Liz Miller on the night shift was the only functioning contact the union had—she was the only nurse in her unit who we were sure had voted in favor of the union. And the night shift of any hospital is always significantly smaller than the day shift because management's *incorrect* assumption is that patients sleep at night and are not in need of nearly the same attention as they are during the day. Of course, anyone who has ever been hospitalized overnight knows that at night, patients are either awake in pain or fear, or are woken up for various tests, IV bag changes, administration of medications needed in short time intervals, lab tests, and so forth.

So one person would talk to us: Miller, who had voted yes for the union. She was a seasoned nurse, thinking about how to retire, working in a unit with many new and young nurses, many of whom were people of color. Miller is a classic case of someone who is a pro-union activist but not a natural leader. She is a songwriter and musician when she isn't working the night shift, selected as the Pennsylvania representative for the National Songwriters Association. She identifies as a feminist, as someone who experienced Second Wave feminism in the 1970s and the changes that women, including registered nurses, had to fight for to secure basic decent treatment and respect. I like Miller a lot: she is funny and exuberant. She makes me want to hear her sing in a smoke-filled Nashville bar. She was interesting and easy to spend time with.

But as the lead on a campaign where my job was to teach the workers to win and, specifically, to overcome the significant crisis of the Tele department, there wasn't much Miller could do to help the cause. She loved her unit and felt very good about her coworkers, except for the vexing issue of how to get them to see what she saw: a union as a good choice for nurses. She was extremely frustrated by her inability to move the younger nurses or most of her coworkers. In my discussions with her, and in a formal interview conducted after the campaign, she explained at length that, to her, voting for a union was obvious: Why wouldn't the workers want a union?

Miller started attending pro-union meetings since the beginning of the unionization effort in December 2015. At that point, there was an uptick in energy for the union because management had made hospital-wide internal changes to sick leave and attendance policies. Interestingly, the policies were being changed, according to the management memo, because of the city of Philadelphia becoming one of the first cities in the United States to affirm a city-wide sick-leave ordinance, a campaign run by progressive activists on the heels of New York City approving a limited policy of three paid days of sick leave per year. Philadelphia's new ordinance was similar to New York City's, and those high up in management at one of the biggest hospitals in Philadelphia decided that if they must amend the sick-leave policy for what they considered low-level employees and contractors, they'd make higher-paid workers foot the bill by taking away and seriously restricting *their* better sick-leave policy. To be clear, we are discussing the prospect of registered nurses losing sick time and having a more stringent attendance policy as a response to progressive social policy.

According to Miller, the imposition of the new policies was an affront to all the nurses. Teams of managers explained to all workers in the hospital that if they were late a few times, management could mark them down for a missed shift. If workers were sick, they had to bring in a doctor's note to prove it. The nurses who had been trying to form the union early in 2015—but who had hit the wall with unwilling nurses in Tele, as well as in other departments—were suddenly having other nurses approach them asking about unionization. Miller, who had always been the one person in her unit who wanted the union, was able to convince one day-shift worker, whom she identified as someone that other nurses listened to, to attend her first union meeting on the heels of the sick- and attendance-leave policy debacle. That day-shift nurse was Marne Payne.

Payne was an energetic, twenty-nine-year-old nurse who, like Miller, loved working in her unit. She had been there for nine years prior to the start of the union discussion. Payne was still finishing nursing school during her first two years of working at Einstein, doing an externship at the hospital. She started as a nurse in the Tele unit in August 2009. For Payne, Tele was a smart choice because there was upward mobility: if you were a Tele nurse, you worked next to the critical care unit (CCU), and you could train to become a cardiac nurse, which was a highly skilled and coveted position. Upward advancement was important to Payne. As she tells it, although her parents didn't go to college, they pushed hard for her and her two siblings to succeed. All three work in health care in Philadelphia, which is not surprising given that health care and education are the backbone of modern Philadelphia's economy. Growing up black in the Philadelphia suburbs, Payne lived in a house that was very academic. She describes how her father, who had not attended college, pressured her in school: "I could get a ninety-two on a test, and my father would say, 'Why didn't you get a ninety-six?' He was never pleased." For Payne, hitting key life milestones, like graduating from high school with good grades, buying a house, and securing a job with decent pay and room for growth, mattered a lot. "Remaining independent and a free thinker mattered, and that's how I approach Einstein, my patients, and the union," she says.

Not long after the hospital imposed the new sick-leave and attendance policies, Payne was convinced that Einstein needed a union. "I remember the first time I said anything about a union, I went running down the hallway at work saying we needed a union," she says. "I started screaming that we needed a union." Payne liked and respected the manager in Tele. She thought she was straightforward and an advocate for the nurses in her unit. But the new sick-leave and attendance policies, in Payne's and many other nurses' minds, were completely disrespectful. She says that her own manager knew it but couldn't protect the nurses from the hospital-wide policy.

This dynamic—when workers realize that even if they like their manager, their manager doesn't control key decisions—is often crucial to worker self-awareness that they themselves might have to do something to restore their dignity.

Not long after Payne expressed the need for a union, she was called into the office by the CCU nurse manager and told she wasn't allowed to talk about a union in the hallway. After having been a loyal nurse for years, and one who by her own description prizes her free-thinking ways, being told that she was forbidden to talk about something probably compelled Payne to attend her first union meeting just weeks after the incident.

At Miller's urging, Payne attended what they experienced as the first union meeting (there had been other union meetings, but a year before, when the effort fizzled out). It was December 2015. The meeting was at Chickie's & Pete's sports bar. Despite the noisy atmosphere, Payne remembers the conversation going decently well. There were nurses from other unionized facilities who talked about how unionizing helped them, and everyone at that December meeting agreed it was time to try unionizing. During the next meeting, Payne listened to a union staffer describe the types of things they could win if they formed a union. After the meeting, Payne began to do research to fact-check the discussion about what a union could and couldn't do. Not long after, hospital management began holding daily anti-union meetings. By Payne's description, her manager was very good at telling nurses why they shouldn't have a union. "My boss was right out there from the starting gate, pushing hard against the union," she says. "Anyone who hadn't made up their minds yet, my manager got them. She did a really good job keeping the atmosphere on our floor very anti-union."

A combination of factors informed Payne's initial turn against the union. She, her manager, and most of her coworkers conceded that they had things okay in their unit at work, and a union might disturb the peace. This is exactly what A-level union-avoidance consultants do: as with the highly paid public relations consultants who are front groups for the fossil fuel industry, their goal is to drive serious doubt about any union claims of workers winning a better life. And if that fails, they resort to fear: fear of job loss and fear of change, of something bad happening. The professional fossil-fuel-doubter industry is somehow better understood by progressives and liberals in the United States, but it created its playbook from the union-busting industry. Doubt, then fear.

In Payne, IRI Inc.—the professional union busters who were by then throughout the hospital—found their natural leader (union busters and union organizers are trained to understand who these workers are). Despite going to a second union meeting, Payne decided that "everyone at the union was a liar" and chose to campaign against the union. It can't be stated strongly enough: there were professional union busters working her hard to suddenly flip her from pro- to anti-union. The union-busting consultants, as Martin Levitt stated in his book many times, lie, lie more, and keep lying. True to Payne's spirit, when she made up her mind that the union was making promises it could not keep, her drive made her all out against the union. It's worth noting that no successful union organizer *promises* workers anything. In fact, a cardinal rule of unions like PASNAP and 1199 is that organizers *never* make promises; rather, organizers explain to workers they will win what they are willing to fight for. That Payne came to believe she had heard union organizers making promises was likely a result of intense penetration of IRI, conducting what Miller described as "nonstop mandatory meetings."

These nonstop mandatory meetings held by IRI were a trademark A-level union-busting strategy: they were long, droning, and frequent. In the lingo of union battles, the consultants from the union-avoidance industry were conducting what are called "captive audience meetings." These meetings were considered *captive* because the meetings take place on the clock and are mandatory. If a worker, even a free thinker, thinks she can refuse to attend when they call her in—even if she is caring for a patient—she is wrong. Refusing to attend mandatory captive audience meetings is considered gross insubordination and an offense that can be grounds for firing. IRI was in full swing in the Tele unit.

According to Miller, "We were getting letters in our mailboxes at work every day from our manager, saying, 'As a personal favor to me, I want to ask you to vote no to the union.' And I was thinking, this was really not fair, this isn't personal, we are doing this because you can't get it done, you can't make things change—we have to." But the manager was working the day-shift nurses hard. Miller explained that the day-shift nurses were "afraid of Maryanne [the manager]. I was arguing with the day-shift nurses, but they were being told if they supported the union, they were going to be considered traitors. And management was pulling everyone away from the patients for these meetings for one hour or more at a time to move the traitor message."

To Miller, the meetings were infuriating. But to most nurses in her unit, they were effective. From Miller's view, the young, new nurses never had to advocate for themselves. They didn't go through the experience years earlier of being told they had to wear dresses every day at work. Miller remembers in the 1970s, when everyone in her unit decided to come to work the next day wearing pants, not dresses. Overnight, they won the right to wear pants to work. Experiences like these separated Miller from the younger nurses who dominated the day shift. Payne, on the other hand, became one of the most vocal and visible anti-union nurses. She says that she would monitor the pro-union Facebook page, and "if PASNAP was on social media pushing something, I went on social media and pushed for the opposite. The people I trusted were against the union, so I went all out and campaigned against PASNAP."

The day before the vote, Payne took to social media, imploring nurses to vote no. She used an analogy about a highly recruited and highly touted star player coming to Philadelphia's storied football team and failing spectacularly. The team was locked into a long contract with a player who just couldn't deliver what everyone promised he would. The nurses were the fans, and they would be humiliated forever by a union, like the fans of the football team. She wrote, "Not all unions are bad, but I believe PASNAP is the devil." She closed the piece by writing, "Service above self!! VOTE NO!! VOTE HELL NO!!!"

How to shift the opinion about the union with the Tele nurses was an important topic in every weekly meeting with the pro-union Einstein nurses. By then the pro-union nurses knew they simply couldn't get to supermajority numbers without moving the Tele department and a few other clusters of anti-union nurses in other units. Our strategy was to act like a union and move forward, for example, deciding to hold elections for which nurses would be elected to the negotiations committee, despite the vexing and frankly terrifying legal charges that, at that point, no one saw a way out of. Thankfully in late May the NLRB dismissed all the employers' allegations of wrongdoing and recommended that the hospital recognize the union. And immediately, as if the union-avoidance law firm had already long prepared for this moment, the employer appealed the decision. So to the nurses, the employer first contested their election, and it was now contesting the first legal ruling. The nurses issued a flier to their coworkers declaring victory, and management put out a long memo to all nurses explaining that they were immediately appealing the ruling and would never recognize the union.

This phase of union-busting operations is called "futility." It's standard in union-busting playbooks. Futility engenders an insidious kind of doubt in workers. Union busters consistently tell workers that, even though they voted to form a union, they'll never actually get one. Management would challenge the union every step of the way, so why don't they just give up now and save everyone's time? And true to the moment, just after the hospital filed the appeal to the next-level court in the appeals process, nurse attendance plummeted at the regular weekly 7 A.M. and 7 P.M. shift-change-based Wednesday meetings. The nurses who limped in to what had been robust evening meetings reported that others throughout the hospital had read the long e-mail from management—which probably explained why they hadn't shown up; they were giving up.

The goal of the union at this stage is to raise expectations and reassert that workers can win, even in the face of futility efforts by management. Figuring out how to successfully message this in the face of formidable management memos was key. The fact that we had one favorable legal ruling on our side wasn't a real comfort because it read just like a legal ruling: the only people who could understand nearly any sentence in the thirty-odd pages of legalese were lawyers. The workers needed a confidence boost.

We knew who could understand the legal language, however: politicians, probably half of whom are lawyers. We knew that someone other than nurses or the nurses' union had to send the message to the nurses that the hospital was going to eventually lose. One of the PASNAP organizers had formerly been a very successful fundraiser to key politicians in the area—likely the most highly valued position to almost any politician. We tasked her with securing a letter, on official letterhead, from powerful Pennsylvania politicians to the hospital CEO, stating that they were aware that the hospital was stalling unionization, that the legal ruling in favor of the nurses would prevail, and that they stood with the nurses. This letter had two objectives: to lift workers' spirits and give them hope, and to have them see people perceived as more important than the hospital CEO challenging his authority.

The CEO of Einstein, Barry Freedman, considered himself a liberal Democrat. He was known to attend fund-raisers for Democrats running for office. We had researched him by talking not only with the nurses but also with key players in unions in New York City, where Freedman had previously been a hospital CEO. We used this research to better understand him and our strategy.

The PASNAP organizer pulled through. On June 7, 2016, ten senators, including ones who hailed from the important Senate Appropriations Committee, signed a letter siding with the nurses and against management. It stated their awareness of the nurses' election and that the NLRB had ruled in favor of the nurses. The final paragraph of the letter stated:

> We support the nurses' efforts to improve the quality of care of their patients by creating an organized, collective voice in their workplace. We believe it is in the best interest of our constituents and the community for [Einstein Medical Center] to respect that decision. Instead of spending healthcare dollars on expensive "union avoidance" consultants, put those funds toward building a partnership with your nurses, who interact with the patients you serve every day.

Within minutes of knowing the letter had been sent to the CEO, the union made hundreds of black-and-white copies of the letter, as well as more expensive color copies showing the official, gold-leaf stamp of the Senate of Pennsylvania. We quickly gave copies to the nurses, and they went floor to floor, handing out the letter as if it were Halloween candy.

It worked. More nurses attended the subsequent Wednesday meetings, and those who came once again believed they could win the fight. It's hard to overestimate the value of important outsiders validating workers' dreams while union busters are convincing them that they'll never come true.

The discussion at the next Wednesday meeting, in mid-June 2016, centered on what needed to happen next. From experience, the staff of the union understood that management, and particularly the CEO, would immediately sow doubt in the minds of the senators that there was actually real nurse support for the union. In fact, we predicted this because the hospital had hired an influx of nurses during the unionization campaign, which was a strategy to make management look as if it was listening to the nurses by lessening the crushing patient load. (In actuality, though, that hiring binge was likely to be temporary.) With this new wave of employees, the CEO was likely to tell the senators there wasn't even majority support for the union: out of the now 1,000 staff nurses, only 463 had voted yes, and Freedman would claim the numbers of support were falling.

To combat what we assumed would be the CEO's message, the nurses needed to quickly get a hand-signed real majority petition to show, rather than tell, the public that the CEO was lying. The nurses in the room were worried about getting a majority of no less than 65 percent (we could not yet set the higher threshold of 80 percent because we still had entire units, like Tele, working with the union busting consultants, so achieving 65 percent would be hard as hell, but it was urgent, too). The nurses had never gotten a majority of their coworkers to do anything up to that point. The discussion was simple: the nurses had to achieve a supermajority or management would get the upper hand.

For the union staff, the hand-signatures-only petition was a structure test that helped all of us, the organizers and the pro-union nurses, understand which nurses had serious support among their colleagues and which were enthusiastic but couldn't persuade colleagues to sign the open-letter petition to the CEO. Structure tests are crucial at every phase of a tough union campaign. Without them, organizers and workers have no idea whether, or where, there's real majority support for the union. Because time was of the essence, we decided not to focus on the Tele department and instead use the petition mostly to reassess how nurses in other units were feeling, given the relentless intensity of the boss campaign. Would nurses who had previously taken any kind of pro-union action quickly sign the petition demanding the employer drop its legal appeal, recognize the union, and come to the negotiations table?

It was late June at that point, and there was still no legal recognition of the union. Every other hospital that had voted yes was already many sessions into their negotiations—this played into Einstein management's futility messaging. There was pushback from some nurses who thought we should take the letter from the senators and hold a press conference. But we explained that nothing other than a supermajority of nurses' signatures would counter Freedman's claim that most Einstein nurses didn't want a union anyway. These moments, where union staff who have experience in many rounds of employer warfare teach the worker leaders—all of whom are new to a union fight—are key to winning in high-risk, high-tension, high-stakes union wars. We understood this petition was a test of the nurses' support for the union, and also that it was urgent for the fight to ultimately get the employer to drop their legal charges and recognize the union. If the nurses could demonstrate a real majority, it would also help in the effort to move Tele and other anti-union departments because management's message to the senators was the same as it was to the anti-union clusters: no nurses really want the union, even if a few accidentally voted for it in April. A petition signed by a supermajority of nurses would prove that wasn't the case.

Weeks later, just in time for the July Fourth weekend—certainly longer than was ideal—the nurses reached a majority, then got more signatures on their petition: 60 percent of nurses signed. Good enough to go, and "go" was the order of the day. The nurse leaders marched the petition to the CEO as a way to directly challenge his authority (it doesn't matter if the CEO is in to receive these type of majority petitions or not; it is still an act of escalation by the workers themselves and they leave the giant, blown-up, hand-signed petition with the secretary to the CEO).

Enabling workers to constantly make acts of defiance is key to building up a credible strike threat—because a strike is the highest act of defiance. But marching the petition into the CEO's office was only the first act. The second act would involve groups of nurses hand-delivering the petition (enlarged to three by six feet) to each member of the hospital's board of trustees. There were a couple dozen community VIPs on the board of trustees, and hand-delivering the giant, signed petition and a packet that contained the legal ruling and the senators' letter would provide an opportunity for many nurses to express their defiance of management's wishes and be certain the board knew that the nurses really did want a union, despite management lies.

In the United States, private hospital boards are typically made up of prominent members of the community—think of philanthropists who donate to the children's cancer wing and get their names on hospital buildings. Board members most certainly do not want negative publicity nor do they want well-loved nurses appearing unannounced at their offices, in cleanly washed scrubs, pronouncing that their hospital is antidemocratic and attacking its employees. The union began to get reports that the CEO was increasingly agitated. He had called the senators to tell them exactly what we had predicted he would—that nurses didn't want the union and that the union was just a money-grubbing special interest group. But when the hospital trustees began calling the CEO to demand that nurses stop coming to their offices—and in the case of a few liberals on the board, questioning the CEO's leadership—the dynamic was shifting. In all the right ways.

WITH PRESSURE MOUNTING and nurses themselves getting stronger and stronger, the next opportunity for action was clear: the national Democratic Party convention in late July, where Hillary Clinton would be anointed as the presidential nominee. We knew this was a key moment. National and international media would be focused on a proudly liberal city. The idea that thousands of nurses, beloved in all opinion polls as the most trusted workers in America—and women to boot—would be potentially walking picket lines, protesting union busting and unsafe staffing conditions, meant a spectacle we were certain that local politicians would not tolerate.

The timeline, however, was moving faster than the nurses' organization was growing. Union busters were still driving futility and fear messages daily. Despite the real pressure hospital management felt from the nurse's actions, they weren't backing down. The nurses needed more leverage: the leverage of nurses walking picket lines during the Democrats' convention. Union president Patty Eakin, herself a nurse who had been part of the 2010 Temple University Hospital strike, was a sitting member of the local Labor Council, where all unions coordinated to support endeavors like political campaigns. We decided that Eakin needed to get a resolution from the Labor Council that called on all unions to support the nurses who would be picketing the Democratic National Convention.

We didn't know until Eakin arrived at the Labor Council meeting in mid-July that months earlier the council had signed an actual no-protest agreement with the official host committee of the

Democratic Party. Despite the foolish "labor peace" accord holding
the council back from taking advantage of labor issues when the
world's media would be in town, we knew that Eakin's proposal to
support the nurses' picket line at the Labor Council was about to
ripple straight into the halls of Democratic Party power. From the
view of the unions who had agreed to the labor peace accord during
the convention, Eakin's description of nurses—most of whom are
female—walking picket lines while the first serious female candidate for president was accepting an already troubled nomination
was about to make its way straight from the Labor Council into elite
Democratic Party circles.

It was the second week in July 2016. I was looking at my watch,
counting the minutes until a strong-arm from the Dems called Eakin to tell her what she could *not* do. I was getting her ready to stand
her ground, and at that moment, had we not already had a supermajority petition hand-signed by the nurses demanding the CEO
drop his legal appeal, the entire effort would have unraveled against
us. This is a superb example of why majority petitions matter. Behind the scenes, different players were back-channeling with each
other: What would it take to get the nurses to back down? Democratic leaders and the male leaders of the Labor Council were concerned. Meanwhile, we were frantically trying to move the nurses
who had just barely pulled off their first majority petition to take a
strike vote, an act way too serious for such an early stage of worker
development. So discombobulated were the politicians and labor
leaders that we realized if we could only get a credible picketing
threat, we would likely have the leverage needed to get the Democratic Party elite to tell—forcibly tell—the CEO that he must withdraw his legal appeal charges.

Nurse organizers in the hospital had put up hundreds of fliers
throughout the hospital calling for an emergency all-nurses vote
about picketing in ten days. One of many quirks of labor law for
health care workers is that workers must submit a legalized, formal

ten-day notice of intent to picket in order to avoid punishment. The clock was ticking: the Democratic convention was ten days away, and the moment of leverage would disappear fast. Could we secure enough votes from the nurses in order to submit a notice to picket?

We knew that we needed to get the plan moving quickly by suggesting a way for the head of the Labor Council to go on record supporting the nurses, even though he was part of signing the accord promising labor peace. We decided to have Eakin ask the head of the Labor Council to fax and send a letter on Labor Council letterhead to the hospital CEO, copied to the Democratic host committee, simply stating his concern about the nurses' plight and how unfortunate it would be if there were labor action during the convention. This was a bit of a dog whistle: six years earlier, recall, PASNAP had conducted a highly successful strike at Temple University Hospital, and so the Democratic Party knew the Labor Council was serious. The affable elected head of the Labor Council liked Eakin, and he and the other unions had supported her and her nearly two thousand colleagues during the Temple strike. In his mind, writing the letter wasn't violating the no-protest agreement. Had Temple workers not previously gone on strike, the threat of action would likely have fallen on deaf, or at least highly suspicious, ears.

With the letter from the Labor Council in place, and even though we had a majority petition demanding that the hospital drop its legal appeal, recognize the union, and start collective bargaining negotiations, we knew that we needed a strong affirmative vote from the nurses to authorize the sending of a legal, formal, ten-day picket notice. We quickly called together a meeting and had to do what real organizers do best: be honest, be straightforward, be clear, explain exactly what the strategy is, make it compelling, and in this case lay the decision squarely on the nurses. Everyone was nervous about the 7 A.M. and 7 P.M. shift change meetings: it was unfortunate that we had to have a night-shift vote first because our top nurse supporters worked the day shift in most units.

Our 7 A.M. meeting, which is the night shift coming off of work, was in a church basement two blocks from the hospital. We were either winning this vote or missing the biggest act of leverage possible. I laid it out exactly as Bernie Minter—of 1199 fame and the author of the manual that taught it was a sin to lie by omission or commission—had instructed. I laid out the options: take a really strong action—an action people didn't feel ready for—and defeat their boss and win the union, or be consumed with fear of direct action and lose our moment of maximum power.

After many questions and much discussion of concerns, the night-shift nurses unanimously voted to picket. We took a picture of all hands raised, and we put it on slides for the 7 P.M. meeting of the day-shift nurses. By then, news was spreading through the day shift that the night-shift nurses had voted to authorize the ten-day picket notice. By the evening meeting, held in the basement of a restaurant near the hospital called Nick's Roast Beef, where we could get maximum turnout, an overflowing crowd of nurses voted to send the CEO a picketing notice.

EVERY POLITICIAN IN TOWN knew the nurses were voting. The Labor Council knew the nurses were voting. By eight the next morning, Eakin, the public face of a massive and successful strike at Temple University Hospital, faxed the letter from the nurses authorizing the ten-day notice to picket to the entire power structure. Exactly three hours later, I received a phone call from the hospital legal counsel—the law firm Fox Rothschild, long entrenched in the Democratic and Republican power structures—offering to meet to see whether we could work out the differences between nurses and the hospital.

The first thing I told the hospital's lawyer was that any actions we would take would have to be ratified by the nurses themselves. I explained that neither I nor PASNAP leadership were the kind of unionists who would make decisions for the nurses—only they could decide their future. I explained, therefore, that if we were to meet, these meetings would not be secret, and the union would cut no deal. The lawyer hung up after telling me that there was "no way, no way in hell" the CEO would agree to meet if it wasn't secret. My nerves were fraying. I called the head of the union and quickly explained that I had refused a secret meeting with the CEO. We were tense about the moment, about my decision, about everything.

Before we could decide whether to give in, just enough time had passed—one hour—before the lawyer called back, saying, "Okay. Give us dates for a meeting." Bingo! That's what happens when the nurses are in serious motion and everyone knows it because they are showing it, with majority petitions, with overwhelming votes for picketing, and with being public about everything they are doing to unionize.

Days later, after three rounds and many hours of high-stakes meetings between CEO Barry Freedman and me, along with the hospital's law firm and the executive director of the union, and done in close consultation with key nurse leaders, we had a deal. Interestingly, despite the fact that the three meetings were premised on my telling the management team that any deal we hammered out would have to be ratified in a formal vote by the nurses themselves, the CEO and his lawyer were furious that PASNAP stuck to our guns and wouldn't agree to a deal until the nurses voted to withdraw the notice to picket. We were three days from the planned picket, which meant we were two days from the day Clinton would make her speech accepting the nomination.

We called an emergency meeting, which was packed with even more nurses than the recent meetings. I explained the deal: if they voted to rescind their picketing action, the employer would withdraw its legal appeal, recognize the union, and start contract negotiations immediately. There was very little discussion, and the nurses voted immediately to accept the deal. Why not? They had a massive victory, surrendering basically nothing and learning the most important lesson of all: by standing strong and taking high-risk action, they had won big. Although negotiations hadn't started, the nurses had won their union after management emphatically said they would never have one.

AFTER TEACHING THE EINSTEIN WORKERS how to build their work-site organization from the narrow vote to unionize back in April to producing a crucial majority petition demanding that their employer drop its legal appeal, it was finally time to focus entirely on the intransigent Tele nurses. In most departments of the hospital, the nurses' exhilaration was palpable. But Tele had its heels dug in. Throughout the summer, with the exception of Miller, Tele nurses refused to talk to any other nurses or union staff. Candace Chewing, who was working on my team and was the staff organizer assigned to Tele, was fearless and fearsome. She hatched a new idea: to have PASNAP president Eakin phone every Tele nurse with a personal message that the union was heading to negotiations and everyone else would be making decisions for Tele if they didn't participate. We took Payne off her call list, deciding that based on a bad interaction between them months earlier, Eakin wouldn't herself be able to persuade her.

Based on our collective years of experience, we devised a multi-step plan to win over Tele. First, we already knew that this group had not decided, as had some others who had also voted no, to simply change their minds post-election and join the winning side. Second, we were using the authority of the union president to call them all and either get them live or leave a voice-mail message. We assumed this would pique some nurses' curiosity. Third, we appealed to the same individuality they thought was threatened by the union: if the Tele unit didn't participate in the union vote, others would vote on their behalf. We role-played and practiced the message with Eakin:

"Every unit has elected negotiations committee members but yours. All nurses are presently reading drafts of the contract and on crucial issues, no one has any idea what nurses in your unit want, so they will just make it up for you if you continue to not be involved."

We added something else: "Management told you over and over and over you wouldn't ever have a union and now you do. Do you still believe them when they tell you nurses can't win raises and improvements through the upcoming negotiations?" We were sowing doubt about management, which was already putting out a message that just because it recognized the union, it would not give in to any demands in negotiations.

We also had Eakin make the calls from her cell phone, not the office, so the nurses in Tele would not know PASNAP was calling. And we knew all the calls had to happen in quick succession so that the union busters wouldn't hear about it and tell nurses not to talk to the union president. Unsurprisingly, Eakin did not get through to most nurses, since they were working. One day-shift Tele nurse, Ian, did pick up the phone. Eakin is charming and sincere, like most nurses. She was reading from her written rap because she wanted to say it all just right. When Ian asked, "Okay, what should I do next?" Eakin answered, "Agree to take a follow-up call from your union organizer, Candace Chewing, and talk the steps through with her." Ian agreed.

Chewing asked Ian to gather some Tele nurses and meet her in the cafeteria the next day. The staff organizers had decided to start sneaking into the hospital cafeteria, blending in with patients' families, and hold meetings there. He agreed. While Chewing and I were planning how to handle the meeting, we debated whether I should go as the chief negotiator or whether a key worker leader should attend with her. We decided she needed to take one of our most effective nurse leaders with her, one who was strong and had a great way of talking about the union all on his own.

The nurse we decided to send was Pat Kelly, who had spearheaded the entire drive back in 2015 and stuck with it all along. Kelly was a single father of three kids who had to work the night shift: he could be home to take his kids to school and be there when they got off the bus to feed them, start their homework, and head off to the hospital. Kelly was definitely the leader of the leaders at this point, and he'd proven persuasive in several earlier tough meetings with nurses who once believed the union to be a bad idea.

I was waiting anxiously by the phone the next day, when Chewing and Ian were scheduled to meet. Who would show? Would they show? What would happen? When my cell phone lit up with the message on the screen saying, "Candace calling," I stared for a minute, hoping for good news.

First, Chewing explained she wanted to give me the good news. Payne and Ian showed up, along with another nurse we had a hunch was also a leader among nurses in the unit, Patricia Graves. Three of them. The bad news was that Payne still hated the union, and she was angry that Kelly was at the meeting. She yelled at him—really yelled at him. "Okay, keep going," I said to Chewing. "Tell me everything you said, everything Pat said, and everything they said." That level of detail is exactly what lead organizers use when we debrief with a more junior organizer. But Chewing wanted to cut to the chase: she told me that the next step—the only next step she could think of in a very tough meeting—was to ask them to return the next day and meet with me, the chief contract negotiator, to hear exactly how negotiations would work. Fair enough.

I called Kelly next because I wanted to hear what he thought about the meeting and to reassure him that no matter what happened, he did a great job. When he answered, he told me, "I am not sure how that meeting went. I didn't play a big role because the first thing that happened was Marne looking at me and said, 'What are *you* doing here?'" He was still shaken: he wasn't used to being yelled at by anyone, let alone the leader of the anti-union effort.

Later, when I interviewed Kelly about the meeting and his entire history with the Tele unit, he said that from the very beginning, Tele had been a problem for him. He said that back in January, before the vote, before management's legal appeals and everything else, "Tele was the first place I came across two nurses who said, 'Absolutely not. No, we aren't interested. The union won't do anything for us. We don't want to pay dues.' It was the first negative response when we were trying to form the union. In other units they were disengaged, but in Tele, they said a very loud *no* to me and to all our attempts."

I asked Kelly what he thought I should do the next day when I met with Payne and Graves. We agreed the entire focus would be discussing the contract, walking through the draft line by line with them.

Chewing and Kelly, at my instruction, had left a draft of the contract marked "confidential" with the Tele nurses, which was risky because we didn't want the contract falling into the hands of management before negotiations. But it was a risk worth taking if we would earn their trust. The draft was in good shape already. If anything would get them to move, it was the realization that negotiations really were about to start and they actually had had no say up to that point.

Chewing and I waited at the table, fidgety. When Payne and Graves entered on their lunch break, they had the contract draft in hand and marked up from the night before. Good sign, I thought: not just that they showed, but they had been reading the draft contract. They were clearly uncomfortable. I made myself more relaxed at that point, friendly but not too friendly, more serious than friendly. There were a couple of other top nurse leaders lingering in the cafeteria, eavesdropping on our conversation. Everyone, every nurse leader, was nervous with me. We had spent so much time talking about Tele, and the importance of Tele with the entire committee, and that we couldn't ever get to a credible strike threat or therefore a great contract without moving Tele. And here they were!

Thirty minutes later, after I had walked them through how negotiations worked in a good union such as PASNAP and how, in a democratic union, all workers were invited and encouraged to attend their own negotiations and that it would be crucial to secure the Tele nurses' participation, the meeting had to end because their lunch break was over. We asked Payne and Graves to take union membership cards and to sign up more than half their unit—the number they would need to hold elections in their unit for seats on the formal negotiations committee. They took the cards, said they'd think about it, and left. All the other pro-union nurses, who had taken lunch at the same time, ran over as soon as Marne and Pat left to ask what happened.

At nine the next morning, less than twenty-four hours later, Payne called Chewing to say she had some signed union membership cards, and her unit had decided whom they wanted to represent them in negotiations. Chewing called me excitedly, but she literally couldn't talk coherently. She kept blurting something out about cards in her hands. I asked her to text me so I could understand. I couldn't tell whether she was crying or sick. The text read: "34 signed union membership cards from Tele." The nurses had done it. They had cracked the "biggest worst."

To keep teaching her, I told Chewing she had to call back Payne and explain that they had to have an election—this was a democratic union; they could not simply appoint their representatives. Neither Payne nor Graves, clearly the two real leaders, were nominating themselves. They had decided that the representatives would be Miller and a male nurse whom we had not met nor knew of. So I told Chewing to add, "Jane said she [Payne] and Patricia Graves actually have to be nominated for their unit to be taken seriously."

Within days, a compromise was reached, and Graves and Miller were elected to represent Tele. And at the opening of negotiations on August 17, when Graves attended the first negotiations, management was astounded, and they seemed to understand the fight was over. We had moved every single unit in the hospital.

OVER THE COURSE OF THE NEGOTIATIONS, Kelly built a solid relationship with Payne and with all the leaders from Tele. I had to leave in November to resume teaching in Cambridge. I handed the negotiations over to the PASNAP organizing director, Mark Warshaw. When I first told the nurses I had to leave and that we had a transition plan, they were nervous. They were terrified, actually, but I knew that by that point they knew, really deeply knew, that they were winning and almost done. They were confident in themselves, and I stressed repeatedly that I was only a tactician in a serious power fight between them and management.

In early December 2016, by the time a real strike vote was needed—not a vote for picketing, but a vote to strike—in order to get management to offer real changes the nurses were demanding, Payne didn't just participate in the strike vote: she helped lead it. Trump had been elected U.S. president, and management was smelling blood. At that crucial moment, Tele stepped in to become central actors in winning a terrific first collective agreement. The workers had forged an unbreakable solidarity bond through their unpaid, all-volunteer, high-participation, open democratic negotiations.

Payne told me that in the final days, actually the final eighteen hours—there were round-the-clock last-day negotiations—"I wouldn't leave. I couldn't leave. I am for fair pay, and I was not letting management *not* give us a fair pay raise." Miller, who was inseparable at that point from Payne, told me:

> I kept saying to people the process is fascinating, a slow chisel away, all the way to the end, with eighteen-hour days, with people saying, "I am not going to leave. I am going to sit right here to the end." I remember when it was finally over, that last day,

we got the wages, we got some remaining little stuff, too, but it was big, and the raises were big. And it's all big—especially when they [management] don't want to give you anything. We were so burnt out. And then I went home thinking, "Oh, my God. I can't believe this shit happened." I even cried when I drove home, I was crying.

On the blackboard, on that final, eighteen-hour day, as she walked out, Payne wrote, "Thank you, Jesus." On December 23, the day the workers voted to ratify their first contract, she sent a text message to Kelly. He gave it to me, and Payne agreed I could include it here in its entirety:

Hey Patrick. I wanted to personally thank you for all the work and time you sacrificed on this contract. Up until the very end, I still did not believe our contract could be this good the first time around. I know myself that I was not easy to deal with. I have very strong convictions. And so does my floor, telemetry. It was hard for myself and the floor to swallow that the union got in. I did not believe in the process. After last night and waking up this morning I have now realized that we are in fact stronger together. And we can accomplish so much in this profession together. Thank you for being one of the lead organizers and helping to push this through. We now have a true voice and damn good contract!!! Enjoy your holidays with your family. I am sure they miss you!

I asked Payne recently what she would say if it were five years from now and someone in a nonunion hospital was asking her opinion about forming a union. She thought for a couple of seconds and said:

I would tell somebody if they need a union, to be patient and be prepared to fight for what you believe in, and, you have to fight for every nurse in the hospital, you can't have a union and be selfish. You can't be I, I, I. It's not about you, it's about the people, the entire population.

In the end, as Payne herself said to Kelly in the pre-Christmas text, she wasn't convinced about the union in the beginning—even after she had first changed her mind about participating (and convinced her entire unit to back the union). Had Tele not completely flipped its position about building a strong union, they would not have won a life-altering contract. That Payne became the strike vote leader—in a department with a 100 percent strike vote and after running the anti-union campaign—is a powerful lesson in how best to build worker agency: through leader identification and structure tests that bolster democratic participation.

* * *

This real-life struggle, set against the backdrop of a horrible 2017 for the working class in the United States, reaffirms that workers can still win and win big and overcome all sorts of obstacles. Unions prove that in today's strategic sectors—chiefly the service sector, where schools, universities, hospitals, and health care systems are growth industries—workers still have power.

Of course, there are many sectors of workers where using the strike weapon is not as reliable, where there are many low-wage workers who are instantly replaceable, like small grocery stores— but that was also true a hundred years ago. The key to rebuilding working-class power is a more intense focus on questions of strategy—the strategy of which workers to focus on, and why, when, where, and how. The mostly female workers who dominate the service sector of the economy—sectors increasingly under attack from accounting firms, hedge funds, and Wall Street investors who attempt to suck the life out of education and health care, to turn students and patients into profit centers—have the capacity to hold the line on corporate greed. They are rebuilding unions like the West Virginia educators in chapter 1, or building new unions like those built in 2016 at Einstein Medical Center and by nurses and techs in a half dozen other hospitals in Philadelphia. Building strong, democratic unions in strategic sectors made up of enough workers who are hard to replace, and workers who have a kind of moral authority in mission-driven work, is a strategic choice of leadership, not something dictated by the constraints of global trade deals.

CHAPTER 6

How to Rebuild a Union: L.A.'s Teachers

THINK ABOUT ALL THE GOOD TEACHERS YOU OR YOUR KIDS EVER had—the really good ones. The teachers who get students excited to learn a subject and eager to do their work. The ones who propel your kids to come home excited to share what they learned about in school that day. The teachers who encourage and allow students to achieve more than good grades, who spark and feed their curiosity, help them shine, and instill a lifelong love of learning. These were the kinds of teachers in Los Angeles who, fed up with a union that didn't work for them, decided to change it from the inside out. They put together a slate of colleagues to campaign for internal union office called Union Power, and they won every top elected office in 2014. These teachers immediately set out to rebuild the union and build real, lasting power. To do so, they hired full-time professional staff who knew how to run and win a *big* strike.

Why did the teachers in Los Angeles assume they had to be ready to strike in blue-as-can-be-blue-state California? Because Democrats have been smashing teachers' unions—the largest single segment of unionized workers remaining in America—as they zeal-ously drive their corporate-backed, pro-charter-school agenda. Arne Duncan, President Barack Obama's first education secretary, took his and the party's big Silicon Valley donor crusade to privatize public schools and made it the national policy of the Democrats—an about-face for the party that once fought to secure a high-quality public education for all children. In doing so, the Democratic Party has directly contributed to the destruction of a significant part of their own electoral base: America's unions. When it comes to public education and teachers' unions, Democrats don't look much differ-ent from red-state Republicans.

It took the teachers in the country's second-largest teachers' union, United Teachers Los Angeles (UTLA), in America's second largest city, exactly four years of serious, determined hard work to win a great contract in a hard-as-hell fight. These teachers fought for nothing less than the life of public schooling in Los Angeles, and in the process, won big for themselves and for their communities. If you can succeed at uniting 34,000 people as diverse as the teachers in the Los Angeles Unified School District, you can unite America.

* * *

In 1970, two big rival teachers' unions in Los Angeles merged, form-ing United Teachers Los Angeles. (The merger also included nearly a dozen much smaller teacher-related unions.) Because so many unions banded together under one organization, the teachers in Los Angeles are affiliated with both national teachers' unions, the American Federation of Teachers (AFT) and the National Educa-tion Association (NEA). The AFT has always considered itself a union, and it has always been a member of the AFL-CIO. The NEA, by contrast, is technically the largest union in America, complete with collective bargaining, but has never been affiliated with the AFL-CIO, viewing itself more as an organization of professionals.

The AFT tends to represent more urban workers, the NEA more suburban and rural. Most local teacher unions belong to one or the other, making the dual affiliation by UTLA somewhat unusual.

The merger was solidified by a massive strike shortly afterward. Unionized public school teachers walked out for twenty-three school days, and the five-week strike proved victorious: the teachers won their first union contract with substantial raises, rights, and benefits. No sooner had they won, however, than right-wing groups sued. The court overturned the entire contract on the grounds that teachers in California weren't covered by a collective bargaining law. (Recall that public-sector workers are governed by state, not federal law.) The teachers fought back, and threw themselves into the fight to win a state law that gave them the right to collective bargaining. In 1975, a young Jerry Brown won the office of governor for the first time and signed the law, granting teachers collective bargaining rights. California and Los Angeles were smoking hot in this era, with a young, unmarried liberal governor dating a rock star (Linda Ronstadt) and the city's first African American mayor, Tom Bradley. The union was hip and groovy, too, and would go on to secure a good union contract after the collective bargaining legislation had passed.

But in 1977, a conservative group that didn't like where their state was headed—including integrating schools—collected enough signatures to place a ballot initiative before California voters. They passed one of the strictest antitax measures in the country, called Proposition 13. A central feature of Prop 13 hamstrings local communities from raising taxes to pay for education, meaning the financial burden for education shifted to the state from the local government. Even though UTLA was strong, the power structure analysis of its future contract fights changed: the state would play a key role in its fights, not just the Los Angeles Unified School Board.

At the same time, other aspects of Prop 13 began to slowly drain the tax base of the entire state, and funds for public education plummeted. The union would have to go on strike again in 1989, for nine days, just to hold on to a decent contract, making a few gains. But over the following twenty-five years, the union, along with the state and country, withered because Prop 13 intentionally starved state and local budgets and funneled funds to the 1 percent. As a result, UTLA's power waned, and it went from consistently fighting hard for good contracts to often grudgingly accepting the massive cuts that were imposed year after year, state budget by state budget. California's public schools were decimated, and teachers lost faith in their union as the number of students in the classroom steadily rose and budget cuts led to cutting nurses, sports and arts programs, guidance counselors, school librarians, and more.

Thirty-one years into Prop 13, the Great Recession of 2008 finally broke California. The state was spiraling downward, fast. Officials were discussing massive cuts to Medicaid and to whatever was left of affordable housing, education, parks—everything that relied on taxes. Finally, a coalition of unions and community-based organizations headed up by longtime and legendary Los Angeles community and political organizer Anthony Thigpenn set out to challenge Prop 13's devastating effects on California. In 2011, the coalition worked with education and health care unions to gather signatures for a Millionaire's Tax Initiative, which required the many millionaires who call the state home to once again pay their fair share of society's needs. The coalition won in 2012 with the passage of Proposition 30. Prop 30 played a major role in flipping the sixth-largest economy in the world, taking it from being billions in the red to restoring billions in cuts and raising enough revenue to even restart a rainy-day fund in California. According to Thigpenn, "Back in 2012, the conventional wisdom was that we couldn't win new taxation. There's a dominant narrative that Americans are anti-tax, but we proved the pundits wrong. When we help people connect decades of tax cuts to their kids' schools falling apart and things like a dearth of affordable housing or health care, they will, in fact, vote to tax corporations again."

Thigpenn and his team had worked with unions across the state. In Los Angeles, however, he worked fist in glove with a big group of smart, motivated rank-and-file teacher activists in Los Angeles. The defy-all-predictions victory on the millionaire's tax (Prop 30) suddenly raised teachers' expectations that maybe—just maybe—their schools could be great again. That team of teachers, disgruntled by their lackluster official teacher union leadership, set out to run for union office and rebuild their union to meet their vision: to help kids, all kids, get the best education possible. The progressively minded people who ran for union office in 2014 were all long-established teachers with stellar teaching records. Alex Caputo-Pearl, who headed the Union Power slate, had twenty-two years in the classroom under his belt, most of them in South L.A., at Crenshaw High School. He is a top teacher who has been awarded with the L.A. Academic English Mastery Program and has always been very active in community issues in the city. Early in his teaching career, Caputo-Pearl also logged upward of twenty-five hours a week as a volunteer community organizer in the city. His equal commitment to teaching and to the broader community would undergird his and his colleagues' decision to include parents in the union's organizing work.

He led an ethnically, racially, and gender-balanced slate of seven teachers to win elected union office. Union Power campaigned on a very specific agenda to rebuild its union and Caputo-Pearl was straightforward about Union Power's goals back in 2014. It's worth quoting him in detail about Union Power's plan after winning their union election.

We very clearly campaigned on, very explicitly, needing an organizing union. Then we actually spelled that out by saying we'd build something our union did not have: an organizing department. We said that if we got elected, we'd get an organizing director—someone who is responsible for making sure that every single school site is engaged with a high-functioning, high-participation structure. Second, we said we were going to build a parent–community organizing arm, which we'd not had before either, and have people on staff who had experience in working with parents. Third, we'd build a research department, which UTLA had not had before, because we need to know the ins and outs of the district budget, and we need to know all of the dirt on the privatizers. Fourth, even though UTLA has always had a communications department, we'd build a badass communications department that is *proactively* shaping the narrative, not just waiting for somebody to call from the press.

ACCORDING TO THE CONSTITUTION and bylaws of their union, Caputo-Pearl and the six other rank-and-file teachers who swept every seat in the election take official temporary leaves of absence from the classroom and become full-time officers of the union for the duration of their three-year terms. They won election in April 2014, and by the summer of 2014, when they were sworn into office, they had a plan in place to do everything they had campaigned on. By fall 2014, the newly elected classroom teachers hired staff skilled in the science of effective struggle.

They quickly moved two women of color into key positions as union-wide co-regional organizers. Cami George, who is African American, had taught in Los Angeles schools for fifteen years, mostly in elementary school. Of the two senior organizers, she'd been working in various capacities in the union since 2008. Jollene Levid, on the other hand, who is Filipina American, had serious union organizing and union strike experience, which she'd developed over sixteen years of full-time organizing with mostly women health care workers. Levid had actually been a social worker in the L.A. schools, too, and jumped back into organizing with the new leadership because, in her words, "The teachers here are seventy percent women and understanding labor, and the value placed on women's work has always guided my decisions about where I put my energy."

Filling out a triumvirate in the brand-new organizing department was an organizer with even more strike experience, Brian McNamara. He also had a background with health care workers in one of California's strongest unions before the vision of the newly elected teachers' leadership persuaded him to head up UTLA's team as the organizing director. The elected teacher leaders set the bar high for the three top organizers: build a fully inclusive union that engages 100 percent of the workforce, which is 34,000 teachers across 900 schools in a region populated by 30 million people.

This can't be emphasized enough: *the teachers sought out full-time union staff who had successful strike experience.* Remember, there hadn't been a teachers' strike in L.A. since 1989—so how would the rank-and-file teachers know how to get strike-ready? It's not like there is a core curriculum class in college called How to Defeat Management by Striking 101. The progressive teachers, such as Caputo-Pearl, had been experiencing the degradation of the public schools for two decades. He and many other educators in L.A. had seen their union go into one set of contract negotiations after another, each time coming out with nothing much, if not less than the contract prior. They had been paying attention to the power structure, their place in it, and the dramatic rise of privately run charter schools and anti-teacher-union, anti-public-education forces. They knew that reversing course would likely require nothing less than a strike.

Over the next several years, it was precisely the close interaction of the highly experienced staff with the committed, progressive rank-and-file teacher leadership that rebuilt the entire union from bottom to top. They didn't have much of a choice, because when they won office in 2014, the union leaders before them had been in fruitless contract negotiations since 2011. This means the newly elected officers inherited a union contract fight that had been lagging along for three years with no strategy and no engagement with the rank and file. And because of constant budget cuts, the teachers in L.A. hadn't had a single raise since 2006. The union leaders knew they needed to land that contract, and that contract needed to include a raise at minimum.

Caputo-Pearl and the newly elected team knew they had completed step one of their plan: build a new organizing department, headed up by strike-experienced staff. The seven officers made their own work plan, which was to visit every school chapter—all nine hundred—as fast as they reasonably could, to take their message of rebuilding a fighting union to the ranks. Chapters are the smallest level of organization within the union. Basically, each school is its own chapter (with a few exceptions, like very small schools that might be part of a neighboring school chapter). According to many interviews with longtime members, no elected leader of the union, nor staff member, had been to all the schools in decades, if ever. To get a dormant union strike-ready, they had to work from the ground up, with structure tests.

The newly hired organizers got to work on their side of the rebuild plan. From day one, according to Brian McNamara, they had a solid plan:

> First, make sure to build accurate worker lists (meaning that there's an accurate list of all 34,000 teachers by school), and make sure there's a chapter leader in every school. When recruiting chapter leaders, try to identify natural leaders, not just people who might want to be in the position because of any number of other reasons. Then begin a system of small actions that get people feeling more comfortable. Begin a system of structure tests tied to those small actions, which means getting chapter leaders to work with the list of teachers in their own school and start assessing who's going to participate in each action. Have those things start with some-

thing basic, like a petition in support of the contract demands, and then maybe the next thing is a school site picket, and maybe the next thing is some sort of a rally where people pre-commit to attend by signing up in advance saying that they're going to come, so that you can follow up with people to be sure they do attend.

To manage this kind of highly detailed information, UTLA created a position called Analytics Director and hired a union researcher with a degree in forensic accounting, Grace Regullano, who created entirely new data systems.

BY FALL 2014, the newly elected teachers and their growing staff were working at a breakneck pace to try to reach a settlement of the 2011 contract. Per the organizing plan, the leadership team, including the most senior organizers and the seven elected leaders, unfurled their first structure test, of which there would be many over the next four years.

The first structure test, in November 2014, was an "I'll be there" hand-signed petition that school-site teacher leaders would use to recruit fellow teachers to what would be the union's first rally in a long time. The second structure test was the actual school-site rallies. By using the "I'll be there" commitment petition before the actual rally, leaders and organizers could begin to understand who their initial activist base was in the union, and which school-site chapter leader was successful at convincing signees to actually come to the rally. That's the nature of a structure test: it's a verifiable assessment of which leaders can get others to take concrete actions—and not just have an opinion on Facebook late at night, for example.

Not surprisingly, those first rallies weren't huge, but they did begin to build an activist corps for the next action, which, if they wanted to get the 2011 contract behind them, would have to be a way, way bigger direct action. They called for a major, city-wide rally in support of their contract to take place in late February 2015. And, keeping to the method and discipline of structure tests, they prepared for the February rally by launching a campaign commitment card the month before, in early January. The campaign commitment card was a hand-sized card that asked the 34,000 teachers what they were willing to do—starting with whether they'd be willing to attend a city-wide rally in February, if they'd take part in more school-site picketing, if they'd be willing to do parent outreach about the unresolved four-year-old expired contract, if they'd be willing to boycott faculty meetings (letting the administrators know things were changing in the union), if they'd protest upcoming mandatory testing, and, most important, if they'd be willing to strike.

Handing out the commitment card in January and the February rally marked two more structure tests and an escalation, since the last question—willingness to strike—hadn't been presented to union members in a long time. Each action helped the central leadership team understand where they were missing chapter leaders altogether—in which case they needed to identify new ones—and assess how effective existing rank-and-file leaders were so they could offer targeted organizing training and better develop them where needed. By February 26, the day of the city-wide rally and just four months into launching the new organizing program, fifteen thousand teachers showed up at Grand Park, outside L.A.'s city hall. There hadn't been a rally that big since the 1989 strike! And it worked. Suddenly negotiations for the long-stalled contract were back on. Weeks later, the new leadership settled the contract, winning a whopping 10 percent raise. Finally the newly elected Union Power slate and the new organizing team could take a nap. But not for long.

The 10 percent raise was enormously important. It proved to the membership that the new program of moving the union from merely handling grievances to actively engaging teachers in a fight was working. This substantial victory, on the heels of the big rally, gave Union Power leadership the time and space to regroup and implement their other plans, like hiring researchers and communicators and launching a meaningful parent-and-community program. By summer 2015, the leadership knew that it would take far more resources to not only redress but *reverse* the downward spiral of public education in Los Angeles. Winning the long-overdue raise was spectacular, but they needed much more power to restore decades of cuts to just about every aspect of the schools. In July, the broader leadership of the union, the elected executive board, and the chapter leaders launched a strategic plan called the Build the Future, Fund the Fight campaign. A key component of this program was asking the 34,000 teachers to vote to raise their dues.

By the start of the school year in fall 2015 and one year into the new organizing department, the leadership launched its fourth structure test: a public petition—a collection of signatures that would be used internally and for public relations work. The signers were declaring they'd vote yes to the Build the Future, Fund the Fight (BFFF) plan, which included a big dues increase. The message union leadership communicated to teachers during the vote was clear: management is trying to privatize the entire education system in Los Angeles. You can choose to enter into contract talks with almost no financial resources available, or you can come in strong, vote to increase your dues, and tell management that the teachers are united. That's called *framing the hard choice* in union-organizer lingo.

In February 2016, more than half of all teachers participated in the vote, with 83 percent voting to raise their dues and build a stronger union. This came not a moment too soon, because they'd quickly be back in a new round of contract negotiations, but the next collective bargaining battle had one topic only: health insurance. This is because the Los Angeles Unified School District (LAUSD) employed more staff than teachers, including janitors, cafeteria workers, bus drivers, and administrators. So, in order to effectively negotiate the health care plan, all the unions needed to come together in a city-wide coalition on this one single issue. The health care negotiations, and more structure tests around them, would occupy most of 2016 and into 2017. Alongside the health care negotiations, the teachers were also thinking about 2017, when the entire teachers' contract would expire and all-new negotiations would begin. To prepare for those contract talks, the teachers launched a radical plan to systematically engage the parents and students. They planned to kick off 2017 by holding a series of big, open meetings, all across Los Angeles, where the teachers would listen to what the parents, and even the students, wanted in their schools.

EVEN THOUGH TEACHERS WERE REBUILDING THEIR UNION, negotiating health care, and achieving some big wins along the way, and in part because they were tied up in negotiations over health care, the teachers were about to be tested in a showdown that they hadn't seen coming. In spring 2017, the Los Angeles school board held its elections, and the results sent shock waves through the union.

In the decade leading up to that spring, there had been a 287 percent increase in privately run charter schools in L.A., which diverted $600 million from the LAUSD school budget into corporate, private-investor run schools. Even though the 2012 Millionaire's Tax had balanced California's budget, there had been a thirty-year disinvestment in education forced by Prop 13, the 1977 antitax measure. The result, according to a 2017 report issued by the Rutgers Graduate School of Education, *In Brief: The Real Shame of the Nation,* was that California ranked 46 out of 50 states in per-pupil funding. The report stated, "In several states—notably Arizona, Mississippi, Alabama and California—the highest poverty school districts fall as much as $14,000 to $16,000 per pupil below the necessary spending levels."

Unbeknownst to the teachers, pro-privatization and charter school supporters had been monitoring the union's growth carefully and plotting to stop the educators in their tracks. The stakes were high for the pro-charter-school forces. They knew there was a new teachers' union that would head into full contract talks for an all-new agreement, and a central pillar in the union's effort would be stopping the growth of the corporate, privately run charter schools. So in 2017, Silicon Valley's pro-corporate-charter school movement and Wall Street aligned with money-hungry developers to win the majority of the seats on the LAUSD board—much to the union's dismay. Given the incredibly broken campaign finance laws in the United States (especially after the Supreme Court rulings in *Citizens United* and *McCutcheon*), the moneyed interests that wanted public school land for private real estate development and profits from school privatization teamed up to funnel a significant amount of money into school board races so it could influence education policy.

The pro-charter-school forces poured $9.7 million into those elections: not a penny was spared to advance the pro-privatization agenda. A headline in the *Los Angeles Times* the day after the 2017 school board election read, "How L.A.'s School Board Election Became the Most Expensive in U.S. History." Everyone in L.A. took notice. As the *Times'* article pointed out, one donor—mega-wealthy Netflix founder, Facebook board member, and registered Democrat Reed Hastings—donated $7 million to the California Charter School Association Advocates between September 2016 and the school board election. To make it appear that there were more groups invested in destroying the schools, the California Charter Schools Association then redistributed Hastings's millions to other groups, such as the Parent Teacher Alliance, an electoral campaign group that seems intentionally meant to confuse people with the actual Parent Teacher Association (the alliance logo even looked suspiciously similar to the PTA's). So Hastings's fortune, earned from

every click of a Netflix movie, along with his lucrative board seat at
Facebook, was central to the school board election, but you won't
see his name in the city's election spending records because current
election laws in the United States allow rich donors to be shielded
by super PACs and other mechanisms that make tracking the source
of donations difficult. Such is the result of election laws in the era of
the viciously anti-worker, anti-union, pro-corporate, and pro-rich
Supreme Court.

TOP CHARTER GROUPS	AMOUNT
Parent Teacher Alliance	$5,144,716
California Charter Schools Assn. Advocates	$2,837,614
LA Students 4 Change	$1,325,324
Major individual donors	$230,785
Speak UP—Supporting Nick Melvoin	$111,547
Students for Education Reform	$95,964
Charter Total	**$9,695,351**

On the heels of the defeat of the candidates who valued the *public*
in public education, a dull depression set in among many teachers in
greater L.A. leading into the 2017 Memorial Day weekend. The rank-
and-file teacher leadership of UTLA went from idly considering
that they might need to strike in order to win their next contract to
understanding that nothing less than an all-out strike would overcome the new management team. In the summer of 2017, without
the pressure of school hours, the union leadership met to strategize
how to win in negotiations with a school board that had just been
taken over by staunchly anti-teachers'-union candidates. Since
their contract talks for a full new agreement had begun, slowly, concurrent to the health care negotiations as they were heating up, they
set up a contract action team (CAT) that brought in an additional

layer of rank-and-file school-site leaders to work with chapter leaders to get all nine hundred schools ready for the fight of their lives.

In the fall, they held rallies that helped win the health care negotiations in January 2018. The health care negotiations were a major victory, too: the unions held every standard they had in a health care plan every American deserves despite a two-year effort by the school board to cut their benefits and raise their costs. But because the health care negotiations wrapped up as the biggest holidays of every year were hitting, when attention shifts from school and unions to baking cookies, decorating trees, lighting candles, and family gatherings, and because there's always lots of small details that take time when typing up a final proposed negotiated agreement, UTLA put off the extensive and time-consuming, school-by-school, secret ballot ratification vote by the membership on the health care contract until everyone would get back from the big holiday vacation.

By early 2018, as the teachers dotted the *i*'s and crossed the *t*'s on the proposed health care settlement for 34,000 teachers to be able to read, understand, digest, and vote to approve or reject, national media was painting a grim picture for public-sector unions—like UTLA—as coverage began of the U.S. Supreme Court *Janus v. AFSCME* case. *Janus,* a case aimed squarely at government workers' unions, was one of the several biggest cases of the entire Supreme Court docket, cases traditionally heard early and decided on the final days of the cycle. As a sign of the tactical savvy of UTLA, the leadership realized they had a perfect opportunity before them: they launched a campaign called "All-In" concurrent with the health care ratification vote, in the same month that the highest court was deliberating *Janus.* Among many threats posed by Janus was that every public-sector union member in the nation would have to re-sign and reaffirm their membership to every union, which would be an incredible drain on time and resources for those unions. These recommitments would likely have to happen fast—and seemed timed to distract unions from the 2018 midterm elections by heaping a huge internal burden on them as they would be campaigning for congressional elections. All-In was UTLA's effort to proactively ask every teacher to sign brand-new union membership cards that its attorneys had anticipated would meet the threshold of what was very likely to be a new law about the language governing dues and membership, assuming the radical right prevailed in the high court. Over just several days, more than twenty thousand of the union's members would sign the new, *Janus*-ready and *Janus*-specific membership authorization cards. (The Supreme Court did hand the decision to the radical right wing in *Janus* in late June, which surprised no one.)

With the success of the All-In effort, the leadership understood it needed to launch one more structure test before school let out for the summer. In late March, the union asked the 34,000 teachers to check boxes on a piece of paper, then print and sign their name, to indicate which of the following actions they were ready to take:

April 19th day of school site–based actions

May faculty meeting boycotts

May 24th city-wide rally downtown

September strike vote if necessary

With a hostile Supreme Court deliberating in the background, the next shoe dropped when the anti-teachers'-union school board, elected in 2017, hired new full-time staff leadership. It's likely that the anti-teacher majority, backed by the pro-charter, anti-teacher Silicon Valley corporate Democrats, would have wanted to change the superintendent the minute they were sworn into office in July

2017. But that would have been difficult because the superintendent who was in place then, Michelle King, was a widely respected African American educator who had risen through the ranks first as a student, then parent, teacher, and principal in the LAUSD. The teachers respected her, and so did the majority of opinion leaders. But lucky for those backers, early in the new Silicon Valley–backed board's tenure, Michelle King had to take medical leave for a serious illness. Because King originally took only a medical leave of absence, the new board could only install a temporary internal high-level administrator to operate in her stead. Early in 2018, King resigned to address her worsening health. Without missing a beat, the new LAUSD school board hired a new superintendent, Austin Beutner. Unlike King, a towering figure in education policy with decades of experience, Beutner was a 1 percent former hedge fund manager who had *no experience* in education. Not to mention that he was a white man heading up a school district whose students, parents, and faculty are people of color and immigrants.

At this point, union leadership saw the writing on the wall. Within two months of assuming his new post, Beutner released a report titled "Hard Choices." Among other findings, it declared that L.A. teachers were overpaid and that their benefits were too good. It's one thing to have ideological differences, but calling teachers "overpaid" in Los Angeles—a city in which many full-time workers must live in their cars and shower at a gym because housing is so expensive—was ludicrous and insulting.

Irony doesn't do justice to the backdrop of all this: in 2018, the media and Democratic Party held fast to the idea that to save U.S. democracy, Democrats must win the midterms. Among the most decisive swing seats that national Democrats "had to" pick up were seven in greater Los Angeles County. Democrats thought these seats were critical to their success because the seats had been won by Republicans by a narrow margin in the previous election, but

Hillary Clinton had eked out a victory in the same precincts in 2016. This made the greater L.A. region ground zero for the national 2018 midterms fight. Imagine. Top-party donors were doing their best to wipe the teachers' union—their biggest electoral base in Los Angeles (and nationally)—off the map. And the unions were being called on to save the country from itself by flipping seven key swing congressional seats in L.A. It's amazing that Democrats wonder why some workers stayed home on election day in 2016.

By July 2018, with hedge funder Beutner leading the charge for the school board management in negotiations, the teachers' contract negotiations had come to a complete standstill. Worse, school board management was threatening to file unfair labor practice charges over important topics in their bargaining discussions. In labor-speak, management and teachers were in a heated debate over permissive versus mandatory subjects of bargaining under U.S. labor law, and therefore most states' public-sector labor laws. One of many aspects of byzantine labor law dictates that management must negotiate with unions, but only over wages, hours, and working conditions, which are deemed "mandatory subjects." "Permissive subjects" are subjects that the employer discusses only if it so chooses (and when the union is strong enough to force them to). Decades into the renewed war against American workers, those "permissive subjects" have been interpreted pretty damn narrowly. In Los Angeles, green spaces, charter school regulation, and mandatory testing regimes—all key issues to the teachers and parents in L.A.—were considered "permissive" and not mandatory subjects of bargaining. Yet these are core issues that define the working conditions for teachers and nurses.

Any decent negotiator can easily recognize the words management lawyers use to signal they will soon drag a union into court. The very cynical conversation usually starts with: "So, Jane, let me get this right. You continue to insist that how many patients a nurse sees is something that you are unwilling to drop from your proposals?" The point of asking, of course, is to both deflate the workers in negotiations and offer a negotiator like me a no-win situation to the most important worker issue. When the boss's lawyers repeat these asinine questions, it's their way of saying, "If you don't drop this, we'll see you in court."

The L.A. teachers quite clearly understood the multiple implied threats from management's negotiators and made the savvy tactical move to remove the topics that could legally be deemed permissive from their list of proposed changes to their contract. They struck proposals for green spaces, an immigrant defense fund (to deal with Trump's Immigration and Customs Enforcement agents arresting undocumented parents as they drop their kids off at school), and charter school restrictions—all demands that had been part of the original contract draft that they enthusiastically submitted nearly a year earlier. Dropping popular items from negotiations would not be easy to explain to the union members, nor to parents and students, who had all come together in robust, open sessions throughout the first half of 2017 to craft a set of pro-student, pro-community contract demands—a de facto social movement contract. At that moment the teachers knew they had to engage in a method called *inoculation:* where organizers describe all the horrible things management will say and do about the union before management does. It's a mechanism to counter the kind of polarization that is intentional in high-stakes campaigns. In this case, they had to explain to members and the parent-community coalition, before management, why they were removing key proposals, because the new management team was already trying to pit some teachers against others, and the community at large against the teachers. It wasn't hard to imagine that Beutner, author of the extraordinarily disingenuous "Hard Choices" report, would start crowing in public that the union was "finally growing up and seeing management's way" by backing down from its demands.

Fortunately, the teachers had already built high levels of what's called *work-site structure* throughout the nine hundred schools. Work-site structure means there are highly respected teacher leaders in every school who can facilitate meaningful dialogue between teachers, parents, and organizers and, much more important, lead *supermajority direct actions*. By summer 2018, union leaders were confident that they could successfully pull off conversations across tens of thousands of teachers and parents in only a matter of days to explain why yearlong cherished proposals, such as green spaces, were being taken off the demands list. This was ambitious: it was summertime and school was out, so teachers and parents weren't convening in centralized locations. But union leaders were confident they could carry this out because the work-site structures had been fully tested *seven* times unionwide since the leadership change in 2014.

Because the results of the previous structure tests had showed that most teachers were actively engaging with the union, union leadership felt comfortable enough implementing a new strategy that they didn't put in writing so they would not risk getting sued. Leaders couldn't withdraw the demand for green spaces, then tell the teachers in a flier, "Hey, don't worry. We will bring this back." That would itself be what's called an unfair labor practice, something prohibited by law, referred to commonly as a ULP. Instead they withdrew key topics to avert a threatened legal injunction, knowing all along that if the rank-and-file teachers went on a massive strike and if parents and students supported the teachers, every one of the withdrawn popular demands would return to negotiations in the context of a substantially different power analysis—enough power to render the law against permissive subjects inconsequential.

The union was playing power and strategy brilliantly, based on real-life experiences that included four years of systematic structure tests, not on wishful thinking and fantasy. For context, see the list of structure tests and how they were implemented by the union on pages 219–20.

By August, despite the teachers cooperating with employers' demands that they withdraw the permissive topics, hedge funder Beutner wasn't budging on their contract negotiations. In fact, he continued to promote his "Hard Choices" report to the media, spending his time trying to give the teachers a bad image as over-paid, overcompensated, and lazy, rather than actually tending to the negotiations process. His unwillingness to engage in collective

UNIONWIDE STRUCTURE TEST	DATE	IMPLEMENTATION OF STRUCTURE TEST
Each of these was done by hand, face-to-face, across nine hundred schools. They were carried out by teacher leaders under the guidance of staff organizers. Each test helps the leadership understand where they are strong and where they are weak, which helps to prioritize their efforts.		
Regional rallies in the contract that had expired in 2011	November 2014	Used an "I'll be there" sign-up sheet in the weeks before these smaller regional rallies, as they planned their first big city-wide rally set for early 2015. This was the contract the new leadership inherited; the people who lost the election had been negotiating it for over three years.
Organizing for February 2016 Stand Up city-wide rally for the 2011 contract	January 2015	Launched a campaign-commitment card with check boxes of what people were willing to do: school-site picketing, parent outreach, attend a downtown rally in February 2015, boycott faculty meetings, protest testing, and strike if necessary.
Stand Up rally at Grand Park, escalating to city-wide	February 2015	15,000 union members attended, making it the largest action since the 1989 strike
The teachers win big, a 10 percent raise (the first raise in ten years), finally settling the 2011 contract and demonstrating to members that the new methods of organizing work.		

UNIONWIDE STRUCTURE TEST	DATE	IMPLEMENTATION OF STRUCTURE TEST
Launch I'll Vote Yes to Build the Future, Fund the Fight	Fall 2015	Over half of the members of the union signed a public petition saying they would vote yes to increase their dues, which they framed as Build the Future, Fund the Fight.
Membership-wide union election to allow the rank-and-file members to vote to increase dues	February 2016	A majority of members actually participate in the ballot, with 83 percent voting yes. Like most union elections, as with most American elections, traditionally only a minority vote. But UTLA was determined to have real union democracy, with an important question going to the members, and they achieved over 50 percent turnout.
School-site-based rallies for health insurance	Fall 2017	Health benefit negotiations took place parallel to the overall contract bargaining (with a coalition of LAUSD unions), because nonteachers and teachers alike negotiate insurance benefits at the same time.
All-In launches and ratification of health care contract	February 2018	Because the union anticipated that the right-wing would prevail in the *Janus* Supreme Court case, it planned ahead and had the entire membership sign new cards with language the court would stipulate.
4 Questions petition launch	April 2018	This petition asked members about their willingness to take four actions, indicated by hand checks on boxes and their signature.
All-In for Respect rally	May 2018	12,000 members turn out at Grand Park rally.
Strike vote	August 2018	84 percent turn out and participate, 98 percent vote yes.
I Will Strike petition	Fall 2018	Over 75 percent sign.

bargaining left the teachers no option but to begin planning for a strike authorization vote. Many teachers said *enough is enough* with this new non-education, seemingly anti-public-education superintendent of schools. Teachers like Julia Lathin, an art history teacher, were fed up: "Our school has over 2,000 students and one nurse, but she was only hired part time. Because of this, I let my students know that I have a cabinet in my classroom that's always stacked with pads and tampons. I need these kids focused on their education, not worrying that they are going to bleed their pants at school because there isn't a nurse on duty."

Not one teacher I interviewed in Los Angeles during the strike vote placed wages at the top of their list. If you asked a teacher "If management offered to meet your salary demands and nothing else, would you still plan to strike?" the response would be a resounding yes. Among the top concerns voiced by teachers was the need to eliminate Section 1.5 of their contract, which institutionalized a teacher-to-student ratio of one teacher—alone in their class without assistance—to up to forty-six students. That's right: one teacher responsible for up to forty-six students. On Section 1.5, Brandon Abraham, an English teacher with eighteen years of teaching experience, said, "When I started teaching in 1999, the teacher to student ratio was 1:20. I had twenty students in my class. These days, because of all the cuts, we don't even have school librarians anymore, we are teaching basic literacy. They keep cutting and cutting and cutting essential services that students need to learn. To do a good job—which we do—is hard enough when conditions are perfect, but when the conditions get this challenging, it's hard to motivate and inspire students, but we do it. The problem is, really good teachers are leaving the profession because the conditions have become so difficult."

From August 23 to August 30, over seven days, the rank-and-file teachers voted school site by school site. They developed daily tracking systems, calculating how many teachers had and had not voted in the secret ballot strike vote election. This approach mimics the best of get out the vote (GOTV) techniques used in the science of civil electoral processes. It proved to be a perfectly orchestrated strike vote: 84 percent of 34,000 teachers participated in the strike vote, and 98 percent authorized a strike if necessary. The strike vote was a hint of things to come in the 2018 midterms: the turnout for the seven key swing seats in greater L.A. directly benefited from the teachers organizing their strike authorization vote. The same type of GOTV techniques create highly effective election work.

Despite the overwhelming unity and high participation in the strike vote at the start of the 2018–19 school year in Los Angeles—which signaled to management that settling the contract would be wise—Austin Beutner and his Wall Street backers still refused to come to the table with any meaningful proposals. Although teachers' unions across the country were walking precincts, knocking on doors, and deploying their strike-ready work-site machine to save the country from total Republican control, L.A.'s local Democrats were virtually silent on the teacher-student-parent crisis in the negotiations.

In late September, management accelerated its slick public relations campaign against the teachers. The Charter Schools Association has front groups—organizations that explicitly try to hide by whom they are funded and whose agenda they are advancing—with misleading names like Parent Revolution. These groups held press conferences in which they demanded that teachers teach and stop demanding "more money." But UTLA had already launched trainings for their chapter chairs on how to build genuine, bottom-up parent and community support. In the workshops the union did with teacher leaders, they were teaching a method to systematize the community organizing work and ground it in real, grassroots organizing. One of the tools they launched was a chart for each teacher to fill in, and, for each parent the teachers knew to also fill in, capturing all the relationships everyone already had in the broader community. The very top of the September 2018 charting tool looks like this:

CHAPTER LEADER COMMUNITY ENGAGEMENT SURVEY

Building support for the improvements we are fighting for in our schools among community organizations, faith-based institutions, and other associations is a critical part of our campaign. Please take a few minutes to list the organizations and associations that you are involved in.

First Name: _____   Last Name: _____

Employee #: _____   School/Chapter: _____

Cell Phone #: _____

Please list all organizations that you are involved with, including labor, faith, education, ethnic, women's, senior citizen, youth, clubs, neighborhood, professional, political, service, parent, issue, and community based groups.

Name of Faith-Based, Community, Political, or Other Organization or Association	Type of Organization	Your Position or Relationship to the Organization

In October, the school board filed charges against the teachers' union with the Public Employment Relations Board, the internal judicial body that governs public service workers in California. When the school district management lost at the PERB, they moved to outside courts and filed a series of charges calling for injunctions against the teachers.

One such attempted injunction claimed that the special education teachers should not be allowed to strike because it would harm the students. This legal maneuver was a transparent power grab; everyone knew that the district had been steadily eroding support for special education students and classrooms for years. Management still underestimated the solidarity within the union. In response to the injunction, the unionized special needs teachers stood shoulder to shoulder with parents at press conferences during this stall tactic. Their message was clear: "If the school board gave a hoot about the special needs kids, there wouldn't be a strike. You'd be funding more teachers to care better for these children!" Each attempt by management was aimed at diffusing and disrupting the momentum of the teachers. This strategy, you'll remember, is called futility; the point is to make people think that no matter what they do, nothing will change. Although Beutner's actions did stall the strike by several months, the four years of serious union building by teachers and their supporters turned out to be far more formidable than the mayor, local elected politicians, or management team at the school board expected.

The teachers had authorized the strike, "if needed," back in August, and the school board management had in fact succeeded in preventing them from actually going on strike all fall using the legal gimmicks and injunction attempts. Management strategists see each union contract as a war of attrition: they think the longer they stall, the more likely everyone will get frustrated and stop participating—this is part of the futility weapon. Plus there's the weather, which is super real in good strike planning. An early October strike takes place in the best weather on the planet; winter is the colder, rainier season. But by early January, the courts had rebuffed management on each claim, setting the stage for the teachers to be able to finally strike.

The strike began on a Monday morning, January 14, when teachers held picket signs at their schools. Perhaps the boldest lie of all told by Superintendent Beutner was in a press release on the first day of the strike. It stated that only 3,500 teachers were striking and that the rest were in school. That number was off by 31,000. Perhaps that was the same sort of faulty math he used in his claim that the city's teachers were overpaid.

The teachers started by picketing at schools in the morning, then by late morning on the first day of the strike, they marched to the park surrounding city hall. They used this same strategy for three of the first five days of the strike. The teachers didn't have the weather on their side; in fact, it was a weather disaster. Though California had been plagued by droughts and wildfires that fall, it rained all week during the strike; the region had some of the most massive rainfall the state had in years. It's not hard to imagine how much bigger the numbers would have been had there been L.A. sunshine.

Each rally and march day, a crowd of 60,000 people packed the plaza—which meant that many parents and students were joining the protest with the teachers, since there were only 34,000 teachers in the district. These were parents who had been brought into the contract proposal drafting process in 2017 by the teachers' union and their allies like Reclaim Our Schools LA (ROSLA), and who had also been educated by teachers about the issues in their contract fight. These were parents like Jsane Tyler, who said,

> For the first time ever, parents were valued as equal partners by the union. Not only were we allowed to participate, but we were strongly encouraged to be a part of the strategizing, calls to action, including this strike, and the decision-making process. Parents, students and teachers worked diligently, in perfect concert, on behalf of the fundamental right of all students to receive a quality education, without criminalizing them through challenging the racist random searches, or under-serving them

by not serving the whole child. The teachers union invited us to be part of the fight for a model of schooling that provides students with a fighting chance at success! This is real community empowerment and we sparked the movement to reclaim our schools and our voices!

Other parents who were participating in the marches expressed similar sentiments, including Jazmin Garcia, whose daughter attended City Terra Elementary School,

The strike is empowering because parents and kids are out in the streets alongside our teachers. We all found it important to fight for workers' rights and resources for our schools. For me personally, it is important to show my daughter how to be out in the streets. It is important for both me and my daughter to take action together. It is important for my daughter to experience a workers' strike, she's read about them, but now she is a part of one. It was an empowering experience.

The media and the political leadership of the city quickly understood the strike's strength as teachers and parents stood in solidarity in the pouring rain, often dancing. The image of their sixty thousand umbrellas echoed the 2014 Umbrella protests in Hong Kong (which, incidentally, was also a fight for democracy). By the fourth strike day, with tens of thousands of people dancing and chanting in the brutally hard rainfall outside city hall, the mayor and the leadership of L.A. had had enough. It was time to do something. They summoned the union leadership and the management team into city hall to find a solution that would get 600,000 students back to school.

As soon as the top honchos were in the room together—the mayor of the second-largest city in the country, the union president, and the hedge fund banker turned school superintendent—Beutner and the mayor suggested that they narrow the bargaining topics to central issues like pay in order to resolve the crisis quickly. But Caputo-Pearl laid out the bare reality: to settle the strike, the topics on the table would need to actually *expand* to include the ones the teachers were forced to take off the negotiations table back in the summer and the fall because of the legal threats and attempted injunctions. Bingo! The teachers' union leaders' careful calculations in summer and fall to avoid legal action for including "non-mandatory subjects of bargaining" in their contract proposals was paying off exactly as they had hoped. The strike had created a crisis for the employer and the entire political elite of the city and county because it affected so many people. Normally, when big power players such as the mayor of the second-largest city and the governor of the state with the sixth-largest economy in the world get involved to help "encourage" a recalcitrant employer to end the strike by negotiating an agreement, they want it over as quickly as possible—and they want to narrow down bargaining topics to the bare essentials. But the teachers had built enough solidarity and organization to reset the entire power structure and expand the topics on the bargaining table over the course of four straight days of negotiation during the Martin Luther King Jr. holiday weekend in nonstop talks.

* * *

At 6 A.M. on Martin Luther King Jr. Day—the twenty-second hour of a twenty-two-hour, marathon round-the-clock negotiation between the teachers' union and the management of the L.A. Unified School District—the teachers finally won their contract, which addressed all of their demands in one fashion or another. For example, they won provisions for an exciting breakthrough program called the Green Spaces Pilot Program, which had been "taken off the table" back in the summer by management's legal threats. The language, in part, read

The Los Angeles Unified School District shall create a Green Space Task Force that includes representatives from LAUSD, UTLA (the union), and the City of Los Angeles. The District will work with UTLA, the City of Los Angeles, the County of Los Angeles, and appropriate nonprofit partners to create to the maximum extent possible, adequate green space for student physical activity. In creating a task force plan, green space shall be studied in order of priority order as follows:

- Schools without any existing green space and not located near parks
- Schools without any existing green space
- Schools with small amounts of green space and communities with limited to no access to parks and recreation.

This Green New Deal–like victory was among many remarkable achievements that resulted from the walkout of United Teachers Los Angles, its first in thirty years. UTLA fought hard and fought smart to build the power required to win a great contract that supported not only teachers, but their communities—a true social justice collective bargaining agreement, started by the teachers. According to Caputo-Pearl, without an all-out strike, "We knew they'd never agree to our big community demands, including Green Spaces, creating an Immigrants Defense Fund"—ICE had been increasingly targeting schools—"a big expansion of school nurses and guidance counselors, or our top demand to reduce the number of kids per class, unless and until we were out on strike with parents standing united behind the demands."

The strike lasted six school days. The locally elected leaders— mostly corporate Democrat types reflecting the priorities of Netflix mogul Reed Hastings, not the income or ethnicity of the parents or students—had interpreted the 2017 victory of the pro-charter-school candidates as their own structure test, incorrectly thinking there was little to no support for public education in the community. They believed that parents would side with the school board *against* the teachers in a strike scenario. If that happened, the strike would not be a success: parents are the decisive factor in an education fight because of their sheer numbers and assumed moral superiority. Imagine parents, in huge numbers and in the news nonstop, cursing the teachers. That would be a public relations disaster. But the school board was wrong.

Because of intense employer opposition, winning the Green Spaces union contract proposal required the full might of the strike. Management fought teachers tooth and nail on the demand that kids have access to outdoor green spaces for recess. After eight years of Michelle Obama's work with the Let's Move program, where one of the five keys to raising healthier children was getting them outdoors for physical activity, Wall Street bankers who call themselves Democrats—the type who backed her husband and who took over the school board in Los Angeles in 2017—dug in their heels against thousands of teachers who were demanding improvements to the physical, emotional, and mental health for more than a half million students.

The union contract also stipulated that the district would remove the supposedly temporary buildings that had occupied city school grounds for decades. The bungalows—ugly, windowless, steel-walled structures resembling train cars or international cargo shipping containers—were the grotesque reminders of the disinvestment in America's public schools and disinvestment in the American public. The bungalows overlooked asphalt playgrounds and freeways, and often didn't offer access to sunlight or fresh air for students. So dismal were the bungalows that dotted the K–12 campuses that Los Angeles mayor Eric Garcetti, who played a key role in helping drive the strike's settlement, quipped at one point during the negotiation that the city considered buying some used bungalows from the school district to use as shelters for the rapidly expanding homeless population (another result of decades of austerity). The city decided against the idea: because they were so derelict, they weren't suitable for homeless people. Yes, structures that were not deemed as an adequate alternative for people sleeping in the rain or with rats were indeed good enough for poor and low-income kids to spend most waking hours in, supposedly learning the ABCs that will prepare them for competing with AI and robots in Silicon Valley. The idea of equality of opportunity would be a joke, if not for teachers fighting through their union, with their heart and feet, to make it so.

The Green Spaces agreement had way more meaning than even the obvious ones of getting kids outside to play and the riddance of inappropriate learning spaces. Beyond offering children the resources to recreate in fresh air, the Green Spaces agreement also defends against further privatization of the nine hundred remaining public schools. By removing the bungalows, greening spaces, and putting kids back inside buildings with heaters that work and windows to let in air and blinds to keep out the sun, the Green Spaces agreement presents a direct challenge to the privately run, taxpayer-funded charter schools because once again, the publicly run public schools will be attractive.

FEW PEOPLE IN THE POWER STRUCTURE in California understood what was happening inside the second-largest teachers' union in America. Conventional wisdom held that teachers' unions were flat on their backs by the time Trump took office and appointed billionaire blunderer Betsy DeVos to finish off what Arne Duncan—himself a proponent of privatization, charter schools, and weakening the power of teacher unions—started under a wildly popular Democrat president.

Lost in the press coverage during the strike—which focused

on wages, the least important issue to teachers in this strike—was that the strike was about the future of public education. The teachers, working with parents, saved nine hundred public schools in Los Angeles from the jaws of an obscenely well-funded pro-privatization, anti-teachers'-union slate of billionaires. Along the way, the teachers' union also helped win back control of the U.S. House of Representatives by throwing its resources into the seven key House races in greater L.A. at the height of their strike preparations. And they made a mockery of the June 2018 Supreme Court *Janus* decision by building a strike-ready union that the members fully owned and engaged in.

Many of us learn best by doing: by taking action, and by experiencing change. The L.A. teachers delivered a master class in how to rebuild a union, how to unite very different kinds of individuals from Latinx in the heart of Los Angeles to African Americans to white members from the San Fernando Valley, how to effectively hold Democratic politicians accountable to their historic base, and how to fight against a stacked deck and win big.

CHAPTER 7

As Go Unions, So Goes the Republic

To abandon the strike is to abandon the concept of wage labor; for the essence of wage labor as opposed to slave labor, is refusal to work when conditions of work become unbearable.

—John Steuben, *Strike Strategy*, 1950

I PIVOTED FROM AN EARLY CAREER IN FULL-TIME ENVIRONMENTAL activism into organizing unions when I was sent to work in Stamford, Connecticut, at the height of the financial boom in the raging nineties. Neoliberalism was at peak success. Bill Clinton and Tony Blair were finishing the work begun by Ronald Reagan and Margaret Thatcher: dismantling society by dismantling unions. They made union-busting look cool. Clinton was young, danced to Fleetwood Mac, and played the saxophone at his inauguration. Fresh-faced Blair, taking the stage to give his victory speech in 1997, smiled and declared, "We are now today, the people's party . . . no matter what people's background or their creed, or their color, the people are uniting behind *new* Labour." They each seemed comfortable around smart people of color and unthreatened by strong women pushing against the glass ceiling.

But the word *new* that Blair added in front of the party's actual name, the Labour Party, represented the same kind of "new" ushered into the Democrats by Bill Clinton. They each brought policies into their political parties that hurt women, people of color, and all workers by slashing taxes on the rich, eviscerating environmental and labor regulations using "free" trade agreements, and declaring that pensions of teachers and other public service workers were no longer sustainable, and forget "big government." They understood that promoting diversity by putting a handful of women and people of color in a few top slots would make others think they could get there, too. Since many unions remain lily white and male on top, it seemed that "new" capitalism was better than "old" unions. Diversity and empowerment schemes without class and unions fall flat. The story of Taylor Hesselgrave and the Hackbright Academy makes this painfully clear. Hackbright promised to "change the ratio by removing any barriers that might stop a woman from wanting to become a software engineer." But merely changing the ratio, or pumping diversity into a rotten system, won't fix it. There's nothing new except the delivery vehicle: a bunch of Democrats in an Uber.

Stamford and Fairfield County, the region in southern Connecticut where I set out with four smart unions to challenge unfettered corporate power and the super-rich, was a microcosm of these dynamics. Stamford was once a booming industrial region, particularly along the Long Island Sound, where major defense contractors and defense-related industries operated. In 1946, those industries were heavily unionized and there was a general strike. By the raging nineties, however, unions had been all but wiped out of the region. The ones that were left were hanging on by a thread and largely ineffective.

These regional New England towns were wealthy suburbs, with

lovely lawns and a burgeoning finance sector, complete with a glitzy trading floor built by foreign global financial titan SwissRe. On a good day, the ambitious mayor of Stamford, Dannel Malloy, was ambivalent about unions. But most days he was downright hostile and engaged in union busting. He had come of age as a young Democratic Party leader under Bill Clinton's reign in a place where unions didn't have political power. They faded with the region's factories decades back. Union members hadn't made up his electoral base when he ran for mayor. Diversity and stock options were in; unions were on their way out. Right?

Malloy came close to saying that in many a confrontation as workers rebuilt unions from the ground up, work site by work site, supermajority strike by supermajority strike, covering health care, real estate, and hospital sectors, winning thirty-one of thirty-two NLRB elections, first contracts, political races, and a big campaign to stop the racist gentrification plan dressed up as revitalization. We warned Malloy that if he wanted to succeed in politics, he'd have to learn to make peace with working people. That included the thousands of people of color who were our new members and lived in the subsidized housing he sought to demolish. Malloy got the same education in 1999 that Los Angeles school superintendent Beutner and Mayor Garcetti got in 2019: that the *not rich* women and people of color workers in the service sector are every bit as capable of building strike-ready worker organizations and joining with white workers—in the worst of times, through the most hostile conditions. And when they do, they win.

As this book goes to print, the official unemployment rate is 3.7 percent, with newspaper headlines boasting about one hundred months of job growth. But the bright economy forecast disguises the real state of the country: 60 percent of Americans not only have no savings, they are in debt. The 2008 financial crash, for example, gutted a huge number of people's retirement plans, devalued the mortgages of those folks who were fortunate enough to own a home, and led to massive layoffs and unemployment. The crash wasn't an accident; it was precipitated by rule changes, by conscious choices driven by Wall Street bankers and the business elite using their politically decisive lobbying muscle in the nation's capital. It enabled and even incentivized subprime lending, reducing conventional lending standards to "low doc" loans and allowing the merger of commercial and investment banks, all with no regard for the impact on the rest of us.

Even if people didn't lose their homes during the housing crash, it soon became impossible for them to get equity from them or sell them. It trapped them in place, making it impossible to move for jobs when companies like General Motors, after announcing massive plant closures and layoffs in late 2018—closures Donald Trump promised would not happen under his presidency—offered a few workers jobs but in different states after its 2019 plant closings. Or companies like Amazon, who in late April 2019 made a surprise announcement informing thousands of workers that the particular warehouses in which they worked would be closing for renovations in less than two months, and offered them jobs in other states. And many of the so-called new economy jobs are being created in the Southwest and West, far from the Rust Belt, where workers have been hit hard by intentional unemployment (or "globalization," as I've explained). For workers stranded by the housing crisis, that means splitting up the family. Busting up families leads to other social consequences for which the rich also refuse to pay. It leads to workers living in their cars.

That's bad, but it gets worse. The same deregulation of banks and financial institutions that led to workers having their homes foreclosed upon or their families split is now fueling the prospect of more people losing their cars, too. An early 2019 report from the Federal Reserve Bank of New York revealed a new record: the number of Americans ninety days behind or more on their car loan payments was a whopping seven million in January 2019. *Wash-*

ington Post reporter Heather Long wrote, "A car loan is typically the first payment people make because a vehicle is critical to getting to work, and someone can live in a car if all else fails. When car loan delinquencies rise, it is usually a sign of significant duress among low-income and working-class Americans." The most jaw-dropping aspect of reading the report, and media coverage of it, was the lack of concern that it's become normal for workers in America to live in their cars. So much for the American Dream.

Despite conditions getting worse every year, in most cases, the national unions—different from their many upstart locals—have actually held workers back from strikes. Instead, they dutifully cling to the promises from one Democrat after another that they will fix national labor law. But mainstream Democrats have been making this promise since Jimmy Carter won the White House, "+ 60." Plus sixty refers to the number of Democrat- versus Republican-held seats in the Senate, and it's shorthand for filibuster-proof (until recently, if forty-one Senators wanted to block a bill's passage, they could talk forever, aka filibuster, to stop legislation). So despite having the actual numbers lined up for the Democrats to pass labor-law reform, they never have: Carter didn't fix labor law; neither did Clinton or Obama, despite herculean efforts by workers through their unions to elect them and get to + 60 in the Senate.

Why does the inequality continue? Because as the Princeton–Northwestern study discussed in the introduction of this book confirms, huge corporations and the people who run them not only have the money that's missing from nonexistent savings accounts of working folks, but they are also the people making the decisions that allow them to continue to plunder the middle and working class and the planet. When you hear pundits blaming workers for not voting, or voting "against their interests," blame the CEOs and corporate Democrats for decimating unions and failing all the working class, black, brown, female, male, white—all of them—for the past fifty years. Blame the Wall Street–Silicon Valley wing of the Democratic Party for electing Donald Trump. By 2016, the biggest problem was that many workers simply gave up. Many were the ones who were sure the first black president would bail them out along with Wall Street—and he didn't. Some pulled the lever for Trump, but most didn't. The actual numbers from 2016 reveal that rich people and the middle class are who elected Trump. Most workers couldn't pull the lever for him, but they lost faith in Hillary "America is already great" Clinton. Because living in your car, forgoing needed medical care because you can't afford it, and having no pension isn't "already great."

If the Democrats field another presidential candidate who is backed by mostly corporate money, odds are that Trump will win again. He delivered what the super-rich wanted: massive tax cuts. He delivered what the corporations wanted: massive tax cuts *and* the wholesale destruction of more regulations than anyone can keep track of. In addition to undoing regulations, he has dismembered the regulatory agencies, replacing their decision-making staff with the very industry leaders who wanted the agencies abolished. The non-decision-making staff in the federal agencies were humiliated, driven to despair by being forced to work without pay. So many outrageous things happen every day at the hands of Donald Trump that most people have forgotten that hundreds of thousands of workers in the federal government were used as pawns by a viciously cruel boss.

According to the Intergovernmental Panel on Climate Change, we have until 2030 to reverse course before we enter a climate catastrophe. Taking that date as a deadline, what's a credible plan to win the change needed? Winning the White House is urgent. The Democrats need a ticket (hint: the VP might actually matter) and platform that unites everyone who has suffered under previous Democratic administrations, not just Trump's. Trump and his backers will double down on every tactic they used to win in 2016. Because so much of how Republicans won mirrors what union busters do in every hard union fight—be it a contract campaign or an NLRB election—learning the lessons of how the workers who are still winning today, overcoming stiff odds, is key to victory if we want a shot at turning our country around.

For starters, assume there will be massive voter suppression. There's no reason to believe differently after two governor races, Georgia and Florida, were stolen in 2018. (And those were only the most publicized races!) No number of lawsuits or legal action will prevent voter suppression in 2020; forget it. (Recall that a less conservative Supreme Court backed a coup in Florida in the 2000 election). And even though poll watchers will help weed out some suppression, like lawsuits, they won't stop it, either. Instead, we must assume voter suppression will happen and plan for it. Planning for it means understanding that there are two major categories of voter suppression: overt and subtle.

Overt suppression includes expunging names from voting rosters (or at the voting station in the NLRB election booth) on election day. Or disappearing ballots between the close of polls and the count (this is made easier by electronic voting systems with no paper backup). Or that big bunches of ballots somehow get damaged. Or making it difficult for people to vote, since voting day is not a national holiday, most people work, and election departments are underfunded leading to lines so long at the voting location that people actually can't stay to vote. The second kind of voter suppression is subtler but no less effective: convincing people not to bother voting, "because they can't make up their mind" or "both parties stink" or "nothing will change anyway."

The solution to overcoming both types of suppression is building supermajority participation before the election, which is exactly what union organizers do to win a hard NLRB election. We assume the boss will shave 20 to 25 percent of the yes-for-the-union vote, which forces us to build *supermajority participation*—we can assume that voter suppression can shave off a substantial percentage of voters. How do we build this supermajority? Think back to the unionization and strike efforts of the Philadelphia nurses described in chapter 5 and the Los Angeles teachers' union and strike efforts in chapter 6. In each instance, the organizers spent endless time gathering the evidence that they have supermajority participation by identifying natural leaders and using structure tests. This gives them a solid, evidence-based understanding of who is willing to take high-risk actions in the face of increasing polarization. This makes all the difference between thinking, or wishing, you have supermajority support and knowing without doubt that you do.

Polling, tweeting, Fakebooking, or other ways of "engaging" with politics done from the comfort of your home are much less effective than participatory, public structure tests. Why? Polling is anonymous, and plenty of social and political science literature verifies that making an anonymous commitment to something or someone is very different from making a public one. Social media keeps people locked inside their own insular silos, where it can seem like most everyone already agrees with you—but that's far from the case. Effective organizers conduct public structure tests—like the various public petitions signed by the L.A. teachers—repeatedly. Each time people engage in them, it deepens their commitment to the action that needs to be taken. It makes people more likely to stand in an eight-hour line at the polling station, go on strike in the snow or pouring rain, or walk through a mass of angry protestors as they head to a polling station.

Each structure test reveals where your unity and organization are strong and weak, allowing you to prioritize your effort on the weakest links. In a union campaign, focusing on weak areas is often called focusing on the "biggest, worst": given limited resources, it's the areas in the biggest trouble that need the most attention. This generally means spending long days finding people who aren't par-ticipating in the structure tests at all, who aren't attending any of your meetings, and who don't want to talk to you. These are what we call having the hard conversations, because having hard conversations is urgent in a hard campaign.

Besides winning an election, learning to build supermajorities has another crucial benefit: it builds *governing power*. If someone decent wins the election, unless the troops in the field stay mobilized to force needed change, it's very easy for the big corporate lobby to take over and prevent anything significant from happening. The country may feel nicer with a good leader at the top, but we need to address inequality and the climate crisis from the bottom up. So building supermajorities wins hard elections and then serves as the basis to win policy changes, too. In unions, building supermajority participation is crucial because for workers, voting to form a union is only the first step. Even if workers win the vote, nothing changes until they negotiate and win their contract. If we use winning a great union contract, with fully employer-paid health care, child care, workers' control of their schedules, fair pay systems, paid parental leave, real pension and more—things that take *a lot* of power to win in a contract—as analogous to winning society-wide policies, voters have to keep up their unity and activism after election day. There's no way to win life-changing legislation like the Green New Deal otherwise.

In the 2020 election cycle and afterward, Democrats cannot play the data-driven, small-margins game; given the current conservative bent of the Supreme Court, voter suppression will trump small margins. The entire practice of the mainstream, corporate-backed Democratic Party has to change because it relies on data geeks zeroing in on minute numbers of voters getting "activated" or "pushed to the polls for one election day," and then putting them back to sleep for four years. That too led to Trump's election in 2016. He had the winning electoral base that the pundits basically all missed, but instead they kept reporting that he "had no staff in key states" and predicted that Clinton's superior staff in those same states, her "ground game," would win. Pundits and Democrats alike underestimated the power of the evangelical church and the National Rifle Association, to name just two core institutions the Republicans have steadily built while the Democrats steadily wiped out their union base.

To build a supermajority base that's rock solid for 2020—and that builds governing power—liberals and progressives must use other elements that are the norm among successful union organizers, too: defeating futility and deploying inoculation. Futility, the tactic union busters use to subtly convince people nothing will change and they should just stay home and not bother voting, is best combatted by having lots of examples at the ready to describe the many real achievements ordinary people have made despite stiff odds. For example, workers helped create Social Security by first electing FDR, then went on strike until policy makers realized it was important to insure people in old age. Workers then fought for Medicare and Medicaid and won them during Lyndon Johnson's presidency.

Inoculation, a tactic wherein organizers preempt all the horrible things management will say and do about the union, is a way to counter the polarization that billionaires want to create. If you don't get ahead of polarization, you run the risk of people getting election fatigue: no one wants to talk to anyone about the election because just talking about it feels so bad. Think about the half year leading up to the 2016 election: neighbors, friends, family, and coworkers all over the country were arguing and having fights like they've never had.

Most people don't see the process of how that kind of polarization is built, but union organizers have been dealing with bosses fomenting division and hatred for a long time. To beat them, smart unions—like PASNAP in chapter 5—have literature pieces ready to give to workers once the union-busting rhetoric has started to kick in. These pamphlets have sections with headings like, "What are the nine things that management will always say when employees talk about organizing a union?" followed with responses like, "Hint: They come directly from the consultant's anti-union campaign manual." But good literature doesn't win the war for either side. Only face-to-face conversations among trusted colleagues can defeat the kind of polarizing campaigns that are the norm in unionization elections, the Jim Crow South, and now, all of America. This means that neighbors, congregants, parents of kids on the sidelines of every K–12 sports team, book clubs, and knitting circles—every place people gather and regather regularly—need to be engaged in the same way workers engage with each other in their workplaces during a union campaign.

WORKERS DID NOT ACHIEVE ACCESS to quality health care; the right to retire and greater safety on the job; the resources to own a home; access to decent, subsidized affordable housing; and the ability to send their kids to college because some wealthy philanthropists donated money to a certain cause. Plainly, none of the most important gains for equality from the mid-1930s through the 1970s would have been possible without workers building strong organizations like the L.A. teachers union and PASNAP and UNITE-HERE, and the success of their recent strikes is testament to the fact that unions still hold the power to change people's lives.

Their success was also mirrored by thousands of Marriott hotel workers in the same period. In the fall of 2018, in the months leading up to the L.A. teachers' strike in early 2019, the workers at Marriott did something academic experts said was impossible: a union of low-wage immigrant workers toiling in so-called unskilled jobs banded together, went on strike in seven big cities against a major *multinational* employer, and set a new, higher standard for hotel workers and other low-wage earners. Similarly, the tactical genius of school bus drivers in rural West Virginia in 2018 teaming up with teachers helped topple a trifecta-red Republican, natural-resource-destroying, corporate-controlled state. Unions have so much value not just to build the power required to undo the rot of democracy and rampant income inequality, but also to teach Americans how to unite again.

Power for ordinary people can be built only by ordinary people standing up for themselves, with their own resources, in campaigns where they turn the prevailing dogma of individualism on its head. They use their collective intelligence and ingenuity to build solidarity and fight for human dignity. Starting in the early 1970s, and for the next four decades, the rise of something known as "liberal philanthropy" advanced a model of change predicated on pacifying the majority while lawyers and specialists "advocated on behalf of others" (thus the advocacy model). This philanthropic agenda also endorsed the end of unions, seeing them as a vestige of a bygone industrial era. It's time to realize that approach was and is a colossal failure. Democracy, it turns out, requires a thinking people.

Robots aren't better than humans, AI isn't supreme, and Peter Thiel isn't going to live to three hundred years old no matter how much of our wealth he invests in cryogenics. The youthful leadership of this country sure as hell can mitigate the tide of climate change. But the foundation of the house of power for progressives are unions, complemented by strong, independent, community-based organizations helping to hold unions accountable to broad societal goals. Newspapers seem old-fashioned, but we are now seeing the results of losing the function of newspapers, which was never simply "the paper," but real news. Unions get billed as last century too, but the point of unions isn't their buildings or bureaucracy; it's the political education, solidarity, and confidence building among the many that comes from people acting collectively, including strikes, for their own betterment.

Nothing can rebuild a progressive, ground-up electoral base like a strike-ready union. The Koch brothers know this. The Democrats don't. The choice is clear: build good unions, undo Taft–

Hartley, and enable robust collective bargaining and strikes—which will force an end to austerity as it did in Los Angeles. Otherwise, democracy ends. We don't need to innovate. From now until the 2020 election day and beyond, we must put the pedal to the metal on the kind of supermajority strikes that began in West Virginia in 2018. Good unions point us in the direction we need to go and produce the solidarity and unity desperately needed to win. We can fight, and we can win.

Acknowledgments

THE BOOK IN YOUR HANDS HAS MANY CONTRIBUTORS. I AM GRATE-ful to each and every person whose stories and actions inspire me and teach me. I feel blessed by the brilliant people who have developed the best of my thinking and who share no blame for my weaknesses.

Starting on a somber note, two people I love and respect, who supported my work on this book specifically and who each challenged me in good ways since I entered the academic arena, died during the very short months I was toiling over *A Collective Bargain*.

Colin Barker, a powerhouse, radical intellectual, but also a very down-to-earth activist, died in February 2019 from cancer. When I finished the first chapter in December 2018, I sent it to him knowing his time for feedback was coming close to the end. He read it immediately, cheering me on, as he always did. I miss him and am so thankful for his sharp additions to much of my thinking.

Likewise, someone amazingly special in his own right and similar in some ways to Colin, someone fundamentally nice and incredibly understated in intellect, died abruptly and without warning, just as we were e-mailing about him vetting a key chapter in this book—the one and only Dan Clawson. Dan was a key member of my Ph.D. committee and directly helped me think about this book in several conversations. He and his fabulous wife, Mary Ann Clawson, had brainstormed some citations and evidence I needed to back up several claims in one of the chapters. By brainstorm, of course, I mean I sent a brief e-mail request for help and, in return, got a perfectly typed, meticulously written, two-page memo from Dan, who made sure to point out that he and Mary Ann had worked as a team to produce the note. I was sick to my stomach when the news of Dan's sudden passing arrived via text, and I miss him often.

Someone who has inspired me since her birth, and even through her death, occupied large sections of my emotions all through this period—my amazing niece, Pella, who at the young age of twenty-seven was already fighting for the rights of immigrant youth, the planet, and all of us. I haven't had the words to describe how painful it was to lose a twenty-seven-year-old who was already a fierce fighter, and I still don't. I sob mostly instead, as I do now while typing these words. But her strong ethical, moral, and legal convictions about what is wrong, and what is right, about this world live on in all of our family and her many young friends.

This book wasn't my idea. In fact for a short period, I didn't think I should write it. After all, I was busy thinking about a different book, one I was already doing with Verso about strikes (before the resurgence of them in 2018!). Within a matter of months, in the summer of 2018, then Ecco editor Emma Janaskie, along with my literary agent, Sam Stoloff, changed the course of my work pretty much entirely. Sam was super supportive as I navigated each aspect of this project. Emma was just the editor I needed; she pushed, pulled, cheered, pushed again, demanded more, undid giant messy piles of words, untwisted early thinking, and helped me rethink how to organize the ten trillion things I was trying to shove into each chapter. She's an amazing editor, a great thinker, and one hell of a person.

When Emma asked me to write a book in several months from

start to finish, I thought, *Damn, she's like an organizer!* Meaning, she essentially wanted me to do what I do: shift into what I call "warrior mode" and write a book on a deadline, much like an NLRB election, in forty-five days, more or less, with some outside interference expected! Emma busted her ass on this, and when I wanted to be done, she wasn't having it, despite my meltdowns. I'd welcome Emma on a union campaign anytime; her perseverance and clarity in the face of adversity were amazing.

When Emma decided to shift her life to a new project, she handed me off at Ecco to Dominique Lear. I was terrified, really, for a few minutes in the scheme of life. But Dominique welcomed me and this book project with an open heart and open arms, guiding a frenetic me calmly through the remainder of this collective effort. On that note, all the staff—some of whom I won't ever know, from the cover design team to the layout people to the production department—everyone at Ecco/HarperCollins is a pleasure!

As soon as I accepted the mission of cranking out a new book in record time, I began to assemble my A team. Two researchers who were absolutely key to getting this book done, who ably and incredibly assisted me with odd, and at times constant, requests for backup, were Jeff Goodwin of New York University and social-movement-thinker fame and John Lacny. Jeff Goodwin is a more recent addition to my life. He and I met when I entered the academy, and he's been a total, smart, funny, great pleasure since the first time I met him. Jeff immediately volunteered to help me with research, and I couldn't be more appreciative of his talent and solidarity. He's also really fun and has an unrecognized talent at billiards.

I've known John Lacny since my first year in the labor movement, when he showed up as part of the Union Summer team in Stamford, Connecticut. He's been a one-thousand-percent reliable human-solidarity machine ever since! When I write, I have to listen to good classical music. It's how I shut out the noise of the world.

And John Lacny is prouder of the classical music suggestions he sent to me than of his responses to my research requests! A short version of the best of the list he sent me, all excellent recommendations, includes Mozart piano concertos (recordings by Alfred Brendel); *Mozart: Clarinet Concerto & Concerto for Flute and Harp;* Beethoven piano sonatas (also Alfred Brendel); Bach's *Goldberg Variations* (played by Glenn Gould—he did one recording in 1955 and another in 1981; you can listen to both, and they're strikingly different); and string quartets by Beethoven, Haydn, Mozart, and Schubert.

Aside from Jeff and John, the dynamic duo research team, the next person who willingly volunteered endless time to help me was Katie Miles. Katie read every version of every chapter twice, and by the end, I think three times; she probably read two of the hardest-to-write chapters four times each! Her smart organizer brain melded to her inherited writing and editing gene was enormously useful as I cranked out this book. Chris Salm, another former researcher, along with recent former researcher Justin Panos, kicked in at odd moments and did some amazing hospital and Amazon research (most of which didn't make it in but did help me clarify things I could and could not assert about two distinct economic sectors!).

Nelson Lichtenstein, historian extraordinaire, reviewed "Who Killed the Unions?" Upon receiving his approval, I slept considerably better afterward. I so appreciate him generally, and for pinch-hitting and reading that one chapter.

The other person who made the pace and readability of this book possible was Webster Williams for his endless, fast, effective copy editing. Webster is extraordinary. A gift to me and the world. I so appreciate his work and his commitment. Occasionally pinch-hitting, when I was handing Webster too much to do at once, was the great copy editor Jane Halsey. I also want to thank Garret Keizer, whom I barely know, for sending me really encouraging handwritten notes all through the months of this book project.

A lifetime friend and ally, Ross Hammond, showed up nearly every single week—which I asked him to do—to take long hikes with me to get my endorphins, and also my brain juices, flowing. There was one particularly crazy weekend, crazy because of climate change, when, despite harrowing and torrential rain storms and branches flying off trees, Ross showed up regardless, and we hiked for hours under the magnificent canopy of Muir Woods. Other friends who kept me sane (or tried to!) include Laura Pandapas and Cori Valentine, for being sure I went to yoga each week and made room for one night out every week for dinner with two great women! In that department—food and human nourishment—Trish McCall and Gary Friedman insisted I come to their house for Warriors game nights and to accept really good meals as they practiced learning how to make vegetarian food for their in-laws. (I've never had a better gig as a guinea pig, sampling gourmet homemade veggie meals!) When I wasn't tracking details at the horse barn, Maureen Pinto, Susy Stewart, and Thea Chalmers paid necessary and endless attention to my trusted steed, Jalapeno. In addition to a gravity dropper for my bike saddle, I got a trainer and mountain bike coach to help keep my body moving. His name is Allan Reeves, and I thank him for reinforcing my sense of daily discipline, keeping my body physically working when it was breaking down from sitting for too long while writing the first draft. Lifetime pal Catherine Banghart helped fill in citations and, at one point, fill in an empty bank account! John Anner, OMG, John Anner. I'd send him a few sentences and exclaim, "This sucks! What am I saying???" and he'd immediately get me unstuck!

Speaking of getting unstuck, when going in circles about the title of this book, I was visiting with Janice Fine, and she decided to gather her household and declare a brainstorm session to help me find a book title. From that very brainstorm, her son, Benjamin Biko Fine-Donnelly, said, "What about *A Collective Bargain*?" The rest is history. My sister, Bri, participated in many other brainstorms on the design, look, and feel of the book. My brother Mitchell gave generous time to this effort on legal matters. And while on the topic of the law, Bill Sokol, whom I have long called my favorite labor lawyer ever, was endlessly on hand to patiently help me understand various aspects of recent U.S. Supreme Court rulings as they came down, including long discussions about the *Epic* and *Janus* cases. Bill Sokol is the exact kind of labor lawyer every worker deserves and every union organizer craves!

Near the end of this process, two women whom I could not pick out of a lineup but to whom I owe my left or right arms are Miriam Gordis and Annie Berman. These two women were interns at the Francis Goldin Literary Agency, and Sam Stoloff asked them to help me with citations work. They were *lifesavers*. Miriam Gordis in particular pored over the manuscript of this book, fixing citations, adding citations, and also fact-checking the entire thing in record time! I can't thank her enough; I can only keep thanking her.

Last but first, in a serious way, are several extraordinary humans who were willing to let me write about their work lives. These include Taylor Hesselgrave, who deserves a medal of honor for what she survived at the hands of unscrupulous employers. (Her coworkers deserve praise and admiration, too.) And definitely thanks to Marne Payne, Liz Miller, Pat Kelly, Jamie Rhodes, and all the Pennsylvania workers with whom I laughed, cried, and struggled day in and day out during the 2016 Philadelphia organizing campaign.

Notes

PREFACE: THIRTY-SIX WEEKS

viii *47.3 percent of the electorate:* Brendan Cole, "Joe Biden's Popular Vote Share Is Third Largest by Presidential Challenger in Election History," *Newsweek,* November 14, 2020, https://www.newsweek.com/joe-biden-donald-trump-popular-vote-1547483.

INTRODUCTION: TWELVE YEARS OF FREEDOM (ALMOST)

3 *in debt:* Edward N. Wolff, "Household Wealth Trends in the United States, 1962 To 2016: Has Middle Class Wealth Recovered?" National Bureau of Economic Research Working Paper Series, Working Paper 24085, November 2017, https://www.nber.org/papers/w24085.pdf.

3 *$13 million per hour:* Chuck Collins and Josh Hoxie, "Jeff Bezos, Bill Gates, and Warren Buffett Have More Wealth than the Bottom Half of the Country Combined," *Los Angeles Times,* November 15, 2017, http://www.latimes.com/opinion/op-ed/la-oe-collins-hoxie-three-richest-americans-inequality-20171115-story.html.

3 *by $2.5 billion each day:* Oxfam Briefing Paper, "Public Good or Private Wealth?" Oxfam, January 21, 2019.

3 *Princeton and Northwestern universities:* Sahil Kapur, "Scholar Behind Viral 'Oligarchy' Study Tells You What It Means," Talking Points Memo, April 22, 2014.

4 *"of organized interests":* Ibid.

4 *even a worker:* Noam Scheiber: "Uber Drivers Are Contractors, Not Employees, Labor Board Says," *New York Times,* May 14, 2019, https://www.nytimes.com/2019/05/14/business/economy/nlrb-uber-drivers-contractors.html; National Labor Relations Board decision, "Advice Memorandum: Case Number: 13-CA-163062," April 16, 2019, https://www.nlrb.gov/case/13-CA-163062.

4 *contradicts their assertions:* Jim Tankersley and Matt Phillips, "Trump's Tax Cut Was Supposed to Change Corporate Behavior. Here's What Happened," *New York Times,* November 12, 2018, https://www.nytimes.com/2018/11/12/business/economy/trumps-tax-cut-was-supposed-to-change-corporate-behavior-heres-what-happened.html; see also *Americans for Tax Fairness,* a blog containing constantly

updating data on how the top five hundred, then top one thousand, corporations are spending the tax cut money, https://americansfor taxfairness.org (retrieved March 28, 2019).

4   *of the super-rich:* Ibid.

5   *three months of 2017:* Ben Brody, "Daily Report for Executives," *Bloomberg BNA,* January 23, 2018.

5   *$59 million:* Ibid.

5   *the two main parties was 16:1:* Center for Responsive Politics, "Business-Labor-Ideology Split in PAC & Individual Donations to Candidates, Parties, Super PACs and Outside Spending Groups," OpenSecrets.org, https://www.opensecrets.org/overview/blio.php (retrieved April 1, 2019).

6   *"a New Paper Says":* Josh Zubrum, "How Estimates of the Gig Economy Went Wrong, Rise in Nontraditional Work Arrangements Was More Modest than Originally Estimated, a New Paper Says," *Wall Street Journal,* January 7, 2019, https://www.wsj.com/articles/how -estimates-of-the-gig-economy-went-wrong-11546857000.

8   *moving this idea forward:* Sarita Gupta, Steven Lerner, and Joseph A. McCartin, "It's Not the 'Future of Work,' It's the Future of Workers That's in Doubt," *American Prospect,* August 31, 2018, https:// prospect.org/article/its-not-future-work-its-future-workers-doubt.

8   *$1,000 per month:* This was one proposal for a guaranteed income made by Andrew Yang. The test guaranteed-income program in Stockton, California, that started earlier this year was only $500 per month. The Roosevelt Institute modeled different numbers for their hypothetical study of its potential effects: Michalis Nikiforos, Marshall Steinbaum, and Gennaro Zezza, *Modeling the Macroeconomic Effects of a Universal Basic Income,* Roosevelt Institute, August 2017, http://rooseveltinstitute.org/wp-content/uploads/2017/08/Modeling -the-Macroeconomic-Effects-of-a-Universal-Basic-Income.pdf.

11 *"No public assistance":* Joshua Murray and Michael Schwartz, "Moral Economy, Structural Leverage, and Organizational Efficacy: Class Formation and the Great Flint Sit-Down Strike, 1936–1937," *Critical Historical Studies* (Fall 2015): 219–59.

11 *cared about "their" workers:* David Leonhart, "The Corporate Donors Behind a Republican Power Grab," *New York Times,* December 9, 2018, https://www.nytimes.com/2018/12/09/opinion/wisconsin -republicans-walgreens-campaign-finance.html.

12 *in American factories:* According to Howard Kimeldorf, union membership increased from just 7.7 percent of private-sector workers in 1910 to over a third of all private-sector workers in the mid-1950s.

In 2013, private-sector union levels were lower than in 1910, hovering at just 6.6 percent. See Howard Kimeldorf, "Worker Replacement Costs and Unionization: Origins of the U.S. Labor Movement," *American Sociological Review* 78, no. 6 (2013): 1033–62.

Lane Windham claims that "In the mid-1960s, more than three-quarters of manufacturing plants were covered by collective bargaining agreements." Lane Windham, *Knocking on Labor's Door: Union Organizing in the 1970s and the Roots of a New Economic Divide* (Chapel Hill: University of North Carolina Press, 2017), 58.

For reported union membership statistics: (1) Go to the old St. Louis Fed report (https://fraser.stlouisfed.org/files/docs/publications/bls/bls_1865_1975.pdf). Type in page 396 of the PDF (it says 382 at the bottom of the page), and you will see a table for union membership in 1956. It says there were 8.839 million union members in manufacturing in that year. (2) Another report from the St. Louis Fed has total manufacturing employment in the United States in every month since 1939. Go to https://fred.stlouisfed.org/series/MANEMP, click on "download" near the upper-right-hand corner, and you can get this data in Excel. Seasonally adjusted total manufacturing employment in June of that year was 15.835 million. Divide 8.839 million by 15.835 million, and you have a 56 percent unionization rate. The figure is for *all* manufacturing employment, so among nonsupervisory employees, the unionization rate would have been higher than 56 percent. But 56 percent is the baseline. Meanwhile in 2018, only 9.7 percent of workers in durable and nondurable goods manufacturing are represented by unions, according to BLS: Bureau of Labor Statistics, "Union Affiliation of Employed Wage and Salary Workers by Occupation and Industry," January 18, 2019, https://www.bls.gov/news.release/union2.t03.htm.

12 *national congressional elections:* Curtlyn Kramer, "Vital Stats: The Widening Gap between Corporate and Labor PAC Spending," Brookings Institution, March 31, 2017, https://www.brookings.edu/blog/fixgov/2017/03/31/vital-stats-corporate-and-labor-pac-spending.

13 *"Ohio, Pennsylvania and Washington":* Patrick J. Wright, "Right-to-Work for the Public Sector Is Here, Now What?" *Heritage Insider,* December 20, 2018, https://www.heritage.org/insider/winter-2019-insider/right-work-public-employees-here-now-what.

14 *are forbidden:* Hon Hai Precision Industry Co., Ltd. (which does business under the name Foxconn) is not owned by Apple. Its largest institutional owners are Vanguard (6.16 percent), BlackRock (4.34 percent), and Fidelity (2.42 percent): https://www.msn.com/en-us

/money/stockdetails/ownership/tai-2317/fi-anb227?ownershipType
=institutional. However, as noted in a 2017 article from *Nikkei Asian
Review,* Hon Hai "is not just a subcontractor. It is a business partner.
And although both sides are taking steps to reduce their mutual de-
pendence, their fortunes remain very much entwined." The business
relationship won an order to produce iMacs in 2000, and "when it
came to the iPhone, Foxconn not only handled production and met
tight deadlines but also played a crucial role in realizing Apple's aes-
thetic vision. . . . It is no exaggeration to say the success of the iPhone
depended on Foxconn, and Foxconn's growth hinged on the iPhone. . . .
Apple manages inventories of core parts at Foxconn's warehouses in
real time, and Apple employees are on hand at the supplier's factories
at all times. In some ways, the companies have practically integrated
their operations." Since 2011, Apple has accounted for more than half
of Foxconn's revenue: Yuichiro Kanematsu, "Foxconn, Apple and
the Partnership That Changed the Tech Sector," *Nikkei Asian Review,*
July 13, 2017, https://asia.nikkei.com/Business/Foxconn-Apple-and
-the-partnership-that-changed-the-tech-sector.

14 *to prevent suicide:* Brian Merchant, "Life and Death in Apple's
Forbidden City," *Guardian,* June 18, 2017, https://www.theguardian
.com/technology/2017/jun/18/foxconn-life-death-forbidden-city
-longhua-suicide-apple-iphone-brian-merchant-one-device-extract;
see also Malcolm Moore, "'Mass Suicide' Protest at Apple Manufacturer Foxconn Factory," *Telegraph,* January 11, 2012, https://www
.telegraph.co.uk/news/worldnews/asia/china/9006988/Mass
-suicide-protest-at-Apple-manufacturer-Foxconn-factory.html; see
also Juliet Ye, "Foxconn Installs Antijumping Nets at Hebei Plants,"
Wall Street Journal, August 3, 2010, https://blogs.wsj.com/china
realtime/2010/08/03/foxconn-installs-antijumping-nets-at-hebei
-plants/.

CHAPTER 1: WORKERS CAN STILL WIN BIG

15 *"in any other way the members see fit":* Bernie Minter, taken from
an internal, never published 1199 manual he wrote about how to run
an effective union.

17 *That's true worldwide:* Even within one national union, or "inter-
national union," there's huge variation. The fact that most U.S. unions
have the word *international* in their names is a bit like Major League
Baseball putting the word *world* in the World Series. Other than the
Toronto Blue Jays—a stalwart team—Major League Baseball is a
U.S.-driven affair, although many brilliant players come from Latin

America and Japan. The number of Canadian members in U.S. unions is small; unfortunately, there's not much serious globally inclusive thinking emanating from most U.S. unions, despite the desperate need for a genuinely internationalist trade unionism, given the globalized economy. Canada's union structures aren't all that different from America's; Canada's labor law was written using U.S. law as a sort of first draft, making the final product similar to that of the United States. What Canada hasn't had yet are the ubiquitous, vicious union busters we have in the United States. In my work in Canada over the past few years, however, I've witnessed plenty of evidence that U.S. employers are doubling down their focus on this particular export.

20 *in the suburbs of Philadelphia:* Jamie Rhodes, author interview, June 8, 2017.

24 *shortly after the election:* John George, "LA-Based Hospital Operator Finalizes Deal for Crozer-Keystone," *Philadelphia Business Journal,* January 11, 2016, https://www.bizjournals.com/philadelphia /morning_roundup/2016/01/crozer-keystone-health-prospect-medical -buying.html.

28 *answered her cell phone:* Wendy Peters, author interview, February 27, 2018.

28 *"poorest household family income":* Wikipedia, "List of Lowest Income Counties in the United States," November 18, 2016, https:// en.wikipedia.org/wiki/List_of_lowest-income_counties_in_the _United_States.

30 *in the next twenty:* Data from Workforce West Virginia, November 26, 2018, http://lmi.workforcewv.org/EandWAnnual/TopEmployers.html. Cf. accompanying Excel spreadsheet.

30 *"before walking out":* Wendy Peters, author interview, several times spanning the strike, beginning February 28, March 2, and March 7.

30 *the American Legislative Exchange Council:* ALEC is a notorious invention of the ideological right-wing, begun in 1973. They are responsible for drafting common, easy-to-use legislation that conservative state legislatures can simply insert their names into, and then vote up or down on in any given state. This includes charter schools and related school privatization schemes, along with lots of nefarious legislation from gun rights to anti-affirmative-action to anti-union measures and fill in almost any blank on the right's agenda. John Nichols, "ALEC Exposed," *The Nation,* July 12, 2011, https://www.thenation .com/article/alec-exposed/.

31 *by any means necessary:* Jennifer Berkshire, "How Education

Reform Ate the Democratic Party," *Baffler,* November 2017, https://thebaffler.com/latest/ed-reform-ate-the-democrats-berkshire.

33   *"everything, which is pretty incredible":* AFT–West Virginia flier announcing the settlement.

33   *Trump took office:* In the same election, Justice won by 48,421 votes (350,408–301,987) over Republican Bill Cole, or 49 to 42 percent, "West Virginia Governor Results: Jim Justice Wins," *New York Times,* August 1, 2017, https://www.nytimes.com/elections/results/west-virginia-governor-justice-cole. Justice attended a Trump rally on Thursday, August 3, 2017, where he announced his party switch. Alana Abramson, "'I Can't Help You Anymore Being a Democrat.' West Virginia Governor Switches Parties at Trump Rally," *Time,* August 4, 2017, http://time.com/4886765/west-virginia-rally-jim-justice-republican-trump.

33   *approve the settlement:* However, Carmichael's opposition to the deal between the unions and the governor was openly stated and covered by both local and national media. West Virginia radio station WSAZ reported (on both February 28 and March 1) that "Senate President Mitch Carmichael speculated Wednesday [February 28] that as many as 22 Republicans in the 34-member Senate will oppose Governor Justice's plan." Carmichael further stated, "It's easy to come in here and just vote for what people want, but that's not what the general citizens expect of West Virginia." Kelsey Hoak, Andrew Colegrove, and Kristen Schneider, "Senate President Wants to Use $58M to Fix Public Insurance Instead of Giving Pay Raises," WSAZ.com, March 1, 2018, http://www.wsaz.com/content/news/WVa-House-Bill-including-new-teacher-raise-passed-by-Finance-Committee-475461093.html. Associated Press reporters John Raby and Michael Virtanen on February 28 noted: "'The Senate is, you know, very fiscally conservative,' Carmichael said. He noted they've already managed to provide pay raises to the people chanting at the Capitol and all public employees. 'We know that we need to raise their salaries but it would be absolutely fiscally irresponsible to write a check that we cannot cash for future generations.'" *Washington Post,* February 28, 2018, https://www.washingtonpost.com/national/striking-west-virginia-teachers-to-return-to-class-thursday/2018/02/27/6564e7a8-1c1d-11e8-98f5-ceecfa8741b6_story.html.

37   *Measure Z:* "Measure Z Fact Sheet," TimesUpOakland.org, October 2, 2018, https://www.timesupoakland.org/measure-z-fact-sheet.

37   *experience sexual harassment routinely:* Holly J. McDede and Kristin McCandless, "Oakland Measure Z Could Raise Minimum

Wage, Bring Harassment Protections to Hotel Workers," KALW, October 30, 2018, https://www.kalw.org/post/oakland-measure-z -could-raise-minimum-wage-bring-harassment-protections-hotel -workers#stream/0.

38 *harassed by a guest:* Unite Here Local 1, "Hands Off, Pants On: Sexual Harassment in the Chicago Hotel Industry," July 2016, https:// www.handsoffpantson.org.

39 *the maximum allowable is fifteen:* Irma Perez, author interview. Irma is what's called a shop steward in her hotel, so she's deeply familiar with her own contract and the standards in her area. She states, "We have to clean 15 rooms a day at my job. But at hotels that are not unionized, workers have to clean 28 rooms a day, or sometimes even 30." From my time working in Las Vegas, the same union versus non-union standard applied to number of rooms cleaned per day, fifteen in a unionized hotel versus upward of thirty in a nonunion casino.

39 *22.71 percent no:* Robert Gammon, "Final Results for the Nov. 6, 2018 Election," *East Bay Express,* November 27, 2018, https://www .eastbayexpress.com/oakland/final-results-for-november-2018 -election/Content?oid=23230633.

CHAPTER 2: WHO KILLED THE UNIONS?

43 *Martin Jay Levitt:* Martin Jay Levitt, *Confessions of a Union Buster* (New York: Crown, 1993).

44 *The primary reason:* The export of this service to Europe and other trading partners is underway, but only recently.

47 *a union label to back their demands:* Howard Kimeldorf, "Worker Replacement Costs and Unionization: Origins of the U.S. Labor Movement," *American Sociological Review* 78, no. 6 (2013): 1033–62.

47 *to name only a few:* Erik Loomis, *A History of America in Ten Strikes* (New York: New Press, 2018).

48 *practice collective bargaining:* William Domhoff and Michael J. Webber, *Class and Power in the New Deal: Corporate Moderates, Southern Democrats, and the Liberal-Labor Coalition* (Stanford, CA: Stanford University Press, 2012).

50 *threat of jail time:* Jeremy Brecher, *Strike!* (San Francisco: Straight Arrow Books, 1972), ch. 5, "Depression Decade"; Loomis, *A History of America in Ten Strikes.*

50 *This change in approach:* The other big exception in that era was the International Ladies' Garment Workers' Union, whose members consisted of mostly women and who, like today's teachers' unions, understood more than one hundred years ago that to win, they had

to bring their families and whole community into their factory-based fights for justice on the job.

51   *in news coverage and in the community:* Leyla F. Vural, "Unionism as a Way of Life: The Community Orientation of the ILGWU and the Amalgamated Clothing Workers of America" (Ph.D. diss., Rutgers University, 1994); and Nancy Maclean, "The Culture of Resistance: Female Institution Building in the International Ladies Garment Workers' Union 1905–1925," Ann Arbor Michigan, Michigan Occasional Papers in Women's Studies, 1982.

51   *workers in industrial disputes:* On an official history website for the Pennsylvania State Police, they admit that their own origins date back to the Coal and Iron Police: "Historical Facts and Highlights, Pennsylvania State Police," PATrooper.com, http://www.patrooper.com/history.html.

52   *from 1906 through 1935:* William Domhoff, *The Corporate Rich and the Power Elite in the Twentieth Century: Why They Won, How Liberals and Labor Lost* (New York: Routledge, 2019).

53   *decades-lasting structural achievements:* See Domhoff and Webber, *Class and Power in the New Deal,* and Charles Payne, *I've Got the Light of Freedom: The Organizing Tradition and the Mississippi Freedom Struggle* (Berkeley: University of California Press, 2007).

53   *from 11.5 percent to 26.6 percent:* Domhoff, *The Corporate Rich.*

54   *maintenance of union membership:* Nelson Lichtenstein, *State of the Union: A Century of American Labor* (Princeton, NJ: Princeton University Press, 2002).

55   *forty-four months of the war:* Brecher, *Strike!,* 226.

55   *non-war-related employment:* Ibid., 227.

56   *nonagricultural workers stood at 34.2 percent:* Domhoff, *The Corporate Rich.*

56   *firing workers for striking:* Clawson and Clawson, Union Decline, 1999 Annual Review article.

57   *the entire community in labor fights:* In my second book, *No Shortcuts: Organizing for Power in the New Gilded Age,* I discuss the strategy of the CIO in greater depth.

58   *both the House and the Senate:* Domhoff, *The Corporate Rich.*

59   *act only out of self-interest:* "Democracy in Chains: An Interview with Author Nancy MacLean," KKFI, August 7, 2018, https://kkfi.org/program-episodes/democracy-chains-interview-author-nancy-maclean/.

60   *"call for independent labor organizations":* Levitt, *Confessions of a Union Buster.*

61 *institutionalized racism and labor law:* Lichtenstein, *State of the Union.*

62 *"wage their war with near impunity":* Levitt, *Confessions of a Union Buster,* 36.

62 *tooth and nail despite the law:* John Logan, "The Union Avoidance Industry in the United States," *British Journal of Industrial Relations* 44, no. 4 (December 2006); and Levitt, *Confessions of a Union Buster,* chapter 2, "Genesis."

63 *Chicago, Detroit, and New York:* Levitt, *Confessions of a Union Buster,* 34.

63 *not management:* Logan, "The Union Avoidance Industry in the United States," 653.

65 *financial, insurance, and hospitality sectors:* Ibid., 653.

65 *"activities behind management and supervisors":* Ibid., 652; and Levitt, "Genesis."

66 *"anyone other than a bonafide management representative":* Hamilton Nolan, "What a Real Live Union-Busting Seminar Looks Like," Splinter News, August 22, 2018, https://splinternews.com/what-a-real-live-union-busting-seminar-looks-like-1828520464.

66 *"Your Future in the Union's Hands":* In my possession is one such hard-to-obtain manual, called *Total Victory, 2nd Edition, The Complete Guide to a Successful NLRB Representation Election,* written by Donald Wilson for LRI, the Labor Relations Institute, in 1997.

68 *long lines for hours hoping to vote:* Ari Berman, "Brian Kemp's Election in Georgia Is Tainted by Voter Suppression," *Mother Jones,* November 16, 2018.

69 *Maquiladora Zone:* "Examples of Maquiladoras in Mexico," according to CorpWatch, do include GM, Ford, Chrysler, Honeywell, Xerox, Zenith, and IBM, https://corpwatch.org/article/maquiladoras-glance.

GM is especially known for operating in the maquiladora zones, e.g., the DelCo division, https://newrepublic.com/article/153467/mexico-brink-labor-revolution.

An article from the *Financial Times* says that "Michigan-based Ford is planning to spend $1.3bn expanding an engine factory in the northern state of Chihuahua and $1.2bn on a new gearbox plant in the central state of Guanajuato. . . . The business case for manufacturing in Mexico is compelling. According to research by Evercore ISI, average hourly labour costs excluding benefits can be as low as $8 to $10. By comparison, Ford, General Motors and Fiat Chrysler Automobiles pay an average $48 to $58 an hour in their US factories. . . . So-called maquiladora factories are allowed to import materials and equipment and export manufactured products duty-free under the North American Free Trade Agreement of 1994 involving the US, Mexico and Canada," https://www.ft.com/content/95lce8ca-e434-1le4-9e89 -00144feab7de.

A 2013 story in *Auto News* reports on Fiat Chrysler's expansion of its Saltillo North engine plant, https://www.autonews.com/article /20131010/OEM01/131019986/chrysler-expands-mexico-plant-to -build-i-4-engines-for-export#axzz2j2IK7gF5.

A 2016 article on maquiladoras in *The Economist* notes that "Honeywell, one of the biggest aerospace firms in the region, employs 350 people in the design, engineering and testing of aircraft components in Mexicali, the capital of Tijuana's home state of Baja California," https://www.economist.com/business/2013/10/26/big-maq-attack.

A 2001 report from the Federal Reserve Bank of Dallas notes that Xerox is "among the companies with new investments in Mexico this year," https://www.dallasfed.org/~/media/documents/research /busfront/bus0101.pdf (see endnote 5). This same report also says that "The maquiladora regime that originated in the 1960s has been replaced with a more comprehensive, madquiladora-*like* regime that supports freer trade and investment for all of Mexico's manufacturing industry, since both NAFTA and the PROSECs apply to maquiladoras and nonmaquiladoras alike. In this sense, the maquiladora label may no longer be warranted, given that the initial program that established the industry has essentially ceased to exist, along with its reason for being. What remains as a viable, increasingly important component of the Mexican economy, however, is the industrial base created by the maquiladoras—one that is intimately linked with the economy across the border," https://www.dallasfed.org/~/media /documents/research/busfront/bus0101.pdf (page 5).

A 1996 report from Human Rights Watch mentions General Motors and Zenith among the companies that "require pregnancy exams as a condition of employment." Zenith stated in a letter to Human Rights Watch that "it is common practice among Mexican and maquiladora employers in Matamoros and Reynosa to inquire about pregnancy status as a pre-existing medical condition," https://www.hrw.org /news/1996/08/17/mexicos-maquiladoras-abuses-against-women -workers.

IBM operates in Guadalajara, Jalisco, according to (among other sources) a 2001 article in *Fortune* magazine, http://archive.fortune

.com/magazines/fortune/fortune_archive/2001/10/29/312481/index.htm.

73 *They pay workers so little:* The national organization Good Jobs First does an excellent job of tracking these insane taxpayer subsidies.

74 *under the weight of the Great Depression:* AFSCME website history section.

76 *compared with 36.1 percent in the public sector:* Julia Wolfe and John Schmitt, a profile of union workers in state and local government, key facts about the sector for followers of *Janus v. AFSCME* Council 31, Economic Policy Institute, June 7, 2018.

79 *to the organization:* Celine McNicholas and Zane Mokhibe, "Who's Behind the *Janus* Lawsuit?" *American Prospect* (February 26, 2018), https://prospect.org/article/whos-behind-janus-lawsuit.

82 *takes its current form beginning in the 1950s:* Logan, "The Union Avoidance Industry in the United States."

CHAPTER 3: EVERYTHING YOU THOUGHT YOU KNEW
ABOUT UNIONS IS (MOSTLY) WRONG

90 *"ethical core of the profession":* Gabriel Winant, "Why Are so Many White-Collar Professionals in Revolt?" *Guardian,* May 27, 2018.

90 *Twenty years later:* Temporary means someone gets a two- or three-year teaching contract, but still, with no path to tenure, like adjuncts, who go semester to semester.

91 *resources to greater academic freedom:* Kristen Edwards and Kim Tolley, "Do Unions Help Adjuncts?" *Chronicle of Higher Education,* June 3, 2018, https://www.chronicle.com/article/Do-Unions-Help-Adjuncts-/243566.

91 *Law 360, to name a few:* Steven Greenhouse, "Why Newsrooms Are Unionizing Now," Nieman Reports, March 21, 2019.

91 *he doesn't believe in unions!:* Laurel Wamsley, "Gothamist Properties Will Be Revived Under New Ownership: Public Media," NPR, February 23, 2018, https://www.npr.org/sections/thetwo-way/2018/02/23/588388525/gothamist-properties-will-be-revived-under-new-ownership-public-media.

94 *"part of the working class":* Bill Fletcher, *They're Bankrupting Us! And 20 Other Myths About Unions* (Boston: Beacon Press, 2012).

96 Industrial Unionism in Meatpacking: Roger Horowitz, *Negro and White, Unite and Fight: A Social History of Industrial Unionism in Meatpacking* (Champaign: University of Illinois Press, 1997).

96 *work with blacks or share eating facilities:* Ibid., 221. "More than

90% of white members objected to working with a black in the same job classification, and 90 percent of Southern whites supported segregated eating facilities."

96 *especially the NAACP:* Ibid., 222.

97 *politeness and friendly negotiation:* Shawn Gude, an interview with Erik Gellman, "When Fighting Racism Means Fighting Economic Exploitation," *Jacobin* (March 25, 2019): https://jacobinmag .com/2019/03/national-negro-congress-jim-crow-gellman.

98 *"more important than ever":* Dorian Warren, author conversation followed by e-mail exchange, March 28, 2019.

98 *"only a high school education":* David Card, Thomas Lemieux, and W. Craig Riddell, "Unions and Wage Inequality: The Roles of Gender, Skill, and Public Sector Employment," Working Paper 25313, Cambridge, MA, National Bureau of Economic Research, November 2018.

98 *$1,041 to $829 weekly:* Bureau of Labor Statistics, 2018 annual press release of union related data, covering data from the previous year.

99 *versus only 51.4 percent:* Elyse Shaw and Julie Anderson, "The Union Advantage for Women" (IWPR #C463), Institute for Women's Policy Research, February 2018.

99 *for their nonunion counterparts:* Ibid.

99 *improvement with a union:* "10 Reasons Why Being Union Helps Women," International Union, United Automobile, Aerospace and Agricultural Implement Workers of America website, March 2, 2017, https://uaw.org/10-reasons-union-helps-women.

99 *of the year before:* Shumita Basu and Mara Silvers, interview with Joi Chaney, "Is Pay Transparency a 'Thing' in Your Workplace?" WNYC, April 10, 2018, https://www.wnyc.org/story/pay-transparency -thing-your-workplace.

102 *labor feminism:* Dorothy Sue Cobble, *The Other Women's Movement: Workplace Justice and Social Rights in Modern America* (Princeton, NJ: Princeton University Press, 2005).

103 Why We Lost the ERA: Jane Mansbridge, *Why We Lost the ERA* (Chicago: University of Chicago Press, 1986).

105 *finally win the law's passage:* Deon Roberts, "NC Attorney General Gives Reasons Why Duke Customers Shouldn't Pay for Coal Ash Cleanup," *Charlotte Observer,* April 26, 2019, https://www.charlotte observer.com/news/business/banking/article229720699.html.

105 *"We have 12 years":* Nato Green, "Why Unions Must Bargain Over Climate Change," In These Times, March 12, 2019, http://inthese

times.com/working/entry/21791/grecn-new-deal-climate-change
-labor-common-good-bargaining-permissive.

108 *"New York State"*: J. Mijin Cha and Lara Skinner, "Reversing Inequality, Combatting Climate Change: A Climate Jobs Program for New York State," The Worker Institute at Cornell University, June 2017, https://www.ilr.cornell.edu/sites/default/files/InequalityClimate ChangeReport.pdf.

109 *they hoard:* Christian Parenti, "Make Corporations Pay for the Green New Deal," *Jacobin* (March 13, 2019), https://jacobinmag.com /2019/03/green-new-deal-private-investment-energy.

111 *and sometimes it works:* Melissa Phipps, "10 Businesses Supposedly Controlled by the Mafia," HowStuffWorks.com, February 27, 2015, https://people.howstuffworks.com/10-businesses-supposedly -controlled-by-the-mafia.htm, January 13, 2019.

111 *America's Industrial Unions:* Howard Kimeldorf, *Reds or Rackets: The Making of Radical and Conservative Unions on the Waterfront* (Berkeley: University of California Press, 1988); Judith Stepan-Norris and Maurice Zeitlin, *Left Out: Reds in America's Industrial Unions* (Cambridge, UK: Cambridge University Press, 2002).

113 *"'structurelessness' does not work"*: Jo Freeman, "The Tyranny of Structurelessness," *Berkeley Journal of Sociology* 17 (1972–73): 151–65; and *Ms.* (July 1973): 76–78, 86–89.

CHAPTER 4: ARE UNIONS STILL RELEVANT?

116 *below minimum wage:* James A. Parrott and Michael Reich, "An Earnings Standard for New York City's App-based Drivers: July 2018 Economic Analysis and Policy Assessment," Center for New York City Affairs at The New School, July 2018, https://static1.square space.com/static/53ee4f0be4b015b9c3690d84/t/5b3a3aaa0e2e72 ca74079142/1530542764109/Parrott-Reich+NYC+App+Drivers+TLC+ Jul+2018jul1.pdf.

118 *"It was so clarifying"*: Taylor Hesselgrave, author interview, January 16, 2019.

119 *"radical, practical change"*: Retrieved from the Ecotrust website January 24, 2008, https://ecotrust.org.

120 *"A Community Is Waiting for You"*: Retrieved from the Hackbright Academy website May 6, 2018, https://hackbrightacademy.com.

121 *partners was Winmore:* A customer relations software firm, Winmore rebranded themselves after the negative headlines they got from firing all their senior, nonmanagement engineers for daring to stand

up for themselves. It seems to me there isn't a coincidence, though obviously I can't prove this assertion. But since this is purely a rebranding, not a new company, I am using the new name throughout. They were called Lanetix at the time they illegally fired all their engineers.

122 The Lean Startup: In his influential book, Eric Ries advises creating cross-functional teams that function like autonomous start-ups within a larger parent company. Each team will see through an experiment before reorganizing into different groups. According to Ries, this forces each group to be more experimental and innovative. Eric Ries, *The Lean Startup* (New York: Crown, 2011), 244–61.

129 *which was a lie:* Complaint and Notice of Hearing, Lanetix, Inc and Washington-Baltimore Newspaper Guild, Local 32035, A/W The Newspaper Guild—Communications Workers of America, AFL-CIO, Case 5-CA–213831, August 22, 2018.

130 *never intimidate them again:* Ibid.

130 *"as their bargaining representative":* Ibid., page 5.

132 *unions from "back east":* AnnaLee Saxenian, *The New Argonauts: Regional Advantage in a Global Economy* (Cambridge, MA: Harvard University Press, 2006), 56.

132 *"the* father *of Silicon Valley":* Tom Wolfe, "The Tinkerings of Robert Noyce," *Esquire* (December 1983): 346–74, retrieved from Stanford University website, January 27, 2019.

132 *Noyce and a handful:* Shockley would later emerge as a eugenicist, but there's no evidence that that is why Noyce fled his shop.

133 *"the enterprise would be finished":* Ibid., 28 of 34 in retrieved Web version.

134 *"inequality in America":* Jonathan Taplin, "Introduction," *Move Fast and Break Things: How Facebook, Google, and Amazon Cornered Culture and Undermined Democracy* (New York: Little, Brown, 2017).

134 *"the White House gate":* From an interview with Jonathan Taplin, "The Massive Monopolies of Google, Facebook and Amazon, and Their Role in Destroying Privacy, Producing Inequality and Undermining Democracy," Alternet, April 17, 2017, https://www.alternet.org/2017/04/move-fast-break-things-jonathan-taplin-tech-interview (retrieved January 28, 2019).

134 *Alphabet, Microsoft, and Facebook:* "The 100 Largest Companies in the World by Market Value in 2019," Statistica, https://www.statista.com/statistics/263264/top-companies-in-the-world-by-market-value (retrieved January 28, 2018).

135 *"firms pay their employees":* Allana Akhtar, "The World's Largest Hedge Fund Breaks Down How the US Workforce Got Screwed over

the Past 20 Years," *Business Insider,* April 17, 2019, https://outline.com/sNwaHw.

136 *some more:* Wolfe, "The Tinkerings of Robert Noyce."

137 *In his book* The Fissured Workplace: Weil outlines everything you need to know about this particularly scandalous corporate swindle, in much greater detail than I can here. David Weil, *The Fissured Workplace: Why Work Became So Bad for So Many and What Can Be Done to Improve It* (Cambridge, MA: Harvard University Press, 2017).

139 *the so-called gig or platform economy:* Christopher Rugaber, "Why the 'Gig' Economy May Not Be the Workforce of the Future," AP News, September 24, 2018, https://www.apnews.com/dee67b607a034699abf4ec14bab5cb1c.

139 *by JPMorgan Chase:* Rugaber, "Why the 'Gig' Economy May Not Be the Workforce of the Future."

139 *the Bureau of Labor Statistics:* "BLS, Contingent and Alternative Employment Arrangements," May 2017, https://www.bls.gov/news.release/conemp.htm, and a subsequent additional post by Henwood on June 13, responding to critics of his original post, https://lbo-news.com/2018/06/13/contingency-a-follow-up.

139 *in September 2018:* Electronically Mediated Employment: BLS added four new questions to the May 2017 Contingent Worker Supplement. These questions were designed to measure an emerging type of work—electronically mediated employment, generally defined as short jobs or tasks that workers find through mobile apps that both connect them with customers and arrange payment for the tasks. Bureau of Labor Statistics, "Electronically Mediated Employment," September 28, 2018, https://www.bls.gov/cps/electronically-mediated-employment.htm.

140 *"than is generally recognized":* Dean Baker, "World Development Report Gets It Seriously Wrong on Inequality and Labor Markets," *Beat the Press,* a Center for Economic Policy and Research blog, May 6, 2019, http://cepr.net/blogs/beat-the-press/world-development-report-gets-it-seriously-wrong-on-inequality-and-labor-markets.

140 *the end of one year:* Rugaber, "Why the 'Gig' Economy May Not Be the Workforce of the Future."

141 *Journalist Bryan Menegus:* Bryan Menegus, "Amazon's Aggressive Anti-Union Tactics Revealed in Leaked 45-Minute Video," Gizmodo, September 26, 2018, https://gizmodo.com/amazons-aggressive-anti-union-tactics-revealed-in-leake-1829305201.

142 *in Fremont, California:* Bob Woods, "Why Elon Musk's Latest Legal Bout with the United Auto Workers May Have Ripple Effects

across Silicon Valley," CNBC, December 7, 2018, https://www.cnbc.com/2018/12/07/teslas-bout-with-uaw-union-may-have-ripple-effects-in-silicon-valley.html.

142 *who would produce the cars:* Jeffrey Rothfeder, "Elon Musk Has Delivery Issues," *The New Yorker,* January 10, 2017, https://www.newyorker.com/business/currency/elon-musk-has-delivery-issues.

143 *"the Davos Elite":* Kevin Roose, "The Hidden Automation Agenda of the Davos Elite," *New York Times,* January 25, 2019, https://www.nytimes.com/2019/01/25/technology/automation-davos-world-economic-forum.html.

144 *is urgent:* Sarita Gupta, "The Most Important Job in the World Is One No One Wants Anymore," Quartz, December 12, 2018, https://qz.com/1490065/the-most-important-job-in-the-world-is-one-no-one-wants-anymore.

144 *a shortage of 450,000 caregivers:* Laura Petrecca, "Technology Is Transforming Caregiving," AARP, October 15, 2018, https://www.aarp.org/caregiving/home-care/info-2018/new-wave-of-caregiving-technology.html.

145 *turn sixty-five years old:* Gupta, "The Most Important Job in the World Is One No One Wants Anymore."

146 *robots are all the rage:* Petrecca, "Technology Is Transforming Caregiving."

146 *"sang, danced and told stories":* Ibid.

146 *leach into the ground:* "E-waste Is the Toxic Legacy of Our Digital Age," iFixit, https://www.ifixit.com/Right-to-Repair/E-waste.

147 *"We need to help with loneliness":* Adam Satariano, Elian Peltier, and Dmitry Kostyukov, "Meet Zora, the Robot Caregiver," *New York Times,* November 23, 2018, https://www.nytimes.com/interactive/2018/11/23/technology/robot-nurse-zora.html.

147 *"has made national headlines":* Ibid.

149 *certain types of jobs, and more:* Liza Featherstone, *Selling Women Short: The Landmark Battle for Workers' Rights at Walmart* (New York: Basic Books, 2004).

149 *"by top Shoney management":* LDF Brief at 9-10, citing *Haynes v. Shoney's, Inc.,* No. 3:89-cv-30093, 1992 WL 752127, at 2, 20 (N.D. Fla. June 22, 1992) (certifying class action); see also *Haynes v. Shoney's, Inc.,* No. 3:89-cv-30093, 1993 WL 19915, at 6-7 (N.D. Fla. Jan. 25, 1993) (approving consent decree requiring, among other things, $105 million in relief to class members and significant corporation-wide reforms), http://www.americanbar.org/content/dam/aba/publishing

/preview/publiced_preview_briefs_pdfs_09_10_09_893_Respondent AmCuNAACPLDEF.authcheckdam.pdf.

151 *on November 1, 2018:* Daisuke Wakabayashi, Erin Griffith, Amie Tsang, and Kate Conger, "Google Walkout: Employees Stage Protest Over Handling of Sexual Harassment" *New York Times,* November 1, 2018, https://www.nytimes.com/2018/11/01/technology/google-walkout -sexual-harassment.html.

152 *"potent social influence":* Richard Freeman, "What Does the Future Hold for U.S. Unionism?" *Industrial Relations* 44, no. 1 (Winter 1989): 25–46.

CHAPTER 5: HOW DO WORKERS GET A UNION?

155 *Bernie Minter:* Bernie Minter, from an unnamed, undated, fifty-eight-page manual containing an assortment of information about the union compiled in the mid to late 1960s, according to my mentors at District 1199 New England, and which I call "The Old 1199 Manual."

156 *belong to one:* Niall McCarthy, "Which Countries Have the Highest Levels of Labor Union Membership?" *Forbes,* June 20, 2017, https://www.forbes.com/sites/niallmccarthy/2017/06/20/which -countries-have-the-highest-levels-of-labor-union-membership -infographic/#264d533133c0.

156 *and most Americans having unions:* Source is Gallup poll results from 2018, Lydia Saad, "Labor Union Approval Steady at 15-Year High," Gallup, August 30, 2018, https://news.gallup.com/poll/241679 /labor-union-approval-steady-year-high.aspx.

161 *and its union:* Michael Winn, author interview, June 2017.

162 *"medical staff members":* No One Size Fits All: Worker Organization, Policy, and Movement in a New Economic Age (LERA Research Volumes), eds Janice Fine, Linda Burnham, Kati Griffith, Minsun Ji, Victor Narro, and Steven Pitts (Ithaca, NY: Cornell University Press, 2018).

163 *"go somewhere else":* "MNA Stands Behind 1,500 Striking Temple U. Hospital Nurses," Massachusetts Nurses Association, April 5, 2010, https://www.massnurses.org/news-and-events/archive/2010/p /openItem/4385.

165 *"another side of his leadership":* Nela Hadzic, author interview, June 7, 2017.

168 *leading up to their election:* In President Obama's second term, he began to make some progressive changes administratively, via rule and regulation changes in various agencies. One bone he threw to

national unions frustrated by lack of progress on anything to do with union elections was to mandate that firms or companies that hire union avoidance consultants had to file monthly paperwork with the National Labor Relations Board naming the basics, the firm or union avoidance consultants, and the amount of money being spent on union busters. I am in possession of the monthly reports that demonstrate that Einstein had hired IRI Inc.

174 *"He was never pleased":* Marne Payne, interview with author, April 2, 2017.

175 *"that we needed a union":* Ibid.

180 *"the patients you serve every day":* Letter in author's possession.

192 *"to all our attempts":* Pat Kelly, interview with author, April 2, 2017.

CHAPTER 6: HOW TO REBUILD A UNION: L.A.'S TEACHERS

200 *teacher-related unions:* The "merger" was really messy, in some ways, because it was so messy trying to put together so many smaller, independent unions; it was more like a "partial merger" legally, though functionally, the organizations did come together. Whoever did the merger language back in 1970 didn't do it well, something the Union Power leadership had to tackle, like so many other things, years later. They had to add a membership-wide vote to change the constitution to make the merger full when they voted on the dues increase in 2016.

201 *UTLA somewhat unusual:* "History of UTLA," UTLA.net, https://www.utla.net/about-us/history-utla.

204 *"to call from the press":* Alex Caputo-Pearl, author interview, August 30, 2018.

205 *"I put my energy":* Jollene Levid, author interview, January 23, 2019.

207 *"follow up with people":* Brian McNamara, author interviews, August 30, 2018 and January 23, 2019.

208 *since the 1989 strike:* Alex Caputo-Pearl, author interview, April 20, 2018.

210 *private-investor run schools:* Jane McAlevey, "Teachers Are Leading the Revolt Against Austerity," *The Nation* (May 9, 2018), https://www.thenation.com/article/teachers-are-leading-the-revolt-against-austerity.

211 *pro-privatization agenda:* Howard Blume and Ben Poston, "How LA's School Board Election Became the Most Expensive in U.S. History," *Los Angeles Times,* May 21, 2017.

211 *As the* Times' *article pointed out:* The Parent Teacher Alliance, an electoral campaign group that seemed intentionally meant to confuse people with the actual Parent Teacher Association (the alliance logo even looked suspiciously similar to the PTA's), received most of its money from the California Charter Schools Association. Hastings earned his fortune from Netflix and his connections to Facebook, but you won't see his name in the city's election spending records because current election laws in the United States allow rich donors to be shielded by super PACs and other mechanisms that make tracking the source of donations difficult. Such is the result of election laws in the era of the viciously anti-worker, anti-union, pro-corporate, and pro-rich Supreme Court.

212 *2017 Memorial Day Weekend:* This story was repeated in the ratification meetings on Tuesday, January 22, 2019, and in the all-staff contract debrief on Wednesday, January 23, 2019, both of which I attended.

215 *Early in 2018, King resigned:* In February 2019, King passed away.

221 *"a nurse on duty":* Julia Lathin, author interview, August 30, 2018.

221 *"have become so difficult":* Brandon Abraham, author interview, August 30, 2018.

228 *"behind the demands":* Alex Caputo-Pearl, author interview, February 3, 2019.

230 *for homeless people:* Alex Caputo-Pearl, author interview, and Jeff Goode, author interview, January 23 and February 7, respectively, 2019 (both were a party to the final negotiations and this conversation).

CHAPTER 7: AS GO UNIONS, SO GOES THE REPUBLIC

233 *"become unbearable":* John Steuben, *Strike Strategy* (New York: Gaer Associates, 1950), 14–15.

234 *"behind new Labour":* Tony Blair, victory speech from 1997 general election, retrieved from YouTube on April 24, 2019, https://www.youtube.com/watch?v=RHXA5GykEbw.

235 *about one hundred months of job growth:* Nelson D. Schwartz, "Job Growth Underscores Economy's Vigor; Unemployment at Half-Century Low," *New York Times,* May 4, 2019, https://www.nytimes.com/2019/05/03/business/economy/jobs-report-april.html.

236 *for the impact on the rest of us:* Erin Coghlan, List McCorkell, and Sara Hinkley, "What Really Caused the Great Recession?" Institute for Research on Labor and Employment, University of California, Berkeley, 2018, http://irle.berkeley.edu/what-really-caused-the-great

-recession/; Sheldon Richman, "Clinton's Legacy: The Financial and Housing Meltdown," *Reason,* October 14, 2012, https://reason .com/2012/10/14/clintons-legacy-the-financial-and-housin.

236 *after its 2019 plant closings:* Jamie L. LaReau, "Economist: Expect General Motors to Lay Off Even More Michigan Workers," *Detroit Free Press,* January 9, 2019, https://www.freep.com/story/money/cars /general-motors/2019/01/09/gms-restructuring-plan-bring-more -jobs-cuts-and-marketshare-loss/2507689002.

236 *jobs in other states:* Krystal Hu, "Amazon Shuffles Thousands of Workers in Its Quest to Revamp Delivery," Yahoo Finance, April 23 2019, https://finance.yahoo.com/news/exclusive-amazon-shuffles -thousands-of-workers-in-its-quest-to-revamp-delivery-175043905 .html.

236 *hit hard by intentional unemployment (or "globalization"):* Rex Nutting, "Half of the New Jobs Were Created in These 5 States," MarketWatch, January 28, 2018, https://www.marketwatch.com /story/half-of-new-jobs-were-created-in-these-5-states-2018-01-26.

237 *low-income and working-class Americans:* Heather Long, "Record 7 Million Americans Are 3 Months Behind on Car Payments, a Red Flag for Economy," *Washington Post,* February 12, 2019, https://www .washingtonpost.com/business/2019/02/12/record-million-americans -are-months-behind-their-car-payments-red-flag-economy.

238 *are who elected Trump:* Kim Moody, "Who Put Trump in the White House?" *Jacobin,* November 1, 2017, https://www.jacobinmag .com/2017/01/trump-election-democrats-gop-clinton-whites-workers -rust-belt; also Guy Molyneux, "Mapping the White Working Class," *American Prospect,* December 20, 2016, https://prospect.org/article /mapping-white-working-class.

Index